"Can We All Get Along?"

Dilemmas in American Politics

Series Editor: **Craig A. Rimmerman,** Hobart and William Smith Colleges

If the answers to the problems facing U.S. democracy were easy, politicians would solve them, accept credit, and move on. But certain dilemmas have confronted the American political system continuously. They defy solution; they are endemic to the system. Some can best be described as institutional dilemmas: How can the Congress be both a representative body and a national decision-maker? How can the president communicate with more than 250 million citizens effectively? Why do we have a two-party system when many voters are disappointed with the choices presented to them? Others are policy dilemmas: How do we find compromises on issues that defy compromise, such as abortion policy? How do we incorporate racial and ethnic minorities or immigrant groups into American society, allowing them to reap the benefits of this land without losing their identity? How do we fund health care for our poorest or oldest citizens?

Dilemmas such as these are what propel students toward an interest in the study of U.S. government. Each book in the *Dilemmas in American Politics* series addresses a "real world" problem, raising the issues that are of most concern to students. Each is structured to cover the historical and theoretical aspects of the dilemma but also to explore the dilemma from a practical point of view and to speculate about the future. The books are designed as supplements to introductory courses in American politics or as case studies to be used in upper-level courses. The link among them is the desire to make the real issues confronting the political world come alive in students' eyes.

BOOKS IN THIS SERIES

"Can We All Get Along?"

Racial and Ethnic Minorities in American Politics

FOURTH EDITION

Paula D. McClain
Duke University

Joseph Stewart Jr.
Clemson University

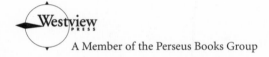
Westview PRESS
A Member of the Perseus Books Group

Dilemmas in American Politics Series

Cover photograph: A member of the Texas Department of Public Safety stands guard as members of the Ku Klux Klan hold a rally Saturday, June 27, 1998, in Jasper, Texas. The KKK held a rally to denounce the dragging death of James Byrd Jr. (AP Photo/David J. Phillip)

Published in the United States of America by Westview Press, a member of the Perseus Books Group, 5500 Central Avenue, Boulder, Colorado 80301–2877.

Find us on the world wide web at www.westviewpress.com

Westview Press books are available at special discounts for bulk purchases in the United States by corporations, institutions, and other organizations. For more information, please contact the Special Markets Department at the Perseus Books Group, 11 Cambridge Center, Cambridge, MA 02142, or call (617) 252–5298, (800) 255–1514 or email special.markets@perseusbooks.com.

Library of Congress Cataloging-in-Publication Data
McClain, Paula Denice.
  "Can we all get along?" : racial and ethnic minorities in American politics / Paula D. McClain,
Joseph Stewart Jr.—4th ed.
    p.   cm.
  Includes bibliographical references and index.
  ISBN-13: 978-0-8133-4321-1 (pbk. : alk. paper)
  ISBN-10: 0-8133-4321-6 (pbk. : alk. paper)
  1. Minorities—United States—Political activity.   2. United States—Race relations—Political aspects.
3. United States—Ethnic relations—Political aspects.   I. Stewart, Joseph, 1951– II. Title.   III. Series.
E184.A1M347   2006
305.8'00973—dc22

                                                                                    2005009838

The paper used in this publication meets the requirements of the American National Standard for Permanence of Paper for Printed Library Materials Z39.48–1984.

10   9   8   7   6   5   4   3   2   1

To Harold M. Rose, friend, colleague, and mentor. You taught me more about research and the academy than you will ever know. But more importantly, you taught me how to be a scholar.

—P.D.M.

To Jewel L. Prestage, for whom I was the "warm-up act" in Black Politics courses a "few" years ago. Without that expereience, my part in this would never have been possible.

—J.S.

Contents

1   America's Dilemmas   1

2   Resources and Status of America's Racial Minorities   29

3   America's Racial Minorities in the Contemporary Political System: Actors   65

Targeting Racial and Ethnic Minorities, 214
VRA: Looking to the Future, 215
Conclusion, 217

List of Illustrations and Maps

Photographs

Mayoral candidates Antonio Villaraigosa, right, and James Hahn shake
  hands May 31, 2001, before their final debate at the Museum of
  Tolerance, Los Angeles, California. (AP Photo: Kevork Djansezian)   202

Maps

Tables

List of Acronyms

AIM	American Indian Movement
APILC	Asian Pacific Islander Legislative Caucus
APSA	American Political Science Association
BIA	Bureau of Indian Affairs
CILS	California Indian Legal Services
COFO	Council of Federated Organizations
CRLA	California Rural Legal Assistance
FBI	Federal Bureau of Investigation
HAVA	Help America Vote Act
HEW	Department of Health, Education, and Welfare
INS	Immigration and Naturalization Services
JACL	Japanese American Citizens League
JCPES	Joint Center for Political and Economic Studies
LAPD	Los Angeles Police Department
LDF	NAACP Legal Defense and Educational Fund
LEAP	Leadership Education for Asian Pacifics
LNPS	Latino National Political Survey
LULAC	League of United Latin American Citizens
MALDEF	Mexican American Legal Defense and Education Fund
NAACP	National Association for the Advancement of Colored People
NARF	Native American Rights Fund
NBES	National Black Election Study
NBPS	National Black Politics Study
NCLR	National Council of La Raza
OCR	Office for Civil Rights
OFCCP	Office of Federal Contract Compliance Programs
PASSO	Political Association of Spanish Speaking Peoples
PNAAPS	Pilot Study of the National Asian American Political Survey
PRLDEF	Puerto Rican Legal Defense and Education Fund
SCLC	Southern Christian Leadership Conference

SNCC   Student Nonviolent Coordinating Committee
UDL   United Defense League
VAP   Voting-Age Population
VRA   Voting Rights Act

Preface

This book is the result of a collaboration that began over a bottle of cabernet sauvignon at the 1992 American Political Science Association (APSA) meeting in Chicago. What started as an evening devoted to reading papers quickly turned into a discussion of the difficulties of teaching a true minority group politics course.

Some universities, depending on their location, have a course devoted to a particular group—for example, black politics, Latino politics, Asian politics, American Indian politics—or even a more specialized course such as Mexican American politics or Puerto Rican politics. Indeed, we have both taught such courses. But more commonly the demand is for an umbrella course that, ideally, compares the politics of the four principal U.S. racial and ethnic minority groups—blacks, Latinos, American Indians, and Asian Americans—and their relationships with the majority. This is the situation at our current institutions.

Such umbrella courses generally take one of two forms. The less-than-ideal alternative is focused on one ethnic group because that is where the interest and expertise of the instructor lie. In such situations, it is possible for a student to take the same course twice from different instructors, never to encounter overlapping patterns and never explicitly to consider interminority group relations. The second, preferable form involves undertaking a comparative examination of the politics of the major racial and ethnic minorities of the United States. This is an idealized alternative because, as we can report from personal experience, it is difficult to implement. One must spend countless hours amassing data from various sources in an attempt to draw out the similarities and the differences among the groups and to develop the depth and nuance that characterize a good course.

Toward the bottom of the bottle of wine, we decided that we had sufficient expertise on black and Latino politics and enough familiarity with the literature of American Indian and Asian American politics to write a book for a true junior/senior-level minority politics class. We mentioned our "prospectus from a bottle" to Cathy Rudder, executive director of APSA, who discussed it with Sandy Maisel of Colby College, the editor of Westview Press's new series Dilemmas in American Politics. Sandy contacted us, indicated that this was the book the series' editorial advisory board had decided was a high priority; McClain, a member of the board, had missed the meeting! Sandy convinced us to write a shorter, less-detailed volume for use as a supplement, primarily in American government courses. The larger, upper-division book is still in our plans.

The words for the title are appropriated from Rodney King's first news conference following the acquittals of his attackers and the subsequent Los Angeles riots. His words crystallize the dilemmas faced by the nation, by members of both minority and majority groups.

Response to the first, second, and third editions have been gratifying. To paraphrase Yogi Berra, we would like to thank everyone who made this fourth edition necessary. Sales for all editions suggest there is an interest in learning more about the nation's racial and ethnic politics (or in teachers having their students exposed to more material on the topic). Racial and ethnic politics, like politics in general, is constantly changing. Thus, for this book to fulfill its role, it is necessary to produce a new edition. The basic structure has not been altered, but materials have been added or updated. Readers will find an analysis of the 2004 elections and data from the updated 2000 census.

We could not have accomplished what turned out to be a larger undertaking than we had imagined—to write the first edition—without the help of numerous people. Steven C. Tauber served as our principal factotum. (Hint: This word appears in the GRE verbal exam. Look it up. Fans of the old TV series, *The Fugitive*, will have already encountered it.) Steve spent countless hours on numerous tasks, with perhaps the worst being an attempt to get the National Black Election Study data file to run again after a transfer from one computer system to another. Steve has served as McClain's teaching assistant for her Minority Group Politics course at the University of Virginia for several years in the early 1990s. His intellectual contributions to the study of racial minority group politics are present throughout the book.

Thanks also to Don Nakanishi of the Asian American Studies Center at UCLA for helping us identify Asian American elected officials; to Larry Bobo of the Department of Sociology at UCLA for sharing his Los Angeles County Survey data with us; to Paul Waddell and his staff at the Bruton

Center for Development Studies of the University of Texas at Dallas for generating the maps in Chapter 2 in the first edition; the research staffs of the Joint Center for Political and Economic Studies and the National Association of Latino Elected and Appointed Officials; and to Paula Sutherland, head of Government Documents, and Linda Snow, reference librarian, McDermott Library, University of Texas at Dallas, for tracking down or pointing us toward valuable information we knew existed somewhere but had no idea where. Our colleagues and students over the years, especially those in McClain's Minority Group Politics class, helped by enduring our on-the-job efforts to fashion a coherent, comparative course by asking questions that forced us to seek more answers, and by answering questions we posed.

We are also indebted to Sandy Maisel; to Jennifer Knerr, our acquisitions editor, Shena Redmond, our project editor, and Cheryl Carnahan, our copy editor, at Westview Press; and to the reviewers of a very rough first draft—Stephanie Larson of Dickinson College, Roderick Kiewiet of California Institute of Technology, and F. Chris Garcia of the University of New Mexico. Each offered helpful comments, some of which we heeded. Ted Lowi also read the rough draft and gets a special nod for pushing us to put more politics in the book. This book is better for their efforts, and none of them is responsible for any errors that remain. We blame those errors, as has become the convention in our discipline, on Paul Sabatier.

The second edition benefited from the encouragement and suggestions of many individuals in addition to those who helped us in the beginning. We cannot remember everyone who provided helpful suggestions, but some people cannot be forgotten. Working with Series Editor Sandy Maisel and our Westview editor Leo Wiegman has been a joy. Hanes Walton Jr., University of Michigan; Todd Shaw, University of Illinois; and Rick Matland, University of Houston, provided us with detailed insights of their experiences in using the first edition and numerous suggestions for what we should change or not change for this edition. We actually paid attention to some of those suggestions! Several graduate and undergraduate students at the University of Virginia—Stacy Nyikos, J. Alan Kendrick, and Andra Gillespie—tracked down items that helped us update the earlier edition. Amy Fromer of the Institute for Public Policy at the University of New Mexico produced the maps of the United States, and David Deis of the Department of Geography, California State University–Northridge produced the Los Angeles map found in Chapter 2.

Stacy, Alan, and Andra are heartened to know that there is life after working with us. Their predecessor, Steve Tauber, now an assistant professor of political science at the University of South Florida, would like us to note that it took three people to replace him.

We were gratified to be able to produce the third edition. We noticed an increasing interest in race, ethnicity, and politics as the demographics of the United States continue to change. The importance of the politics of the groups examined in the book cannot be understated. Several graduate students at Duke University—Shayla Nunnally, Monique Lyles, and Jen Merrolla—found much of the information used to update this edition. We thank them for all of their help. We would also like to thank those individuals who reviewed the second edition and offered us valuable suggestions for the third edition; their names remain anonymous to us. Our thanks as well go to David Deis of Dreamline Cartography for producing all of the maps in this edition.

In the publication of this fourth edition, we continue to be buoyed by the tremendous increasing interest in race, ethnicity, and politics. Yet, we are surprised that *"Can We All Get Along?"* is still the only book that examines America's racial minority groups from a comparative perspective. Putting together a book of this type is not an easy task and requires many people to do so. Several graduate students at Duke University—Efren O. Perez, Michael C. Brady, and Niambi M. Carter—found the data and updated most of the tables in this new edition. We owe Mike Brady a tremendous thank-you for finding the picture that appears on the cover of this new edition. He included it in pictures of multiracial groups and its sense of irony, authority, and power jumped out at us. We also must thank our editor, Steve Catalano, and our marketing manager, Michelle Mallin, of Westview Press for their continued support and belief in this book. They are our champions and we are truly appreciative.

Perhaps most importantly, we thank Don Lutz, University of Houston, for giving us the bottle of wine that began this process, and we also thank our families. Paul C. Jacobson, Kristina McClain-Jacobson Ragland, Jessica McClain-Jacobson, and Paula Sutherland have patiently, lovingly, and supportively endured this lengthy and, at points, contentious (between the authors) process.

Finally, the book is dedicated to two individuals who have had a great deal of influence on our personal lives and professional careers. Harold M. Rose, an urban geographer at the University of Wisconsin–Milwaukee, has shared two decades of research collaboration on black urban homicide with McClain. They are now intellectual partners, but in 1977 Rose befriended the new assistant professor, shared his ideas for a major collaborative project, mentored her in the ways of the academy, and taught her the importance of maintaining one's intellectual integrity, of paying attention to detail, and of being thoughtful and reflective in one's scholarship. McClain affectionately dedicates this book to him.

Stewart's efforts are another step in a process that began when, as an assistant professor at the University of New Orleans, he decided he wanted to teach the sophomore-level Black Politics course. Jewel L. Prestage, who had been teaching the class, may have seen this as an opportunity to avoid those long drives across the bridges from Baton Rouge and to free her to teach other, more interesting upper-division classes. Whatever the reason, she approved of Stewart being her "warm-up act" and was supportive and helpful, as she has been in the years since. Had she not been so, Stewart's career would have probably taken a different track. He would have missed interesting intellectual endeavors. Jewel Prestage made Stewart's efforts on this project both possible and necessary, and he is grateful.

Paula D. McClain
Durham, North Carolina

Joseph Stewart Jr.
Clemson, South Carolina

1

··

America's Dilemmas

On November 2, 2004, Alabama voters voted on
Amendment 2 that would have removed language from
the state constitution requiring segregated schools for
"white and colored children" as well as removed a
passage—inserted in the 1950s in an attempt to counter
the *Brown v. Board of Education* ruling declaring
segregated schools unconstitutional—that said
Alabama's constitution does not guarantee a right to a
public education. Amendment 2 was supported by the
Republican governor, most of the legislators, and the
state newspapers. Opponents of the removal of the
language used the argument that was ridiculed by most
of the state's newspapers and legal experts that
removing the language against guaranteeing a right to
public education would open the doors for "rogue"
federal judges to order the state to raise taxes to pay for
improvements in the public school system. Amendment
2 was rejected by a margin of 1,850 votes, thus insuring
that the racist and segregationist language remains in
the Alabama State Constitution.

—Alabama, November 2, 2004[1]

ON APRIL 29, 1992, RIOTING ERUPTED in Los Angeles after the announcement that a predominantly white jury in a suburban municipality had acquitted police officers who had been videotaped beating black motorist Rodney King. These activities were widely reported as black reactions to an obvious injustice perpetrated by whites against blacks. Indeed, Americans are used to interpreting political and social relations in white-versus-black terms. The facts are more complex. The brunt of property crimes was borne by Korean retailers; the majority of those arrested during the civil disorders were Hispanic (Morrison and Lowry 1994). As the United States proceeds through the twenty-first century, the variety and identity of the actors are changing, but racial and ethnic conflict is an old story.

In his *Democracy in America*, published in 1835, Alexis de Tocqueville, an early French visitor to the republic, notes that the treatment and situation of blacks in the United States contradicted the American passion for democracy. He saw slavery and the denial of constitutional rights and protection to blacks as the principal threats to the U.S. democratic system: "If there ever are great revolutions there [in America], they will be caused by the presence of the blacks upon American soil. . . . It will not be the equality of social conditions but rather their inequality which may give rise thereto" (Tocqueville 1834 [original], Mayer and Lerner 1966:614). This same disparate treatment was noted more than a century later by sociologist Gunnar Myrdal, who published the first comprehensive scholarly examination of the oppression of blacks in the United States, *An American Dilemma* (1944). Myrdal argues that the contradiction within American society between an allegedly strong commitment to democratic values on the one hand and the presence of racial oppression on the other creates a moral dilemma for white Americans and is the root of the U.S. race relations problems.

Although many doubt that Myrdal's argument is correct—that is, that most white Americans are terribly cross-pressured by the presence of both democratic ideals and racial discrimination—the use of the term *dilemma* is invaluable in an examination of racial minority group politics in the United States. This book focuses on two dilemmas. The first dilemma harkens back to the founding of America, is the subject of de Tocqueville's concern, and continues to resonate today: *How does a governmental system that professes in its Constitution and its rhetoric to be democratic and egalitarian handle the obvious reality of its systematic denial of basic rights and privileges to its own citizens based on color? When forced to confront and correct the inequalities, how does it provide for and protect the rights of identifiable racial and ethnic minority groups?* The questions this reality-versus-rhetoric dilemma engenders are amazingly similar over time: How shall blacks be counted when apportioning congressional seats (1787)? Is it impermissible to draw "funny-shaped" congressional districts in an attempt to enhance minority group representation (2001)?

The second dilemma is less often articulated, perhaps because it exists within the perspective of the minority groups: *What strategy—coalition or conflict—should be used by minority groups in dealing with other minority groups and with the majority group?* In essence, this dilemma poses the "what do we do about it?" question, given the political realities of the first dilemma. In many, if not most, considerations of this second dilemma, members of minority groups are treated as passive subjects in a majoritarian system and as natural allies against members of the majority. The present volume challenges this perspective and considers a broader range of strategic choices that are available to members of racial and ethnic minority groups as actors within the polity.

In focusing on these dilemmas, this book addresses the importance of race and ethnicity in American politics—the decisions about who gets what, when, where, and how—in general and in the politics (historical, legal, attitudinal, and behavioral) of the four principal racial minority groups in the United States: blacks (African Americans), Latinos, Asians, and Indian peoples in particular. These groups are the focus because unlike other ethnic minorities—for example, the Irish, Italians, and Jews—who have also suffered from social discrimination, blacks, Latinos, Asians, and American Indians have lived in the United States *under separate systems of law* for varying periods of time. Because each has a history of differential legal status and because this history has led to special attention in contemporary law in an attempt to remedy the effects of historical discrimination, these groups require special attention in political analysis.

There is a tendency in the political science literature to assume that all racial minority groups within the United States share similar experiences and political behaviors. Consequently, blacks, Latinos, Asian Americans, and American Indians are often merged under the rubric "minority group politics." But the increasing recognition of differences among and within these groups has generated debate over whether the concept of minority group politics is useful in thinking about and studying the political experiences of all nonwhite groups in the United States. Although these groups share racial minority group status within the United States, there are fundamental differences in their experiences, orientations, and political behaviors that affect the relationships among the four groups as well as between each of the groups and the dominant white majority. Similarities in racial minority group status may be the bases for building coalitions, but they may also generate conflict. Consequently, this book focuses on the groups separately at times and comparatively at other times.

Terms Used in This Book

Before proceeding, it is important to define the terms used throughout the book. The way individuals identify themselves and how they are identified by others in the polity is of more than semantic interest. Self-identification, often referred to as **group political consciousness**, and other-identification can promote or thwart nation building and can affect, as we shall see later, people's ability and willingness to participate in the political system.

First, the terms *black* and *African American* are used interchangeably. Recent survey data indicate that seven of ten African Americans prefer the term *black* (Gomes and Williams 1992). We also prefer the term *black* for theoretical reasons. It concisely describes an identity and a status within American society that are based on color. The black experience in America differs markedly from that of the white ethnics, and the use of African American may convey the impression that blacks are just another ethnic group similar to Italian Americans, Irish Americans, or Polish Americans. Blacks have been subjugated and segregated, on the basis of color, from *all* whites regardless of their ethnic backgrounds. Further, after one generation, white ethnics have been able to shed their ethnicity and blend into the mainstream of white America, but blacks, because of their skin color, remain identifiable generation after generation. We also use *black* because it is a convenient proxy term for an insular group that is more or less politically cohesive, that has historically been stigmatized, that is generally depressed economically, and that remains socially isolated.

Similarly, we use *Latino* and *Hispanic* interchangeably as umbrella terms when we cannot distinguish among subgroups of the nation's Spanish-origin population. The largest of the Latino groups are Mexican Americans, Puerto Ricans, and Cuban Americans. The term *Hispanic* is eschewed by many intellectuals because it is Eurocentric—the term literally means "lover of Spain"—which, given the national origins of the overwhelming majority of U.S. Latinos, is inappropriate. Moreover, *Hispanic* is a term devised by the U.S. Census Bureau for classifying individuals and is devoid of any theoretical or political context.

The Latino National Political Survey, discussed more fully in Chapter 3, suggests that Latinos do not primarily identify themselves as members of a Hispanic or Latino community. Although *Latino* is the preferred identifier among the intelligentsia, few Mexican Americans, Puerto Ricans, or Cuban Americans self-identify themselves with either pan-ethnic term. The preferred identification terms are *Mexican* or *Mexican American* among Mexican Americans, *Puerto Rican* among Puerto Ricans, and *Cuban* among Cuban respondents (de la Garza et al. 1992).

Third, we use the term *Indian peoples* or *American Indian peoples* rather than *Native Americans*. The reasons for this choice are simple yet profoundly important. The term *Native American* was used during the nativist (anti-immigration, antiforeigner) movement (1860–1925) and the antiblack, anti-Catholic, and anti-Jewish Ku Klux Klan resurgence during the early 1900s (Higham 1963). The rhetoric of these groups was couched in terms of "native-born" white Protestants vis-à-vis those of "foreign" origin, for example, Catholics. There was even a political party known as the Native American Party. Thus, whereas popular culture may refer to Indian peoples as Native Americans, we feel it is important to separate this group from the white supremacist terms used by the nativist movement. Moreover, we seek to defuse the specious argument made by some that if one is born in the United States, one is a native American, thereby dismissing the unique situation and status of American Indian peoples. Indian peoples encompass a variety of tribes, each with its own history and different structural relationships with the U.S. government. Finally, many native Hawaiians consider themselves Native Americans. Although not grouping native Hawaiians with American Indians in the 2000 census, the U.S. Census Bureau, after years of grouping native Hawaiians with Asians, put them in a new category with Pacific Islanders. Native Hawaiians are not included in our discussion here, so our terms separate American Indians from native Hawaiians.

The question of who is an Indian is central to any discussion of American Indian politics. The essence of the "Indianness" issue rests not with Indian peoples themselves but with the federal government. One of the inherent powers of Indian tribes as sovereign nations is the power to decide who belongs, and historically tribes have focused on allegiance as the deciding factor. Over time, the federal government has increasingly tried to answer the question to decide who is or is not covered by legislation. As a result, more than thirty different definitions of who is legally an Indian have been produced depending on "blood quantum," federal tribal recognition, residence, descent, self-identification, and miscellaneous other factors. Moreover, the question of who is subject to Indian law also depends on the relationship of the tribe to the federal government and on whether the federal government recognizes the tribe. Federal recognition occurs in a variety of ways: congressional action, presidential executive order, administrative ruling by the Bureau of Indian Affairs (BIA), or judicial opinion. In addition to federally recognized Indians, there are more than one hundred groups who used to be recognized as Indians but have had their status "terminated" by the federal government and more than 50 tribes recognized by state, but not federal, governments (Wilkins 2002:13–27).

Finally, the term *Asian American* envelops a multiplicity of ethnic origin groups—Japanese, Koreans, Chinese, Filipinos, Southeast Asians, Pacific Islanders, and East Indians (Kitano 1981). Each of these groups has a different history of entrance into the United States, but "Asian Americans have been here for over one hundred and fifty years, before many European immigrant groups" (Takaki 1993:7). The Chinese arrived first in significant numbers, followed by the Japanese, Koreans, Filipinos, Asian Indians, and, later, Southeast Asian refugees. We find no local, contemporary survey data that address ethnic identity for Asian Americans, but the historical record suggests a situation even less unified than that of Hispanics. National rivalries often survived the immigration process, so that, for example, early Japanese immigrants were as anti-Chinese as any of their non-Asian counterparts (Ichioka 1988). Furthermore, unlike Latinos, first-generation immigrant Asians have not shared a common language, a situation that provides a formidable barrier to any pan-Asian identification (Espiritu 1992).

Race and Ethnicity

Although this is not a book about **racism**—the belief in and practice of using race as a justification for discrimination among individuals—per se, each of the groups considered has been affected by racism, albeit differently. Some of this racism is on an individual level, in which individuals discriminate against other individuals because of their membership, real or perceived, in a racial group. More problematically, some of the racism is institutionalized, which is more complex, less obvious, more routinized, and more difficult to eradicate than discrimination based on individual racism. Individual racism is usually more conscious, and perhaps more blatant, whereas discrimination based on institutional racism is more likely to be subtle, unconscious, and rationalized on the basis of nonracial criteria (Feagin and Feagin 1978). Furthermore, social class and gender differences are variables that both compound the effects of racism and affect the way group members can and do respond to the situations in which they find themselves. When information is available to allow us to take these factors into account, we shall do so. But over and above class and gender, race has been and continues to be a central theme of the American polity and society.

Race—initially construed in terms of white, black, and Indian—has never been a benign concept in the United States. We should remember that the first Africans to arrive at Jamestown, Virginia, in 1619 were indentured servants, not slaves. Slavery was not instituted on a broad scale until 1661 in Virginia (20 years after slavery had first been incorporated into colonial law in Massachusetts) as the need for labor increased and whites found Indian servitude and slavery inadequate and the supply of white indentured servants insufficient. The permanent enslavement of Africans and African Americans was the answer to a "vexing" labor problem. The supply of blacks appeared to be endless, and "if they ran away they were easily detected because of their color. If they proved ungovernable they could be chastised with less qualms and with greater severity than in the case of whites, because Negroes represented heathen people who could not claim the immunities accorded by Christians" (Franklin 1969:72).

With the institution of slavery and the mass importation of black slaves, whites—although solving their labor problems—began to fear the mixture of races and to be concerned that growing numbers of blacks would rebel against the institution of slavery. These fears and the whites' disdain and contempt for blacks created a dynamic of white oppression that manifested itself in a multiplicity of ways. Many states, concerned about the purity of the white group, codified into law the degree of black ancestry that qualified one to be legally defined as black and thus subject to legal restrictions. Louisiana and North Carolina used the one-sixteenth criterion (one great-great-grandparent); one-eighth (one great-grandparent) was the standard in Florida, Indiana, Maryland, Mississippi, Missouri, Nebraska, North Dakota, South Carolina, and Tennessee; Oregon used a one-quarter standard (one grandparent) (Spickard 1989:374–375).

This obsession with "black blood" was also codified into legal restrictions on marriage partners, which were referred to as **antimiscegenation laws.** Throughout most of their history, 29 states maintained laws forbidding interracial marriage between blacks and whites. Over time, many of these laws were amended to include a prohibition on marriages between other racial combinations in addition to blacks and whites. The 14 states with additional prohibitions included California, between white and Mongolian; Georgia, between white, American Indian, Asiatic Indian, or Mongolian; Nebraska, between white and Chinese or Japanese; and Arizona, between white and Mongolian or Indian. The penalties for interracial marriages ranged from maximum imprisonment of more than two years in 14 states to no penalty in California. These antimiscegenation laws were not nullified until the U.S. Supreme Court decision *Loving v. Virginia* in 1967 (Spickard 1989:374–375). Clearly, the black-white dynamic is the most ingrained in the American political system and is the relationship that has formed much of our thinking about race in the United States. Although the importance of the black-white dynamic cannot be diminished, issues of race and the complexity of the racial dynamic extend beyond black and white today.

We are also concerned with issues of ethnicity—in a specific sense of the term. We use the term **ethnicity**—generally meaning the grouping of people on the basis of learned characteristics, often associated with national origin—because we recognize that within the four groups addressed in this book there are different ethnic origin groups that may have different political attitudes and behaviors. Issues of ethnicity are particularly pertinent within the Latino, Asian, and Indian groups. The U.S. Census Bureau used five racial categories for the 2000 Census—white, black or African American, Asian, American Indian or Alaska Native, and Native Hawaiian or other Pacific Islander. Those who do not feel that they fall within the five racial categories could check a sixth category—"Some other race." It also allowed people for the first time to check more than one race, which resulted in the addition of 57 additional racial categories, for a total of 63. Hispanic, however, was used as an ethnic, rather than a racial, category. Although many Hispanics view themselves as a separate non-white race, they are forced to classify themselves as one of the five races listed above. This practice has caused consternation among several of the groups, particularly Mexicans, who are a mixture of Indian, African, and European—principally Spanish—races. In the 2000 Census, 42.2 percent of Hispanics checked the "some other race" category. Until Hispanic is deemed to be a racial category, we will continue to use ethnicity in conjunction with racial minorities in recognition of the idiosyncratic situation of Latinos vis-à-vis the U.S. Census Bureau.

Such formal identification may define who is included in and who is excluded from the political system. In official terms, the issues are citizenship and voting rights. We now consider the key values in the foundation of the U.S. Constitution, including citizenship and suffrage, and their application to the nation's original minorities—blacks and American Indians.

American Government Foundation and Racial Minorities

April 13, 1993, marked the 250th anniversary of the birth of Thomas Jefferson, the third president of the United States and author of the Declaration of Independence. Despite all of the celebrations around the world, the contradictions and inconsistencies between Thomas Jefferson the man and Thomas Jefferson the statesperson were not lost. The man who wrote in the Declaration of Independence that "all men are created equal and are endowed by their Creator with certain inalienable rights . . . and among these are life, liberty, and the pursuit of happiness" was also a slave owner. The tension that existed between the venerated values of the American political foundation—democracy, freedom, and equality—and the enslavement of a sizable segment of its population was not limited to Thomas Jefferson. It is an ever-present tension and a continuing struggle for the citizens of the United States and the values contained in the organizing document, the Constitution, which is the nation's foundation.

The political values contained in the Declaration of Independence in 1776 and spelled out later in the U.S. Constitution, drafted in 1787 and ratified in 1789, have their origins in classical liberal theory. **Classical liberalism** refers to a particular body of Western European political thought that sought to justify the liberation of the individual from feudal positions and to deride those who benefited from feudalism. In classical liberal theory, private interests are given priority over public or governmental authority, and the economy receives priority over the polity. Liberalism finds expression in the writings of John Locke and others, writings with which Thomas Jefferson was very familiar. The free individual in Locke's liberalism was free from the confines of the state—free to seek private ends. States and governments were coercive; despite declarations that they should be representative, their main purpose was to control and to regulate the conduct of individuals. To paraphrase Locke, if individuals are to be free, mechanisms must be developed to limit government's powers and to ensure that those limits will be preserved. Classical liberal thought runs throughout the *Federalist Papers*, the essays written to justify the ratification of the Constitution. Government's responsibility to protect private property and to provide an environment in which the pursuit of private property can be facilitated is a fundamental principle of the papers.

Given the emphasis on property in classical liberal theory in general, and in the *Federalist Papers* in particular, it is not surprising that the 1787 Constitution was explicitly intended not to apply to blacks and Indians. Article I, Section 2, of the original Constitution states: "Representatives and direct Taxes shall be apportioned among the several States which may be included within this Union, according to their respective Numbers, *which shall be determined by adding to the whole Number of free Persons, including those bound to Service for a Term of Years, and excluding Indians not taxed, three-fifths of all other Persons*" (emphasis added). "Other Persons" refers to the 92 percent of the black population held in slavery in the United States in 1790, the year the government began the census; the remaining 59,557 blacks were free individuals (Pohlman 1991:34; Jarvis 1992:21). In fact, there was no ambiguity regarding the founders' views on slavery or their position regarding the legal status of blacks within the United States.

Jefferson's original draft of the Declaration of Independence included an indictment of King George for "violating the most sacred rights of life and liberty in the persons of a distant people who never offended him, captivating and carrying them into slavery in another hemisphere or to incur miserable death in their transportation hither" (quoted in Jarvis 1992:20). However, this indictment of slavery was unacceptable to both southern and northern delegates because the southerners argued that slavery was fundamental to the economy of the new nation, and the northerners viewed slavery as a business that needed to be regulated.

The issue of slavery and the ensuing debate influenced the final compromise contained in Article I, Section 2, of the Constitution quoted earlier. The framers were cognizant of the fact that slavery would affect the "issues of representation, apportionment among the states, direct taxation, and commerce" (Jarvis 1992:20). Compromise was the watchword of the individuals who drafted the Constitution, and several important compromises were struck over the issue of slavery and suffrage requirements. Whereas Article I, Section 9, mandated a 20-year time period before Congress could limit the importation of African slaves, Article IV, Section 2, maintained that escaped slaves would not be freed from slavery but should be returned to their owners (the fugitive slave clause). The **three-fifths compromise**, in which the delegates decided to count a slave as only three-fifths of a person, resolved the issue of how to count slaves for representational and direct taxation purposes.

Although blacks were counted for representational and taxation purposes, they were not considered citizens of the United States: "Slaves were persons, but they were also property, which meant that a Negro's right to liberty conflicted with his master's right to property. In the colonial ideology, the right of property was central" (Robinson 1971:86). The compromise was momentous because

> it gave Constitutional sanction to the fact that the United States was composed of some persons who were "free" and others who were not. And it established the principle, new in republican theory, that a man who lived among slaves had a greater share in the election of representatives than the man who did not. With one stroke, despite the disclaimers of its advocates, it acknowledged slavery and rewarded slave owners. It is a measure of their adjustment to slavery that Americans in the eighteenth century found this settlement natural and just (Robinson 1971:201).

"This twisted logic satisfied the issue of apportionment but failed miserably in setting the right of blacks, particularly those who were not enslaved, to vote" (Jarvis 1992:21).

The Constitution and Black and Indian Citizenship

After ratification of the Constitution, two important issues remained to be addressed—suffrage and citizenship. Issues of **suffrage**—voting eligibility—were left to the states because reconciling differences in voting qualifications at the national level was thought to be too difficult. Moreover, and critically important, the criteria for **citizenship**—determining who was and was not a citizen of the United States or of a state—were also left to the states. The fact that these two important issues were left up to the states set the stage for the systematic exclusion from the political process of blacks, Indian peoples, women of all colors, and other racial minority groups.

Prior to the Declaration of Independence, the Continental Congress defined the colonies' citizens as "all persons abiding within any of the United Colonies and deriving protection from the laws of the same owe allegiance to the said laws, and are members of such colony" (Franklin 1906:2). Several events surrounding the institution of the Declaration of Independence and the Articles of Confederation indicate that initially "the right to citizenship was to be opened to all white people who were willing to identify with the struggle against the King" (Robinson 1971:135). Among the complaints against King George contained in the Declaration was that "He has excited domestic Insurrections amongst us, and has endeavoured to bring on the Inhabitants of our Frontiers, the merciless Indian Savages, whose Known Rule of Warfare, is an undistinguished Destruction, of all Ages, Sexes, and Conditions." After the advent of the Articles of Confederation, the committee—consisting of Benjamin Franklin, John Adams, and Thomas Jefferson—that had been appointed to devise a new national seal proposed that the seal be representative of the countries from which the peoples of the new nation had originated: England, Scotland, Ireland, France, Germany, and Holland. "Apparently neither the Africans nor the Indians were thought, even by this cosmopolitan committee, worthy of representation" (Robinson 1971:135).

Another event that lends credence to the contention that citizenship was reserved for whites was the manner in which a committee of Congress under the Articles of Confederation, of which Thomas Jefferson was also a member, wrestled with the issue of Indian inclusiveness in the new country. The initial committee report advised Congress to urge the states to make it easy for Indians to become citizens. After all, the colonists had enjoyed generally friendly relations with the American Indian nations with which they had come into contact. Most Indians traded with, protected, and supported European settlers until conflict erupted over control of land. The support of the Iroquois Confederacy, a government that at the time was more than 700 years old, in the French and Indian War had been crucial to the English victory. Likewise, two of the six tribes—including the most powerful, the Oneidas—had sided with the colonists against Great Britain in the Revolutionary War.

This report, however, was tabled. A subsequent report by a different committee "referred to the Indians, not as potential citizens, but as possible allies" (Robinson 1971:136). These events, combined with others, led to the conclusion "that the 'one people,' to whom Jefferson referred in the opening paragraph of the Declaration of Independence, were the white people of the thirteen colonies" (Robinson 1971:136). In addition, the Articles of Confederation, when discussing privileges and immunities, continually referred to "free inhabitants" and "free citizens" (Franklin 1906:1–18).

Although the U.S. Constitution, which replaced the Articles of Confederation, used the word *citizen* in several places, it did not confront citizenship directly; it assumed it. The assumption was that if individuals met the conditions of citizenship developed by the states, they were entitled to the rights and privileges extended in the Constitution. For example, Article I, Section 2, when discussing voting qualifications for election of members to the House of Representatives, states that if an individual meets the voting requirements in the state in which he resides, he is eligible to vote for members of the House of Representatives. Article IV, Section 2, states that "the Citizens of each State shall be entitled to all Privileges and Immunities of Citizens in the several States." The result was that each state was free to determine citizenship as well as voting requirements.

Following the ratification of the Constitution, Congress passed the **Naturalization** Act of 1790 in response to the Constitution's granting congressional power to pass a uniform rule to deal with the process by which foreigners could be "admitted to the rights of citizens" (Franklin 1906:33). This act granted citizenship as a matter of right to free white aliens who had lived in the United States and had shown good behavior for two years, who expressed the intention of remaining in the United States, and who took an oath of allegiance. Between 1790 and 1854, Congress passed 15 laws concerning naturalization and retained the phrase "free white person" in all of these laws without discussion: "The reason for the adoption of the phrase 'free white person' was manifestly the conviction that Indians and slaves, since they did not understand our life and political system, were not freemen and, therefore, were not fitted to be members of the body politic, nor to exercise the duties and responsibilities of citizenship" (Gulick 1918:55–56). Only after the Civil War, in the Naturalization Act of 1870, were naturalization laws "extended to aliens of African nativity and to persons of African descent" (Gulick 1918:56).

Although it could be argued that the Constitution, as it was framed, only excluded enslaved blacks from being citizens, the citizenship status of free blacks was debatable. Whatever doubt existed about the citizenship status of blacks under the Constitution was clarified with the Supreme Court decision in *Dred Scott v. Sanford* (1857). Writing for the majority in its attempt to settle the most explosive political issue of the time, Chief Justice Taney said the question was

> whether the provisions of the Constitution, in relation to the personal rights and privileges to which the citizen of a State should be entitled, embraced the negro African race, at that time in this country, or who might afterwards be imported, who had then or should afterwards be made free in any State; and to put it in the power of a single State to make him a citizen of the United States and endue him with the full rights of citizenship in every other State without their consent? Does the Constitution of the United States act upon him whenever he shall be made free under the laws of a State, and raised there to the rank of a citizen, and immediately clothe him with all the privileges of a citizen in every other State, and in its own courts? . . . It becomes necessary, therefore, to determine who were citizens of the several States when the Constitution was adopted (*Dred Scott v. Sanford*, 19 Howard 393, 406–407).

Taney argues that on the surface the words of the Declaration of Independence that state "that all men are created equal" and "are endowed by their Creator with certain unalienable rights" would appear to apply to blacks. Yet, he concludes, "it is too clear for dispute, that the enslaved African race were not intended to be included, and formed no part of the people who framed and adopted this declaration" (*Dred Scott v. Sanford* 1857:393, 410) and that this exclusion extended to the Constitution when ratified. Taney argues that two clauses in the Constitution, the right of the states to ban the importation of slaves after 20 years and the return of fugitive slaves (property) to their owners, provide evidence that the framers of the Constitution excluded blacks as "people" or citizens of the states in which they reside and thus as citizens of the United States. The Supreme Court thus declared that Dred Scott was not a citizen of the state of Missouri "in the sense in which that word is used in the Constitution" and that blacks, whether free or enslaved, "had no rights that the white man was bound to respect" (*Dred Scott v. Sanford* 1857:454, 407).

The issue of defining national citizenship and citizenship for blacks was not confronted directly until the ratification of the Fourteenth Amendment to the Constitution in 1868. Section 1 of that amendment says, in part, that "all persons born or naturalized in the United States, and subject to the jurisdiction thereof, are citizens of the United States and of the State wherein they reside." Thus, the issue of the citizenship status of African Americans was resolved, and national citizenship was added to the Constitution. Yet the rights, privileges, and immunities granted to blacks by this amendment were illusionary, as is discussed later. (The ratification of the Fourteenth Amendment to the Constitution also modified the three-fifths provision in Article I, Section 2. The Fourteenth Amendment implied that blacks would be counted equally with whites for purposes of representation.)

Although the Fourteenth Amendment established the citizenship status of blacks, American Indian peoples were still not considered citizens. In *Cherokee Nation v. State of Georgia*, the Supreme Court had ruled that Indian tribes "are in a state of pupilage [a minor child under the care of a guardian], and the relationship between the Indian tribes and the United States government [is] likened to that of 'a ward to his guardian'" (1831:16). Based on this wardship status, Indian peoples were considered to be "domestic subjects" and were not entitled to be thought of as citizens. Thus, they could be denied civil, political, and economic rights because "the framers of our constitution had not the Indian tribes in view, when they opened the Courts of the union to controversies between a state or the citizens thereof" (*Cherokee Nation v. Georgia* 1831:16). In fact, the Supreme Court in *Elk v. Wilkins* (1884) refused to extend the right of citizenship conferred in the Fourteenth Amendment to Indian peoples. The decision said, in part:

> Indians born within the territorial limits of the United States, members of, and owing immediate allegiance to, one of the Indian tribes (an alien, though dependent, power), although in a geographical sense born in the United States, are no more "born in the United States and subject to the jurisdiction thereof," within the meaning of the first section of the Fourteenth

Amendment, than the children of subjects of any foreign government born within the domain of that government or the children born within the United States, of ambassadors or other public ministers of foreign nations (*Elk v. Wilkins* 1884:102).

The Court ended its decision by stating:

The plaintiff, not being a citizen of the United States under the Fourteenth Amendment of the Constitution, has been deprived of no right secured by the Fifteenth Amendment and cannot maintain this action (*Elk v. Wilkins* 1884:109).

Thus, Indian peoples were left in a status much like that of slaves prior to the Civil War—they were neither aliens nor citizens.

Citizenship came to Indians only in piecemeal fashion. In response to a Supreme Court ruling that Indian peoples who left their tribes voluntarily were not U.S. citizens, Congress passed the Dawes Act in 1887, which granted citizenship to those who received individual allotments of tribal land (a new procedure meant to destroy the tribes and make Indians private property owners) and to those who voluntarily left their tribe. Tribal Indian peoples remained noncitizens.

In 1901, Congress formally granted U.S. citizenship to the "five civilized tribes," originally of the Southeast—Cherokee, Chickasaw, Choctaw, Creek, and Seminole—who had been displaced to "Indian territory," centered in Oklahoma.[2] In 1919, citizenship was granted to American Indians who had served in the U.S. armed forces in World War I. It was not until the Indian Citizenship Act of 1924, however, that citizenship was conferred on all American Indian peoples.

Citizenship and Later Minorities: Latinos and Asians

Although citizenship denial was the most egregious in the cases of blacks and Indian peoples, an exclusion purposely crafted in the Constitution and upheld by the Supreme Court, other racial groups faced similar situations as they entered the United States. Citizenship for the various Latino groups—Mexicans, Puerto Ricans, and Cubans—came at different times and in different ways. In 1836, Anglos and dissident Mexicans in Texas revolted and seceded from Mexico, creating the Republic of Texas. Hostilities between

Texas and Mexico continued for nearly a decade until 1846 when the United States declared war on the Republic of Mexico. The Treaty of Guadalupe Hidalgo in 1848 officially ended the war, and Mexico ceded what are now the states of Arizona, New Mexico, California, Colorado, Texas, Nevada, Utah, Kansas, Oklahoma, and Wyoming to the United States. Mexican citizens living in the territories that were ceded who chose to stay on the land and live under U.S. rule had one month from the date the treaty took effect to state their preference either for retaining Mexican citizenship and living under U.S. rule or for becoming U.S. citizens. The treaty supposedly guaranteed Mexicans who decided to become U.S. citizens all the rights, protections, and guarantees of citizenship, but the reality was quite different. Problems with the citizenship status of Mexicans arose as early as 1849, when California, in trying to deal with blacks and Indians who were citizens of Mexico prior to the treaty and entitled to U.S. citizenship under the provisions of the treaty, decided that Mexicans were not citizens of the United States and that further action from Congress was necessary to confer citizenship (Griswold del Castillo 1990). The property rights of Mexicans also were unprotected. Boards were set up to determine the validity of Mexican land claims, routinely resulting in Mexicans losing their land to the Anglo newcomers. (The unfulfilled promises of the Treaty of Guadalupe Hidalgo were central to the Chicano movement, discussed in Chapter 2.)

Spain granted autonomy to the island of Puerto Rico in 1897, but when the Spanish-American War began in 1898, U.S. troops landed on the island. With the ratification of the Treaty of Paris in 1899, which ended the Spanish-American War, the United States annexed Puerto Rico. The 1900 Foraker Act made Puerto Rico an unincorporated U.S. territory with a presidentially appointed governor. Puerto Rico remained an American colony until 1952 when it became a commonwealth of the United States. Immediately after the U.S. acquisition, Puerto Ricans were in a political netherworld; they were not citizens of the United States nor of Spain nor of an independent nation. However, with the passage of the Jones Act in 1917, Puerto Ricans became citizens of the United States, although citizenship was conferred over the objections of the island's legislature (Hero 1992). Puerto Ricans residing on the island are subject to the military draft, when there is one, but do not pay U.S. income taxes and do not participate fully in federal social service programs (Moore and Pachon 1985). But Puerto Ricans who live on the mainland are not distinguished from other U.S. citizens for taxation and government assistance purposes.

U.S. involvement with Cuba can be traced to the Monroe Doctrine of 1823. In 1895, with the help of the United States, Cuba launched a war of independence against Spain. Intense U.S. involvement, as with its involvement with Puerto Rico, stems from the time of the Spanish-American War, after which Cuba achieved its independence from Spain although it was still under U.S. military rule. In 1901, Congress passed the Platt Amendment, granting Cuba conditional independence, with the United States reserving the right to intervene—militarily and otherwise—on "Cuba's behalf."

Although many think Cuban Americans first came to the United States after 1959, the 1870 U.S. Census indicates that just over 5,000 persons living in the United States had been born in Cuba (Boswell and Curtis 1983:39). In the 1860s and 1870s several Cuban cigar manufacturers relocated their operations to the United States, settling principally in Key West, Tampa, and New York City. However, the majority of Cubans arrived in the United States after 1959. Census data indicate that in 1960 there were approximately 124,500 Cubans, just over one-third of whom were second- or third-generation Americans. Just a decade later the Cuban population had increased to more than 560,000 persons, slightly over 78 percent of whom had been born in Cuba.

Little is known about the naturalization of the early Cuban immigrants to Florida, but until the 1980s 96 percent of the Cuban immigrants were considered to be white (Boswell and Curtis 1983:102). Thus, it is possible that they were also considered white under the naturalization acts and thus were eligible for citizenship. Cubans entering the United States after Castro's rise to power in 1959 generally enjoyed handsome financial support from the U.S. government and were encouraged to seek U.S. citizenship.

The citizenship status of Asian Americans—primarily the early Chinese and Japanese immigrants—although similar to the Latino case, also has close parallels with the legal status of blacks and Indians under the various naturalization acts. Two events—the Treaty of Guadalupe Hidalgo (1848) and the California gold rush—precipitated Chinese immigration to the United States, which began in 1848. With the annexation of California under the treaty, a plan was sent to Congress for expansion of the railroad to the Pacific coast. The plan proposed that Chinese laborers should be imported to build the transcontinental railroad as well as to cultivate the land in California. At the same time, gold was discovered in California, thus generating the need for both Mexican and Chinese miners who were seen as the best source of cheap labor. Consequently, the 1850s saw a substantial increase in the number of Chinese immigrants to the United States, principally, but not exclusively, to California. By 1870 there were 63,000 Chinese in the United States, 77 percent of whom lived in California (Takaki 1993:192–194).

At first the Chinese were welcomed because their labor was essential to the expansion into California and the development of the territory. But in 1850, the California legislature enacted, then quickly repealed, a foreign miners' tax designed to eliminate Mexican miners (Takaki 1993:194). In 1852, the legislature passed another foreign miners' tax, this one targeted at Chinese miners. This tax required that every foreign miner who did not wish to become a U.S. citizen pay a monthly fee of three dollars. "Even if they had wanted to, the Chinese could not have become citizens, for they had been rendered ineligible for citizenship by a 1790 federal law that reserved naturalized citizenship for 'white' persons" (Takaki 1993:195). The exclusion barred most Chinese from citizenship, but the interpretation of who was "white" was left to administrative officials. Thus, a small number of Chinese were able to be naturalized. The first Chinese applied for citizenship in 1854, another was naturalized in New York in 1873, and 13 applied for citizenship in California in 1876 (Gulick 1918:59).

But anti-Chinese and Chinese immigration antipathy and nativist sentiments were on the rise. President Rutherford B. Hayes warned Americans about the "Chinese problem," saying that "the present Chinese invasion . . . should be discouraged. Our experience in dealing with the weaker races—the Negroes and Indians . . . —is not encouraging. . . . I would consider with favor any suitable measures to discourage the Chinese from coming to our shores" (quoted in Takaki 1993:206). Acceding to anti-Chinese agitation and violence in the 1870s and 1880s, Congress passed the Chinese Exclusion Act in 1882, which reduced Chinese immigration to a trickle (Higham 1963:25; Takaki 1993:200). Additionally, part of the act mandated "that even those Chinese who might otherwise qualify should not be given citizenship privileges" (quoted in Gulick 1918:59). Section 14 of the Chinese Exclusion Act stated that "hereafter no State Court or Court of the United States shall admit Chinese to citizenship; and all laws in conflict with this act are hereby repealed" (quoted in Gulick 1918:59).

As a result of World War II and the participation of Chinese Americans in the war effort, in 1943 Congress repealed the Chinese exclusion laws and extended the right of naturalized citizenship to Chinese immigrants: "At last after almost one hundred years in America, Chinese immigrants could seek political membership in their adopted country" (Takaki 1993:387). Although Chinese immigrants were initially denied citizenship, their children who were born in the United States were considered U.S. citizens. The Supreme Court decided this issue in *United States v. Wong Kim Ark* in 1898 when it ruled that a child of Chinese immigrants was entitled to U.S. citizenship under the *jus soli* (by birth) clause of the Fourteenth Amendment. The Court found that the constitutional prescription of citizenship by birth superseded the Chinese Exclusion Act of 1882 (Ueda 1997).

The first known Japanese immigrants arrived in the United States in 1843, yet the need for labor on Hawaiian plantations in the mid–1860s precipitated the search for labor from Japan. (The United States officially acquired the Hawaiian Islands in 1898 as a territory.) The first Japanese contract workers arrived in Hawaii in 1868, and in 1885 the Japanese government officially allowed Japanese workers to migrate to Hawaii and to the U.S. mainland. Between 1885 and 1924, "200,000 [Japanese] left for Hawaii and 180,000 for the United States mainland" (Takaki 1993:247). On the mainland, Japanese were initially employed as migrant workers in agriculture, railroad construction, and canneries (Takaki 1993:267).

Eventually, the Japanese—primarily those in California—became farmers with extensive land holdings, and their success and increasing presence engendered great animosity. In 1908 the U.S. government pressured Japan to prohibit the emigration of Japanese laborers to the United States, and in 1913 the California legislature passed the California Land Act, which prohibited aliens—principally the Japanese—from owning and leasing land. Other states passed similar legislation. Drawing on the 1790 act, which limited naturalization to "white" persons, these restrictive alien land laws were based on the Japanese ineligibility to become naturalized U.S. citizens: "In 1922, the United States Supreme Court affirmed that Takao Ozawa, a Japanese immigrant, was not entitled to naturalized citizenship because he 'clearly' was 'not Caucasian'" (Takaki 1993:273). Moreover, in 1924 Congress passed the Immigration Quota Act—which was aimed specifically at the Japanese but also covered other Asians—that excluded all aliens who were ineligible for citizenship (those who were not "white," as stated in the 1790 and subsequent naturalization laws, or "African," as the naturalization laws were amended after the Civil War). Once again, however, although Japanese immigrants were denied citizenship, their children born in the United States were citizens. Only with the passage of the McCarran-Walter Act in 1952 were the racial restrictions contained in the 1790 Naturalization Act rescinded and Japanese immigrants allowed naturalization rights.

The Constitution and Black and Indian Suffrage

The Constitution left voting requirements to the individual states and did not specifically prohibit free blacks from exercising the franchise (Foner 1992:57). Moreover, the concepts of citizenship and voting were not linked in colonial and the postrevolutionary America (Kleppner 1990). Because the 13 original colonies were settled primarily by the British, it is not surprising that they adopted the British system of restricting the franchise to property owners. Voting qualifications varied from colony to colony and were based on criteria such as property ownership, status ("freeman"), race (white), gender (male), age, religion, and length of residence (Jarvis 1992:18). Although only Georgia and South Carolina adopted state constitutions that expressly limited voting to white males on the basis of race, voting restrictions based on race were soon instituted in other states as the number of black slaves increased following the introduction of slavery. At the time the Constitution was framed, "free black men could vote in some of the original states, including the southern one of North Carolina" (Davidson 1992:7).

As the black slave population increased in the South, white colonists became concerned about their ability to control slaves and prevent slave insurrections. Thus, numerous slave codes were introduced. As a result, free blacks in the South saw their political and social access restricted and eventually curtailed. Free blacks were forced to carry certificates of freedom or risk being captured and sold as slaves. In addition, "they could no longer vote (except in Tennessee until 1834 and North Carolina until 1835), hold public office, give testimony against whites, possess a firearm, buy liquor, assemble freely (except in a church supervised by whites), or immigrate to other states" (Jarvis 1992:19). Free blacks in the northern regions fared better and lived under less restrictive conditions, but they were regarded as inferior and undesirable, and their employment opportunities were limited. In some instances, northern jurisdictions prohibited their immigration to other regions through the threat of punishment or enslavement (Jarvis 1992:19). By the time of the Civil War, free blacks were denied suffrage everywhere in the United States except in New York and the New England states (except Connecticut).

Following the Civil War and in response to the southern states' refusal to extend suffrage to blacks, numerous actions were taken by the Radical Republican-dominated Congress. For example, the Civil Rights Act of 1866 "anticipated the Fourteenth Amendment by making United States citizens of all native-born people except untaxed Native Americans, and guaranteeing to all citizens regardless of race or previous servitude the right to enforce contracts, file lawsuits, testify in court, own property, and enjoy all benefits of law to which white citizens were entitled" (Jarvis 1992:25). However, neither these laws nor the Fourteenth Amendment explicitly prohibited racial discrimination in the area of voting. This prohibition was not achieved until the ratification of the Fifteenth Amendment in 1870, which states, "the right of citizens of the United States to vote shall not be denied or abridged by the United States or by any State on account of race, color, or previous condition of servitude."

Although in theory the Fifteenth Amendment provided a constitutionally protected guarantee of black male suffrage, resistance—often violent—by white southerners to black voting was evident. Although three Enforcement Acts (1870, 1871, and 1875) were passed in an attempt to put teeth into the amendment, white resistance was not overcome (Davidson 1992:10). Moreover, two Supreme Court decisions undercut the effectiveness of the Fourteenth and Fifteenth Amendments. In *United States v. Cruikshank* (1876), in a case involving white defendants who had killed approximately 100 blacks in a mob attack, the Supreme Court ruled that because these individuals were private actors and were not acting on behalf of the state, the Fourteenth and Fifteenth Amendments did not apply to them. Although it did not find the Enforcement Act of 1870 unconstitutional, the Court severely limited the act's application.

In the other decision, *United States v. Reese* (1876), in a case involving Kentucky election officials' refusal to accept the votes of a black person in a municipal election, the Court ruled that Congress could protect against interference only in congressional elections and not in state elections. Thus, Sections 3 and 4 of the Enforcement Act of 1870 were ruled unconstitutional because they went beyond the Fifteenth Amendment's prohibition against the denial of suffrage. The end of a national commitment to protect the suffrage and other constitutional rights of blacks came with

A group of bystanders views the body of Rubin Stacy, lynched by a white mob in Fort Lauderdale, Florida, July 19, 1935. (AP Photo: APA2817290)

the compromise of 1877 in which Rutherford B. Hayes, to gain the support of the southern states in the contested presidential elections of 1876, agreed to remove federal troops and protection from the former states of the Old Confederacy and then leave the South free to deal with "the Negro problem" as the states saw fit.

After the removal of federal protection, the southern states moved quickly to disenfranchise blacks. This disenfranchisement was achieved through a combination of structural discrimination (e.g., gerrymandering, annexations, at-large election systems, and appointive offices), violence, voting fraud, and eventually through disenfranchising conventions that rewrote state constitutions with clauses to prohibit blacks from voting or participating in politics. By the 1890s, blacks—primarily in the South but in some northern jurisdictions as well—had been legally and very effectively removed from the electoral process (Kousser 1992).

Additionally, in 1896 the Supreme Court, in *Plessy v. Ferguson*, upheld Louisiana's practice of racial discrimination, essentially declaring that separation of the races was allowable under the U.S. Constitution as long as the facilities were "equal." This reasoning became known as the **separate**

but equal doctrine. The end of the nineteenth century and the beginning of the twentieth century constituted the nadir of black political history (Logan 1954).

Although American Indians were the first "Americans," they were the last large group to be granted voting rights and citizenship (Sigler 1975:156). The ruling in *Elk v. Wilkins* (1884) that Indians were not citizens of the United States under the Fourteenth Amendment kept "all Indians unable to prove that they were born under United States jurisdiction from registering to vote" (McCool 1985:106). Moreover, because Indians were not made citizens until the Indian Citizenship Act of 1924, the Fifteenth Amendment, which extended the right to vote to all male citizens regardless of race, did not apply to Indians until that time.

Even after the conferring of citizenship, many states—including Arizona, New Mexico, and Utah—through their state constitutions continued to deny Indians the right to vote. These states argued that because Indians were in a "guardianship" relationship with the federal government and were subject to federal rather than state jurisdiction, Indian reservations, therefore, could not be considered part of the state in which they existed. Therefore, Indians were not state citizens and were not eligible to vote in state and local elections. Beginning in 1927, federal as well as state courts began to reject this argument, but many states continued to find mechanisms to deny Indians the right to vote. The twin issues of state residency and federal guardianship were used in a long series of court cases in various states in attempts to keep Indians from voting. Indians in Arizona, through a series of court challenges, won the right to vote in 1948, and Indians in New Mexico won their case shortly thereafter.

Challenges continued. For example, in 1956 the Utah state attorney general issued an opinion based on an 1897 state law "that withheld residency from anyone who lived on an 'Indian or military reservation' unless that person had previously established residency in an off-reservation Utah county" (McCool 1985:109). In effect, this ruling denied Utah Indians the right to vote. The Utah Supreme Court upheld the attorney general's interpretation of the law, so the state legislature had to amend state statutes to allow Indians to vote. In another case in 1962, a defeated non-Indian candidate in New Mexico challenged the validity of Indian voting rights, claiming Indians were not residents of the state. In this instance, the state Supreme Court upheld the right of Indians to vote (McCool 1985:109).

Structure of This Book

This chapter has articulated the dilemmas we address in this book. Furthermore, it shows that the roots of the first dilemma, the clear presence of racial inequality in a nation that promises equality, precede the founding of the current constitutional system. The remainder of the book elaborates on this dilemma and sets the stage for a consideration of the second dilemma, the choice between coalition or conflict as a strategy.

Chapter 2 provides a brief survey of some of the political resources and the status of each of the groups treated in this book. Several key variables—relative size and geographic concentration, socioeconomic status, degree of participation in a civil rights movement, and coverage by contemporary voting rights legislation—are highlighted to provide both comparable data and a context within which to discuss the contemporary political situations of racial and ethnic minorities, both as individual groups and comparatively. The chapter also discusses the importance of the Voting Rights Act of 1965 and its extensions for the ability of various racial and ethnic groups to gain elective office.

Chapter 3 explores the attitudes that members of racial and ethnic minority groups bring to the public policymaking process and the ways they choose to participate. The aspects of political participation we address are (1) perceptions of discrimination; (2) political ideology; (3) partisan identification; (4) voting behavior; and (5) interest group activities. For each of these areas, when applicable, class and gender differences are noted.

When a government chooses to undertake a purposive course of action in an effort to address a problem, that decision can be affected by whether members of racial and ethnic minority groups are present in policymaking positions. Furthermore, the effect of that decision is unlikely to be uniform across all racial and ethnic groups. Chapter 4 employs a sequential model of the policymaking process to explore the ways members of racial and ethnic minority groups can affect what government does and does not do and what difference these policies make for these groups. The representation of these groups within policymaking institutions offers another perspective on the continuing manifestation of the first dilemma. Analysis of the efforts made to achieve policy goals should provide evidence to help articulate a response to the second dilemma.

Chapter 5 uses the question posed by Rodney King at his first postverdict news conference, which we have appropriated for the title of this book, in an attempt to address squarely the second dilemma. This chapter focuses on the increasing tensions among minority groups and between minority groups and the majority. What options are available to members of minority groups within the American political system, and what are the consequences of pursuing each of these options? The bulk of the discussion compares the viable alternatives of coalition and competition and the arguments, both theoretical and practical, for and against each position. The consequences for both the nation and minority groups of following either track are explored. The last chapter discusses the future of American minority groups' politics and the authors' perspective on the resolution of the dilemmas.

Conclusion

This chapter shows that certain groups have been treated differently in our legal system based on their race or ethnicity. Thus, who is identified as being a member of one of these groups has had important legal implications, at times extending so far as to classify individuals as property rather than as citizens and to impose restrictions upon whom one could marry. This unequal treatment began before the current Constitution was adopted, with the nation's original minorities—blacks and American Indians. The treatment was applied as other racial and ethnic minorities—Latinos and Asians—immigrated, and it continues despite a common rhetoric of equality.

2

....

Resources and Status of America's Racial Minorities

In January 2001, three white teenagers drove into downtown Anchorage specifically to shoot paintballs at Native Alaskans. The youths made a videotape of the drive-by shootings. They shot some of the victims in the face and spewed racial epithets at their victims. A 20-year-old man was sentenced to six months in jail, fined $6,000, and ordered to perform 300 hours of community service. Similar attacks occurred in November 2003 on two Alaska Native women. In one instance, a woman was repeatedly shot with paintballs as the three or four white men in the car shouted "Natives suck" and "Natives should die."

—Anchorage, Alaska, January 14, 2001,
and November 4, 2003

THE FACT THAT ALL AMERICAN racial and ethnic minority groups have not been treated according to the rhetoric of the nation's founding principles has resulted in differences in these groups' contemporary political status based on differential resources, histories of political activism, and levels of access to political participation. The size, economic well-being, and geographic concentration of the group's population; the extent to which the group has participated in a civil rights movement; and the amount of protection that is provided under contemporary voting rights law all affect the way members of each of the groups will be treated within the American polity, what kind of role members of the group will be expected to play in the political system, and what kind of strategy—cooperation or conflict—will be chosen. A consideration of these factors identifies the commonalities and the differences among the various groups that are often lumped together under the rubric "minority group politics."

Population Size, Socioeconomic Status, and Concentration

The number of people and where they are located are important pieces of data in the U.S. political system. The population of a certain location affects important factors such as the number of members each state will have in the U.S. House of Representatives, the way electoral districts will be drawn, the number of votes each state will have in the Electoral College to choose the president, and the way some government resources will be distributed. The latest population surveys (which vary in date by group) provide a detailed picture of the populations with which we are concerned. Tables 2.1, 2.2, and 2.3 present these data and provide basic information about the populations of each group, the groups' age structures, and some indicators of **socioeconomic status**—the general social and economic conditions of these groups—a variable that is related to political participation. In addition, we are able to see the variations that exist within the Latino and Asian communities.

31

TABLE 2.1   Selected Characteristics of the Black, Asian American, American Indian, and Non-Latino White Populations, Latest Estimates

	Black (2000 Census)[a]	Asian American (2000 Census)[a]	American Indian (2000 Census)[a]	Non-Latino Whites (2000 Census)[a]
Population (in thousands)	33,677[b]	11,604[b]	1,863[b]	191,769[b]
% of Total U.S. Pop.	11.9[b]	4.1[b]	0.7[b]	67.8[b]
Median Age (Yrs.)	30.2	32.7	28.0	38.6
% > 18 Yrs. Old	68.6	75.9	66.1	77.9
% H.S. Grad (of Pop. > 25 Yrs.)	72.3	80.4	70.9	85.5
% Unemployed (of Pop. > 16 Yrs. Old)	6.9	3.2	7.5	2.8
Males	7.3	3.5	8.4	3.1
Females	6.4	3.0	6.6	2.4
Median Family Income (In 2003 dollars, except Am. Indian in 1999 dollars)	$34,369[b]	$63,251[b]	$33,144	$59,937[b]
% Owning Home	46.6	53.3	57.5	72.5
% Living in Poverty	23.7[b]	10.7[b]	23.2[b]	8.0[b]

[a] All figures reflect 2000 census figures unless noted.
[b] These figures reflect 2003 data from the American Community Survey and Current Population Survey.
Sources: U.S. Bureau of the Census, "Age: 2000" (October 2001); U.S. Bureau of the Census, "Educational Attainment: 2000" (August 2003); Unemployment (found or computed from): U.S. Bureau of the Census, "Summary File 3, 2000," Tables, P150B, P150C, P150D, P150I, P155B, P155C, P155D, P159B, 159C, 159D, 159I (September 25, 2002), http://factfinder.census.gov/home/en/sf3.html (NB: The data in this Sample File are created from a 1 in 6 weighted sample to reflect the entire population and are not representative of 100% data); U.S. Bureau of the Census, "Summary File 4, 2000," Custom Table Creation (July 30, 2003), http://factfinder.census.gov/home/en/sf4.html; U.S. Bureau of the Census, American Community Survey, 2003 Data Profile, "Table 1. General Demographic Characteristics" (September 9, 2004); http://www.census.gov/acs/www/Products/Profiles/Single/2003/ACS/Tabular/010/01000US; U.S. Bureau of the Census, Current Population Survey, "2004 Annual Social and Economic Supplement," Table FINC-02 (June 25, 2004), http://ferret.bls.census.gov/macro/032004/faminc/toc.htm; U.S. Bureau of the Census, "Income, Poverty, and Health Insurance Coverage in the United States: 2003," Table 4, p. 12 (August 2004).

Despite the growth in the populations of the various minority groups, non-Latino whites constitute a little more than two-thirds of the nation's population. Latinos, as of the 2000 Census, are the next largest single group, composing approximately one-eighth of the nation's population, although blacks are slightly less than one-eighth of the population as well.

TABLE 2.2   Selected Characteristics of the Latino Population and Selected Subgroups, 2000[a]

	Puerto Rican	Mexican	Cuban	Total Latinos[#]
Population (in thousands)	3,718[b]	25,288[b]	1,364[b]	39,195[b]
% of Total U.S. Population	1.3[b]	8.9[b]	0.5[b]	12.5[b]
% of Total U.S. Latino Pop.	9.5[b]	64.5[b]	3.5[b]	—
Median Age (Yrs.)	27.7	24.4	40.3	26.0
% > 18 Yrs. Old	66.4	62.9	81.7	65.2
% H.S. Grad (of Pop. ≥ 25 Yrs.)	63.3	45.8	62.9	52.4
% Unemployed (of Pop. ≥ 16 Yrs.)	6.3	5.7	4.0	5.7
Males	6.7	5.8	4.0	5.7
Females	6.0	5.6	4.0	5.6
Median Family Income (in dollars)	$32,791	$33,516	$42,642	$34,272[b]
% Living in Poverty	25.1	23.0	14.2	21.9[b]
% Owning Home	34.3	48.4	57.6	45.7
% of Total Population Noncitizens	0.8	32.3	27.1	29.0

[#]Total Latino includes data on Central/South Americans and "Other Latinos."
[a] U.S. Bureau of the Census, "Summary File 4, 2000," Custom Table Creation (July 30, 2003), http://factfinder.census.gov/home/en/sf4.html.
[b] These figures reflect 2003 data from the American Community Survey and Current Population Survey.
Sources: U.S. Bureau of the Census, American Community Survey, 2003 Data Profile, "Table 1. General Demographic Characteristics" (September 9, 2004), http://www.census.gov/acs/www/Products/Profiles/Single/2003/ACS/Tabular/010/01000US; U.S. Bureau of the Census, Current Population Survey, "2004 Annual Social and Economic Supplement," Table FINC-02 (June 25, 2004), http://ferret.bls.census.gov/macro/032004/faminc/toc.htm; U.S. Bureau of the Census, "Income, Poverty, and Health Insurance Coverage in the United States: 2003,"Table 4, p. 12 (August 2004).

Latino attainment of the status of the nation's largest racial/ethnic minority has occurred over a relatively short period of time—increasing 63 percent between 1970 and 1980, 53 percent between 1980 and 1990, and 58 percent between 1990 and 2000. Thus, in any political issue in which raw population counts matter, from a national perspective whites will clearly maintain an upper hand for the foreseeable future. Even with rapid Latino population growth, and with Latinos projected to be the primary component of national population growth for the next century, Latinos are

TABLE 2.3   Selected Characteristics of Selected Asian American Population Subgroups, 2000[a]

	Chinese	Japanese	Korean	Filipino	Asian Indian	Vietnamese
Population (in thousands)	2,763[b]	855[b]	1,212[b]	2,104[b]	2,227[b]	1,291[b]
% of Total U.S. Population	1.0[b]	0.3[b]	0.4[b]	0.7[b]	0.8[b]	0.5[b]
Median age (in years)	35.5	42.6	32.7	35.5	30.3	30.5
% age 18 and older	78.6	87.9	75.7	77.9	75.2	73.1
% H.S. graduates (of population ≥ 25 Yrs.)	77.0	91.1	86.3	87.3	86.7	61.9
% Unemployed (of pop. ≥ 16 Yrs.)	2.8	2.1	3.2	3.4	3.3	3.5
Males	3.0	2.5	3.5	4.1	3.1	4.0
Females	2.6	1.9	3.0	2.9	3.6	3.1
Median Family Income (in dollars)	$60,058	$70,849	$47,624	$65,189	$70,708	$47,103
% Living in poverty	13.2	9.5	14.4	6.2	9.6	15.8
% Owning Home	58.4	60.8	40.1	60.0	46.9	53.2
% of Total Population Noncitizens	33.3	29.4	38.2	26.1	45.8	32.1

[a] U.S. Bureau of the Census, "Summary File 4, 2000" Custom Table Creation (July 30, 2003), http://factfinder.census.gov/home/en/sf4.html.
[b] These figures reflect 2003 data from the American Community Survey and Current Population Survey.
Sources: Population Data: U.S. Bureau of the Census, American Community Survey, 2003 Data Profile, "Table 1. General Demographic Characteristics," (September 9, 2004), http://www.census.gov/acs/www/Products/Profiles/Single/2003/ACS/Tabular/010/01000US.

predicted still to be a clear minority—25 percent of the population by 2050, and 33 percent of the population by the turn of the next century (Population Projection Program 2000).

At the same time the Latino population has been growing, it has been diversifying. Immigration from Central and South America and the Caribbean has reduced the proportion of Latinos of Mexican, Puerto Rican, and Cuban origins among Latinos, and Colombians, Dominicans, Ecuadorians, Guatemalans, Salvadorans, and those from other countries now comprise more than one-quarter of the Latino population in the United States (Therrien and Ramirez 2001).

Electoral politics, however, depends not just on the number of bodies but also on the number of those who vote. The one consistent legal restriction on the right to vote is age. In no U.S. jurisdiction can one vote until one is 18 years old. If each group's age distribution is approximately the same, the translation of the potential power of numbers into the actual power of votes becomes an issue of mobilization. But as the tables show, there are broad variations in age structures. In general, the non-Latino white population is older than the other groups, and a higher proportion of its population is over age 18. The only exceptions to this pattern are the Cubans, Chinese, and Japanese—who cumulatively account for only about 1.8 percent of the nation's population. Thus, whites not only continue to constitute the overwhelming majority of the population nationwide, but they also maintain an advantage over most other racial and ethnic groups in the proportion of their population that is old enough to vote. Minority groups' numerical disadvantage is therefore exacerbated by the relative age distributions.

Beyond the numbers and age structure, socioeconomic status has been found to be important in determining levels of participation. Simply put, people who fare better economically have a greater stake in the system and are more likely to be able to afford the time to participate in politics, to engage in activities that stimulate political participation, and to have peers who are politically active. If one is struggling to subsist, political participation—even the simple act of voting—may be perceived as a luxury, a not very profitable investment of one's time and energy.

Tables 2.1, 2.2, and 2.3 also present some selected indicators of socioeconomic status taken from the latest data released by the U.S. Census Bureau. These indicators reflect a number of different perspectives on such status, and the picture that emerges from these data is clear. Only Asian Americans approximate the educational attainment levels of whites, and as Table 2.3 shows, there is significant variation within the Asian American community. Blacks are the next closest group, but even they only come within 13 percentage points of whites' educational attainment levels.

Only Asian Americans somewhat approach whites' unemployment levels. The rate for Japanese is lower, and the rate for Chinese is equal to that for whites, but the rate for other Asian American groups is higher than that for whites. The rates for other groups, however, are noticeably higher than the rate for whites. Thus, it should not be surprising that the median white family enjoys at least a $17,000 advantage over any other group, with the exception of Asian Americans. Asian Americans report a median family income almost $3,314 higher than that of whites. This difference, however, is less than the $5,327 difference measured in the original 2000 Census.

In spite of the family income advantage enjoyed by Asian Americans, a smaller proportion of whites live below the poverty line than any other major group. Asians are about one-third more likely, Cubans are slightly more than twice as likely, and each of the other groups is three or four times as likely as whites to live in poverty. Whites clearly overshadow all of the other groups when we look at homeownership. White homeownership is 1.5 times the rate of black homeownership, 1.3 times the rate of Asian American homeownership, 1.26 times the rate of American Indian homeownership, and 1.59 times the rate of homeownership for Latinos in general. Clearly, by whatever measure one wants to use, the numerical and age distribution disadvantages of racial and ethnic minority groups in the United States are generally compounded by the lack of resources that may be used to compensate for these disadvantages. Only Asian Americans and Cubans have some apparent equity with or advantage over whites on some of the variables, but there are several areas of disadvantage. Further, Asian Americans and Cubans make up only 4.1 and 0.5 percent of the U.S. population, respectively. Additionally, for Latinos and Asian Americans the high proportion of noncitizens in the various subpopulations reduces their ability to use what resources they may have available to them.

Despite these apparently cumulative disadvantages, there are clearly examples of each of these communities mobilizing for political success. How is this possible? The answer lies in looking lower than the national level. Just as the population figures must be considered in light of age structure and socioeconomic resources, we must also look at the way these groups' populations are distributed geographically. Although the figures suggest that minority groups are certain to be overwhelmed in any type of national contest, if former U.S. House Speaker "Tip" O'Neill's dictum "all politics is local" is correct, we should be looking at the subnational level.

Maps 2.1 through 2.4 report the concentration by county within the United States of each of the groups considered here. These maps confirm that each of the minority groups has very different geographic distribution patterns and that areas exist in which each of the "minorities" is either a majority or has the potential to be an important political player.

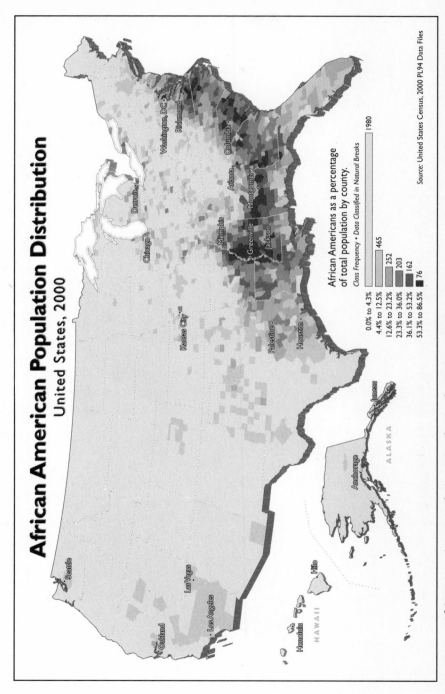

African American Population Distribution
United States, 2000

Washington, DC
Richmond
Columbia
Atlanta
Montgomery
Detroit
Memphis
Greenville
Jackson
Chicago
Kansas City
Palestine
Houston
Seattle
Las Vegas
Oakland
Los Angeles
Juneau
Anchorage
ALASKA
Hilo
Honolulu
HAWAII

African Americans as a percentage of total population by county.
Class Frequency • Data Classified in Natural Breaks

0.0% to 4.3%		1980
4.4% to 12.5%		465
12.6% to 23.2%		252
23.3% to 36.0%		203
36.1% to 53.2%		162
53.3% to 86.5%		76

Source: United States Census, 2000 PL94 Data Files

MAP 2.1   African American Population Distribution by County, 2000

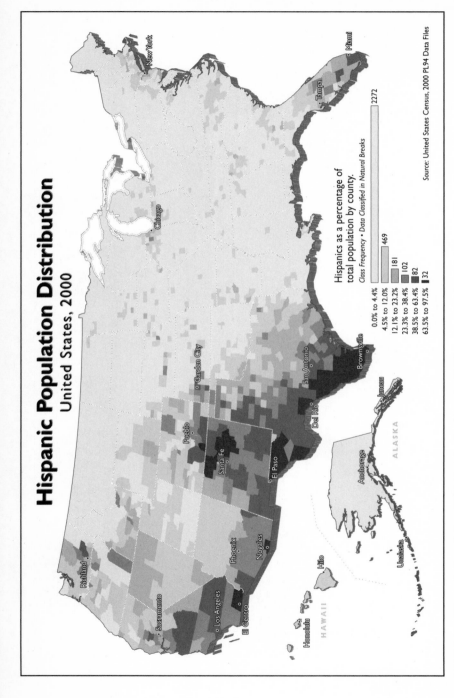

MAP 2.2 Hispanic Population Distribution by County, 2000

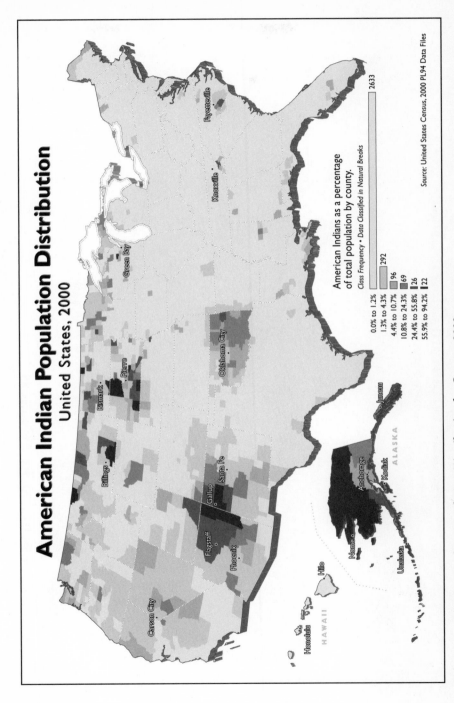

American Indian Population Distribution
United States, 2000

American Indians as a percentage of total population by county.

Class Frequency • Data Classified in Natural Breaks

0.0% to 1.2%	2633
1.3% to 4.3%	292
4.4% to 10.7%	96
10.8% to 24.3%	69
24.4% to 55.8%	26
55.9% to 94.2%	22

Source: United States Census, 2000 PL94 Data Files

Fayetteville

Knoxville

Green Bay

Bismarck   Pierre

Oklahoma City

Billings

Santa Fe

Gallup

Flagstaff

Phoenix

Carson City

Juneau

ALASKA

Anchorage   Kodiak

Nome

Unalaska

Honolulu   Hilo

HAWAII

MAP 2.3   American Indian Population Distribution by County, 2000

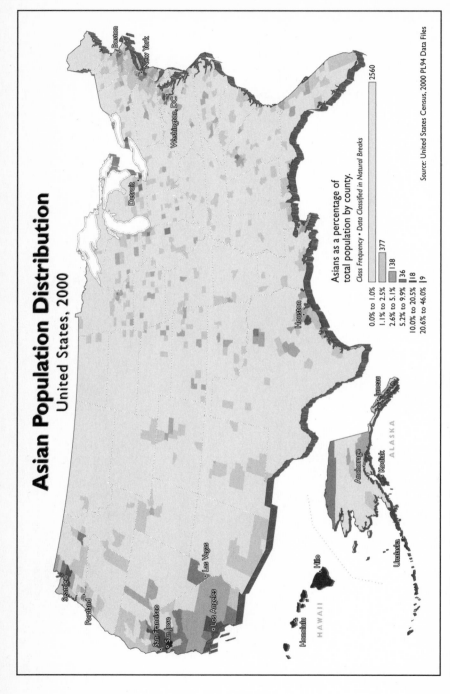

MAP 2.4   Asian Population Distribution by County, 2000

For each of the groups, on a separate map, we have identified areas in which it is totally or virtually nonexistent (because the maps use natural breaks in the population, the scales differ for each group, but <5 percent of the population for each group would be indicative); in which the group is small but represents more than a "token" presence (ranges from 5 percent for Asians to <25 percent for blacks, Indians, and Latinos); in which the proportion is sufficient to be perceived as a potential ally or threat in electoral politics (25 percent–50 percent for all groups); in which a "minority majority" exists in population if not in voting-age population (50 percent–80 percent for blacks, Indians, and Latinos); and in which overwhelming minority majorities are found (>80 percent for blacks, Indians, and Latinos). Because our data are aggregated at the county level, it is possible and even likely that subcounty-level jurisdictions (e.g., cities, school districts) exist in which minorities may constitute majorities but do not appear on our maps. Likewise, there are areas within what appear on our maps as heavily minority that maintain a majority white population. Still, these maps give us some sense of where minority group members are most likely to be found in our nation and where potential minority group political power exists.

Map 2.1 reveals that the African American population is concentrated in a crescent that runs from Maryland down the Atlantic seaboard across the Deep South to east Texas. The heaviest concentrations of black population are found in the traditional "Black Belt," where blacks were concentrated during the days of slavery. The overwhelmingly black counties in the nation are found in rural Alabama and Mississippi. There are, however, more than token populations of blacks scattered throughout most U.S. regions, with the exception of the upper Great Plains. Much of the non-South concentration of blacks consists of residents in predominantly black central cities ringed by "whiter" suburbs; therefore, the county populations depicted here do not adequately reveal the black concentration.

Map 2.2 shows a similar pattern for Hispanics but in a different area of the country. The Hispanic crescent runs along the United States-Mexico border from the Rio Grande Valley in south Texas through New Mexico and Arizona and into southern California. An appendage of this crescent juts up through New Mexico into southern Colorado, and separate pockets of significant concentrations appear in central Washington state. The overwhelmingly Hispanic counties in the nation are found along the Rio Grande in south Texas and in northern New Mexico. The only significant

Hispanic concentrations east of Texas are found in urban areas, particularly around New York City, and in south Florida. This pattern reflects the different settlement patterns of the three major Latino groups. Although Hispanics of different origins are found in each of the three major areas of concentration, in general Mexican Americans are concentrated in the southwestern states that were added after the Mexican War, Puerto Ricans are concentrated in the New York metropolitan area, and Cubans are concentrated around Miami. Indeed, a majority of Cuban Americans in the United States live in Dade County, Florida. Of particular note is the increasing numbers of Latinos in such states as Iowa, North Carolina, and Alabama. These are states that had extremely small Latino populations in the 1990 Census, but because of increased Latino immigration coupled with jobs in the poultry, meat-packing, and farming industries are finding significant increases in their Latino population as demonstrated by the 2000 Census. This has also resulted in a dispersion of the Hispanic population. In 1990, the Hispanic population topped 5 percent in only 15 states and were the largest minority group in 16 of the 50 states. The 2000 Census reveals that in 23 states, Hispanics exceed 5 percent of the population and are the largest resident minority group.

The distribution of the American Indian population, shown in Map 2.3, reflects the effects of the group's push westward. Although there are pockets of Indian concentration in the eastern states, the areas of greatest concentration are found in the Great Plains and westward. This map shows the continuing effects of putting Indians on reservations in rural areas where whites showed little demand for the land. Because of the numbers, however, the map hides the fact that over one-half of American Indians live in metropolitan or suburban areas. Table 2.4 shows the populations of the five largest American Indian tribes and the states in which they are primarily concentrated. Also listed are the states with the highest number of American Indians as a proportion of the state population. Cherokees, concentrated largely in Oklahoma, are the largest tribe, accounting for 19 percent of all American Indians. The Navajo, whose nation occupies the corners of Arizona, New Mexico, Colorado, and Utah, are concentrated in Arizona and New Mexico and are the second largest, with 11.6 percent of the total American Indian population. Alaska has the highest proportion of American Indians (including Eskimos and Aleuts) of any of the U.S. states—16.4 percent of its total population. New Mexico and South Dakota are next, with 9.5 and 8.2 percent of their populations being American Indians.

TABLE 2.4 Population Size and Percent of Five Largest American Indian Tribes and States of Primary Concentration[a], States with American Indians as Highest Percentage of Population[b], and States with Largest Number of American Indians[b], 1999

Total All American Indian Tribes (1990)	1,937,391	% of Total	States of Primary Concentration
Cherokee	369,035	19.0	Oklahoma, California
Navajo	225,298	11.6	Arizona, New Mexico
Sioux	107,321	5.5	South Dakota
Chippewa	105,988	5.5	Wisconsin, Minnesota, Michigan, North Dakota
Choctaw	86,231	4.5	Oklahoma, Texas, California

States with Highest Percentage of Population (1999)	% of State Pop.	Ten States With Largest Number of Indians (1999)	Size of Pop.
Alaska	16.4	California	313,642
New Mexico	9.5	Oklahoma	262,581
South Dakota	8.2	Arizona	261,168
Oklahoma	7.8	New Mexico	165,944
Montana	6.5	Washington	104,819
Arizona	5.5	Alaska	101,352
North Dakota	4.8	North Carolina	99,277
Wyoming	2.3	Texas	97,412
Washington	1.8	New York	76,755
Nevada	1.8	Florida	60,358

Sources: [a] U.S. Bureau of the Census (August 1995), Table 1; www.census.gov/population/socdemo/race/ indian/ailang1.txt; U.S. Bureau of the Census, "Characteristics of American Indians by Tribe and Language, 1990" CP-3-7, Table 1.
[b] "States Ranked by American Indian and Alaska Native Population, July 1, 1999," www.census.gov/ population/estimates/state/rank/aiea.txt.

Finally, Map 2.4 illustrates the intense concentration of the Asian American population. Except for some pockets in eastern urban areas and areas just outside Chicago and Houston, Asian Americans are concentrated in the Pacific coast states, particularly in California and Hawaii.

County-level data obscure the fact that blacks, Latinos, and Asian Americans are concentrated in urban areas. An overwhelming 95 percent of Asian Americans, 82 percent of Latinos, and 86 percent of blacks reside in urban areas compared to approximately 77 percent of the non-Latino

TABLE 2.5   Cities with the Largest American Indian Population, 1990

City	Size of Population
Los Angeles, CA	87,500
Tulsa, OK	48,000
New York, NY	46,000
Oklahoma City, OK	45,700
San Francisco, CA	40,800
Phoenix, AZ	38,000
Seattle/Tacoma, WA	32,000
Minneapolis/St. Paul, MN	24,000
Tucson, AZ	20,000
San Diego, CA	20,000

Source: Arlene Hirschfelder and Martha Kreipe de Montaño, *The Native American Almanac: A Portrait of Native America Today* (New York: Prentice-Hall General Reference, 1993), p. 28.

white population (U.S. Bureau of the Census 1994; 1996). Asian Americans are the most urban of any racial group (Barringer, Gardner, and Levin 1993). In 1940, only 5 percent of American Indians lived in urban areas. In the 1950s, the federal government instituted a program to relocate reservation Indians to urban centers. The Bureau of Indian Affairs (BIA) offered employment assistance to Indians who would voluntarily leave their reservations and relocate in urban communities where job opportunities were more plentiful. The Voluntary Relocation Program, renamed the Employment Assistance Program in 1954, provided a one-way bus ticket, temporary low-cost housing, and new clothing to Indians willing to relocate. As a result of this program, in 1990, 51 percent of American Indians lived in urban areas (Hirschfelder and de Montaño 1993). Table 2.5 shows the ten cities with the largest American Indian populations as of 1990; the 2000 American Indian census data have not been released at this point. Los Angeles heads the list, with a little less than twice the number of the next city, Tulsa, Oklahoma, which has the second largest number.

Historically, cities have been magnets for new immigrants, offering greater employment prospects than rural areas, as well as established immigrant communities into which newcomers can integrate. Between the 1860s (the Civil War) and World War I, the populations of major U.S. cities swelled as Europeans from Scotland, Ireland, Germany, and England—and later, southern and eastern Europeans, such as Poles, Czechs, Slovaks, Greeks, and Russian Jews—immigrated and settled en masse in these urban areas (Lineberry and Sharkansky 1978). During this period, early Asian immigrants settled primarily in cities on the West Coast, particularly in California. More recently, Asians, Latinos, and the overwhelming majority of other newcomers have continued this pattern of predominantly urban settlement. As a result, U.S. cities today have large populations of these immigrant groups.

However, it was not only immigrants who were drawn to cities by the promise of greater economic opportunity. Large numbers of native blacks, Latinos, and Asians also migrated to urban areas in search of economic and political advancement. Between 1910 and 1930, nearly one million blacks—one-tenth of the black population in the South—moved to cities in the North (Judd 1979). The migration of blacks to northeastern states was followed by another black migration to selected manufacturing centers of the Midwest, which continued into the post–World War II era. Many of these migrants were seeking increased economic opportunities as well as escape from the harsh conditions of segregation and racial discrimination in the South. By 1960, socioeconomic trends had resulted in a concentration of blacks in most of the nation's urban centers outside the South (Rose 1971). Coupled with this migration of blacks and other racial minorities into the cities was the exit of a sizable number of whites to the newer suburbs surrounding the cities.

Yet urban centers were not the havens of opportunity that immigrants and migrants had envisioned. Blacks, Latinos, and Asians routinely encountered racial discrimination in employment and housing. Many cities enacted racial zoning ordinances to ensure that racial minorities would be confined to "separate cities" within the larger city, making it virtually impossible for these groups to move out of these areas (Silver and Moeser 1995; Sugrue 1996). Lenders, real estate agents, school boards, city governments, and the federal government, among other individuals and institutions, participated in segregating blacks, Latinos, and Asians not only from whites but from each other. Los Angeles is an example of the racial segregation present in many U.S. cities. Map 2.5 shows the racial and ethnic geographic distribution of blacks, Latinos, and Asians in the city and county of Los Angeles. Yet in many cities the concentrations of minority populations in certain areas could be used by these groups as powerful political and economic resources. How well have these population resources been mobilized? We now turn to this question.

46

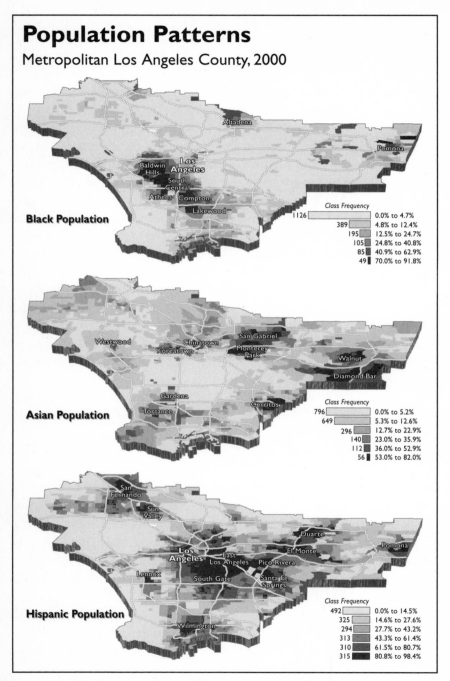

MAP 2.5   Population Patterns, Metropolitan Los Angeles County, 2000

Participation in a Civil Rights Movement

With the level of resources just described, even without a knowledge of the history depicted in this text in the timelines, one would guess that these minority groups are at a disadvantage in the political system. They fit under the rubric "**dominated groups**"—groups that have generally been excluded from participation in the decisionmaking process by which society's benefits are distributed. "Because of this exclusion, dominated groups at different times attempt to change their situation of powerlessness by engaging in nontraditional and usually nonlegitimized struggles with power holders" (Morris 1984:282). These overt efforts by groups to empower themselves constitute **social movements.**

Certain prerequisites appear necessary for a social movement to have a chance to enhance the group's power. First, successful social movements generally tap a reservoir of social organizations for experienced leaders, potential followers, communication networks, money, and labor. The ability to draw from preexisting organizations minimizes start-up costs and provides stability in the early, tenuous days when the movement is vulnerable to a serious countereffort by the dominant group.

Second, successful social movements require catalytic leadership—social activists who create or recognize opportunities to protest the groups' subordinate status. Furthermore, they must be able to organize and motivate people to engage in the effort over what may be an extended period of time.

The movement will be stronger if these two prerequisites are combined—that is, if the leadership is taken from preexisting organizations. These organizations have already demonstrated their ability to raise money and to organize people sufficiently that, at the least, they still exist. If the leadership arises from such organizations, the task becomes one of redirecting energies toward a new goal rather than of having to create an entirely new organization.

Third, successful movements tap outside resources. They elicit money and personnel from the environment that is not immediately affected by their struggle. These resources, although they may be sporadic and may come with strings attached, can be valuable in sustaining the movement and in expanding the scope of conflict. As part of a dominated group, people active in social movements have little to lose by getting others involved. The existing social, political, and economic decisionmaking apparatus does not yield positive results for them. They see change—any change—as likely to yield an improvement.

Finally, the social movement must have a plan—a set of tactics and an overall strategy it can use to confront the existing power structure. An effective set of tactics and strategies will disrupt the existing order; educate others about inequities, injustices, and civil wrongs; provide some sense of hope or efficacy for movement participants; and push the system—if at times imperceptibly—toward change.

Each of the groups considered in this book has participated to some extent in a social movement in an attempt to improve its situation. But the level, scope, and forms of activity have varied across groups. We now discuss the movements of the respective groups.

The Black Civil Rights Movement

The black civil rights movement of the 1950s and 1960s is the best-known and most studied of such movements, and in many ways it has served as a model for other groups. As with most movements, it was not one overall movement led from the top but instead constituted a collection of local movements that when added together produced massive social change. In recognition of the localized nature of the black civil rights movement, this section examines two small but vital parts of this movement as illustrations of the way it operated and what it was and was not able to achieve.

Baton Rouge.   The Baton Rouge bus boycott, which began on June 19, 1953, is often used as the starting point of the modern black civil rights movement. The boycott sought to have the city enforce its ordinance allowing black riders to be seated in city buses on a first-come, first-served basis—in essence, to force the city to make reality match rhetoric. The city refused to discipline drivers who failed to enforce the ordinance, so Reverend T. J. Jemison, minister of Mt. Zion Baptist Church—the city's largest black church—broadcast a radio appeal for blacks to boycott the city bus system.

The United Defense League (UDL) was formed to direct the mass boycott. This confederation of organizations held mass rallies, which drew up to three thousand people, each of the seven nights of the boycott. A move-

Hundreds of black youths are arrested after civil rights demonstrations in Selma, Alabama, in 1965. (Photo courtesy of UPI: Bettman)

ment "police department" was organized to patrol the black community and to provide security for movement leaders. A free car pool was organized with volunteer drivers to help boycotting blacks get to and from work. Even the black community's drunks and winos were organized to "open up the car doors of movement participants as they arrived" at the mass meetings (Jemison, quoted in Morris 1984:19).

Such an effort, of course, is not free of cost. Reverend Jemison asked for and received permission to redirect $650 he had been given for a business trip to help support the boycott. Following his example, his church gave an additional $1,500 to the effort. Other churches in the community followed, donating $3,800 to give the movement its initial capital. The nightly mass meetings provided an opportunity to collect operating expenses. As a result, all of the volunteer drivers' expenses were covered, and the expenses of the movement's police department, as well as the costs of miscellaneous goods and services necessary to run the boycott, were paid as they were incurred.

The dominant white power structure in Baton Rouge quickly offered a compromise, reserving only the two front side seats for whites and the long bench seat in the rear of the bus for blacks and leaving all other seats open on a first-come, first-served basis. After much debate, and with the approval of a mass meeting of eight thousand blacks, on June 25, 1953, Reverend Jemison announced the end of the boycott and the dismantling of the free car pool.

Although the subsequent Montgomery bus boycott became more famous, probably because the recalcitrance of the white power structure there resulted in a more extended and complex effort, the Baton Rouge boycott is instructive. First, this boycott drew on the black churches for the masses of people needed to implement and carry out the boycott, communications networks, leadership, and money. But the successful operation of the boycott also necessitated the creation of an umbrella organization. Without the UDL, there was too much danger that the purposes of the individual churches would have superseded those of the movement.

Second, in Jemison the movement had an educated, articulate leader who had the ability to recognize the potential for effective social action and to organize and motivate people to take advantage of that opportunity. In a pattern that was repeated with Dr. Martin Luther King Jr. in Montgomery, Reverend Jemison was a relative newcomer to Baton Rouge and was unencumbered by any history of personal or organizational conflicts with other potential leaders or by any residual level of distrust.

Third, in the Baton Rouge movement the movement leader was an insider in an existing social organization—the largest black church in town—whose resources the movement needed to tap. The advantage this gave the movement was best exemplified by the ease with which Jemison redirected the $650 from the canceled business trip to the movement coffers. His dual status as both a movement and a church leader placed him in a unique position to make an almost effortless, yet vitally important, contribution to the initiation of the movement.

Fourth, there is limited evidence that external resources were tapped (Jemison reported that "a few whites" contributed; see Morris 1984:23), but the brevity of the boycott made these resources less necessary than would have been the case in a prolonged effort. It is important to note, however, that if the movement had been dependent on external resources, it is doubtful that they could have been amassed quickly enough to allow the leadership to mobilize against this grievance.

Finally, the tactic chosen in this case—an economic boycott—was well suited for its task of disrupting the status quo. It allowed—in fact, re-

quired—the concerted effort of the masses, giving them a feeling of solidarity while simultaneously inflicting great financial losses on the bus
company. This tactic demonstrated the economic clout of the black community to both whites and blacks and also served to broaden the conflict
and perhaps to recruit some unwilling, or unwitting, allies. Individuals
who had never thought about the seating arrangements on buses, or who,
if they had thought about the issue, might have preferred the status quo,
may have been willing to tolerate change if their insistence on continued
segregation would have meant the loss of bus service or the loss of a job if
the bus service had been forced out of existence.

The Baton Rouge bus boycott was only the opening skirmish in the
black civil rights movement, but it provided some valuable lessons. The
leaders of other, later bus boycotts—Martin Luther King Jr. and Ralph
Abernathy in Montgomery (1955–1956), Reverend C. K. Steele in Talla-
hassee (1956), Reverend A. L. Davis in New Orleans (1957)—were all
church-based movement leaders who were keenly aware of the experience
of Reverend Jemison in Baton Rouge (Morris 1984).

Of course, the black civil rights movement continued to evolve, new issues were addressed, other leaders emerged. One major area in which the
Baton Rouge boycott is not very instructive is in promoting a movement
over time. The experience in Mississippi from summer 1961 through summer 1964 sheds more light on the way the black civil rights movement was
able to accomplish what it did.

Mississippi.   It is an understatement to say that Mississippi was the
stronghold of segregation. As late as 1964, a black attorney who was active
in the civil rights movement saw the movement as a "no-fail" situation because "it was impossible for things to have grown worse" (Holt 1966:13).

The black civil rights movement came to Mississippi in 1961 in the
form of Freedom Riders, individuals who challenged the state's refusal to
desegregate buses and bus stations and who viewed the state through bus
windows and jail bars. Late that summer field secretaries from the Student
Nonviolent Coordinating Committee (SNCC) also arrived, led by Robert
Moses, a Harvard-educated schoolteacher from Harlem. Moses sought to
organize black Mississippians based on the idea that they would need to
be self-reliant when SNCC left. Rather than taking an obvious leadership
role, Moses worked to develop local leaders and to discourage "outside"
involvement. His fear was that outsiders who played a major role in the

movement would leave at some point without having equipped indigenous leaders for the continuing struggle.

The development of leadership is a slow process, and there is a risk of stalling or stopping the movement if such development is arrested. Continued and increasing white resistance threatened to do just that. With the assassination of the National Association for the Advancement of Colored People (NAACP) field secretary Medgar Evers in June 1963 and the continuing violence against civil rights workers with no protection from federal authorities (local and state authorities were often involved in perpetrating the violence or allowing it to continue), Moses began to reconsider his opposition to outside, episodic assistance. In particular, he thought the presence of northern white students might insulate civil rights workers from the most blatant discrimination and might raise northern white consciousness about the racist system that existed in the South. It had become clear to Moses that violence against, and even murders of, Mississippi blacks had been insufficient to arouse national sympathies, much less to inspire protest or action.

Local white officials generally argued that blacks did not vote because they did not want to, because they were apathetic. The first tentative use of white students occurred during a fall 1963 "Freedom Vote," which was designed to reveal the state's hypocrisy and to puncture the apathy myth. Essentially, the idea was to put forth a slate of candidates and to have black voters cast "votes," not at the normal polling places but at less threatening locations and not for any official candidates but for individuals who supported the civil rights movement; further, the blacks knew these votes would not count. If black Mississippians bothered to cast "ballots" under these conditions, the apathy myth could be dispelled.

Allard Lowenstein, a white activist and attorney, organized white students—mainly from Stanford and Yale—to assist in this project. The project accomplished four things. First, with a turnout of more than 80,000 black "voters," no one could seriously argue that black Mississippians were apathetic. Second, and as a result of the first accomplishment, local blacks gained confidence. Not only had they taken a courageous step but so had many of their fellow black citizens. Third, white Mississippians became hysterical over both the idea of a Freedom Vote and the presence of the white students in support of the black civil rights movement. America's best and brightest students were threatened, beaten, shot at, and arrested for the heinous crime of attempting to attend a performance of the

Jackson Philharmonic as part of an interracial group. Thus, and fourth, the student volunteers came to understand clearly what life was like in Mississippi, and they communicated this reality outside of the state. The white volunteers wrote to their parents, friends, and representatives in Congress; national attention became focused on Mississippi, and news coverage of the movement increased. The symbolic exercise, therefore, was not meaningless (Chafe 1993).

Based on the Freedom Vote experience, Robert Moses became convinced that bringing in more students from prominent white northern families would either restrain white violence or highlight it for national attention, thus increasing pressure on federal authorities to become involved. An umbrella organization, the Council of Federated Organizations (COFO), was formed to coordinate the civil rights movement efforts. Under COFO auspices, more than one thousand college student volunteers were brought to Mississippi for the 1964 Summer Project. The underlying logic was correct but disheartening. The movement had discovered a tactic that would help it to expand the audience for its struggle and, it was hoped, bring federal intervention on its behalf. The bad news was that the tactic was predicated on the notion that threatening, beating, and shooting at affluent white northern students was a serious offense but that doing the same to black Mississippians was not.

This logic proved all too true. At the very beginning of the Summer Project, three participants—James Chaney, Michael Schwerner, and Andrew Goodman—disappeared while on a trip to investigate the bombing of a black church. Their disappearance prompted a massive investigation by the Federal Bureau of Investigation (FBI) that eventually led to the discovery of the men's bodies. The important lesson for the movement was that the murder of white civil rights workers (Schwerner and Goodman) resulted in federal attention whereas the numerous attacks on black Mississippians that had been reported previously had not done so.

Although the Summer Project did not change Mississippi overnight, it provided an important first step in the process. For example, "freedom schools" enhanced the academic skills of black children, better preparing them for future political and economic participation. And building on the Freedom Vote, a racially integrated Mississippi Freedom Democratic Party, which pledged allegiance to the national Democratic Party ticket, was formed to challenge the still segregated regular Mississippi Democratic Party. Although it was unsuccessful in achieving its goal of replacing the "regulars" as the official Democratic Party, the project's efforts foretold a major increase in black political participation in the state that had been the most resistant to any such participation of any state in the nation. Perhaps because of the length of their effort, or perhaps because of the more resistant environment, the movement leaders in Mississippi—unlike those in Baton Rouge—used outside resources to further their cause. The lessons of the black civil rights movement were not lost on other racial and ethnic minority groups.

The Chicano Movement

Social movements among Latinos have been limited, and there has been no overarching pan-Hispanic effort. Young Puerto Ricans in New York and Chicago have participated in a Puerto Rican nationalist movement. César Chávez emerged as a leader of the National Farm Workers Association, which joined with Filipinos to protest pay inequities in the agricultural labor force. But the most wide-ranging, significant Latino movement was the Chicano power movement of the 1960s among Mexican Americans in the Southwest.

The Chicano movement was influenced both directly and indirectly by the black civil rights movement. The direct influence came through the participation of a few Mexican Americans in that movement. Individuals such as Maria Varela and Elizabeth Sutherland Martinez gained both valuable experience and a realization that the black movement was not concerned with the plight of Mexican Americans. Indirectly, however, the Chicano movement emerged from the general activism of the 1960s, which was spearheaded by the black civil rights movement.

At the core of the Chicano movement were Mexican American students, male and female, who sought more attention for the needs of their people. They wanted to move beyond the efforts of the more conservative Mexican American interest groups. The movement's most dramatic early political success came in Crystal City, Texas, in 1963 when the Political Association of Spanish Speaking Peoples (PASSO) was formed and coalesced with a predominantly Mexican American local chapter of the Teamsters Union to defeat all of the white candidates for the city council, replacing them with Mexican Americans. This "Crystal City Revolt" was important because it demonstrated the possibilities for local Mexican American political mobilization. This was the first time Mexican Americans had taken political control of a municipal government in the U.S. Southwest. Furthermore, it highlighted the important role young people were to play in the movement.

This role was further highlighted in the March 1968 Mexican American student walkout at Lincoln High School in East Los Angeles. Acting on an idea of Sal Castro, a teacher at the school, more than one thousand students staged a week-and-a-half-long strike that was "the first major mass protest explicitly against racism undertaken by Mexican Americans in the history of the United States" (Muñoz 1989:64). This action served as a catalyst to increase political awareness, revitalize existing community organizations, generate new political organizations, and mobilize young Mexican Americans, who became the heart of the Chicano movement.

Unlike the black civil rights movement, the Chicano movement relied less on established organizational resources and more on the energies of young people. By doing so, it found an energetic reservoir of leaders and skilled organizers—including Rodolfo "Corky" González, José Angel Gutiérrez, and Reies López Tijerina—who minimized the need to tap outside resources. Furthermore, by emphasizing the need to win local political and economic control of Mexican American communities, the movement adopted a strategy in which there was a possibility of a visible payoff in an effort to attract new supporters.

The spirit of the Chicano Movement is best expressed in the autobiographical writing of José Angel Gutiérrez (1998:11).

> My generation of Chicano activists made events happen. We were determined, motivated, political actors in the Chicano movement. As proud militants and ready activists . . . we sought group ascendancy; we wanted to uplift our people, *la raza*, as a group. . . . [We] were in solidarity with one another. . . . We asserted our right to a homeland, Aztlan. My generation began the struggle to make a reality of Aztlan, building community in a serious way. Nation building begins at the neighborhood level, and we were the epitome of community development. To date, our generational struggle and creativity is manifest in the numerous Chicano institutions we created while making community. We took the Chicano movement from sporadic unrest to social protest to social movement to political party to governance and left Chicano institutions in place to keep vigil and shepherd over our gains.
>
> We created more organizations and programs for all Chicanos than any previous generation of activists. Our record as builders of the Chicano

community remains unmatched and unchallenged by the present generation of Hispanics.

The Asian American Movement

The Asian American movement is a clear example of a civil rights movement that was spawned by the black civil rights movement. Until the time of the black movement, each group of Asians in the United States had organized, litigated, and participated in politics when such participation was permitted, but they had done so as Japanese Americans, Chinese Americans, Filipino Americans, Korean Americans, or whatever their country of ancestry rather than as Asian Americans. The example of the black civil rights movement, which heightened sensitivity to racism, in combination with the anti-Vietnam movement, changed that situation. A generation of middle-class college students was suddenly aware of its "Asianness" as it questioned the nature of the Vietnam War. The students were in a unique position to raise questions about the racial implications of U.S. military policy. Thus, much like the Chicano movement, the Asian American movement was youth-oriented and drew less on established organizations than did the black movement.

Perhaps because of the attempt to bridge such a broad spectrum of diversity, no single national leader or strategy emerged. Leaders were prominent only within a specific geographic area or a particular Asian ethnic group. Thus, it is not surprising that no single plan of action was ever formulated. The unifying principle of the various localized movements seems to have been the pursuit of equality (Wei 1993).

The American Indian Movement

The 1960s and 1970s also marked the reemergence of American Indian activism from the 70-year hiatus that had followed the Wounded Knee Massacre of December 28, 1890. The group that came to symbolize this renewed activism was the American Indian Movement (AIM), a protest group modeled after black protest groups, formed in Minneapolis in 1968 to deal with the problems faced by urban Indians, especially the problem of police brutality. Within two years, AIM had expanded its concerns and addressed tribal and Indian issues regardless of the Indians' place of residence. Unlike other social movements, AIM and related Indian interest groups have sought "to retain their political and cultural exclusion from absorption or incorporation in the American polity" (Wilkins 2002: 201).

Leadership of AIM came not from established groups but from Clyde Bellecourt and Dennis Banks, two of the cofounders of the movement, and Russell Means—the most outspoken of the AIM leaders, who became a symbol of American Indian resistance. This leadership allowed AIM to attract bright, energetic young Indians from all parts of the country.

AIM became best known for its participation in dramatic events to highlight injustices. For example, in 1972 AIM was a major actor in the takeover of the headquarters of the Bureau of Indian Affairs (BIA) in Washington, D.C. And in 1973, AIM activists protested tribal government corruption on the Pine Ridge Reservation, U.S. violations of the 1868 Fort Laramie Treaty, and continuing federal controls over American Indians by seizing the village of Wounded Knee and holding it for ten weeks against a force of hundreds of federal officers. But AIM's use of confrontation triggered the concerted opposition of the BIA, the FBI, and other federal agencies. These agencies engaged in an effective, organized campaign of surveillance, infiltration, and intimidation against American Indian activists—including AIM—which diverted their energies from pursuing policy changes to squabbling internally.

Summary

One of the goals of each of these movements has been to attain political power. Casting a vote is the most basic formal act of participation in a polity. We now consider the contemporary status of voting rights for minority groups.

Voting Rights Law

The simple act of voting has important symbolic and potentially important practical ramifications. The right to cast a ballot separates the insiders (citizens) from the outsiders (noncitizens) and dependents (the underaged). When aggregated, votes determine who the nation's public policymakers, the people who allocate public resources, will be. In short, the vote is seen as a tool for protecting other rights and achieving other goals—as a means rather than an end.

For most Americans the right to vote is assumed, and Americans assume all other citizens have the same right. After all, in the wake of the

Civil War, the Constitution was amended to ban intentional discrimination by public officials based on race or previous condition of servitude (the Fourteenth Amendment) and to prohibit the denial or abridgment of the right to vote by officials at all levels of government on the basis of race, color, or previous condition of servitude (the Fifteenth Amendment). But within a few years, the Supreme Court declared much of the legislation designed to enforce the Fifteenth Amendment unconstitutional, and Congress repealed other such legislation. Thus, when federal supervision of southern elections ended in 1877, the states were effectively free to structure and operate their electoral processes as they saw fit.

What followed was the systematic disenfranchisement of the black electorate. Through a variety of devices—discriminatorily administered literacy tests, poll taxes, white primaries—southern states passed some of the most effective legislation ever enacted. For example, between 1896 and 1900, the number of black Louisianans registered to vote dropped from 130,334 to 5,320. Likewise, at the end of the nineteenth century, only 9 percent of Mississippi's black voting-age population was registered to vote; three decades earlier the figure had been 70 percent (U.S. Commission on Civil Rights 1968).

In the early part of the twentieth century, some legal progress was made in attacking various methods of disenfranchisement. In 1915 the Supreme Court, in *Guinn v. United States*, declared unconstitutional the **grandfather clause**—a device used by southern states to deny the vote to those whose grandparents were slaves—which circumvented the Fifteenth Amendment. In 1944, in *Smith v. Allwright*, the Court invalidated Texas's **white primary** as a violation of the Fifteenth Amendment. This primary had been based on the logic that the state's Democratic Party was a private organization and, thus, that its means of nominating candidates—the "white primary"—was not covered by the equal protection clause of the Fourteenth Amendment. The Democratic Party was the dominant party in Texas, and the individual who won the primary was the predetermined winner of the general election. If the Democratic Party were a private organization, and if only members of the party could vote in the primary, black voters were effectively blocked from participation. In spite of these victories, the Supreme Court rarely changed day-to-day realities for black citizens.

It was against this backdrop that the black civil rights movement pressed for the right to vote as a top priority. The belief was that the ballot could be a tool for achieving other changes sought by the movement.

The federal legislation that was passed at least partially in response to the black civil rights movement was the Voting Rights Act (VRA) of 1965, which was amended in 1970, 1975, and 1982. Basically, the act, as amended:

1. prohibits "tests or devices" that had been used in the past to disenfranchise racial minorities—for example, literacy tests, education requirements, tests of good character, racial gerrymandering, and English-only elections in jurisdictions in which a single linguistic minority constitutes more than 5 percent of the voting-age population;
2. requires that "covered" jurisdictions gain federal assent for any changes in election laws or procedures to assure that such changes do not abridge the right to vote on the basis of race, color, or language minority status; and
3. makes clear that if the effect of a practice is discriminatory, it is unlawful, regardless of the intent of its originator.

The second, "preclearance" provision applies in only those political jurisdictions in which fewer than one-half of those who were eligible to vote were registered or voted in the 1964, 1968, or 1972 presidential elections *and* in which a discriminatory "test or device" was used in registration or voting. Thus, the states of Alabama, Alaska, Arizona, Georgia, Louisiana, Mississippi, South Carolina, Texas, and Virginia, as well as 5 counties in California, 5 counties in Florida, 2 towns in Michigan, 10 towns in New Hampshire, 3 counties in New York, 40 counties in North Carolina, and 2 counties in South Dakota are covered jurisdictions.

Legislation has been fairly effective in dealing with vote denial. Although gaps still exist between the political participation rates of the various racial and ethnic populations and the rate of the white population, these gaps have narrowed since the passage of the VRA. And, as is detailed in Chapter 4, the number of successful office seekers from groups previously denied the vote is increasing—particularly for blacks, somewhat less so for Hispanics, and less noticeably for Asian Americans and Indians.

More work remains, however, in the area of **vote dilution**. Vote dilution involves "the impairment of the equal opportunity of minority voters to participate in the political process and to elect candidates of their choice" (McDonald and powell 1993:27). Drawing on Supreme Court decisions that mandate that voting power must be apportioned equally based on population (the one person, one vote decisions), the logic has been extended to mandate that voters have the right to cast ballots that have the potential to elect candidates of their choice. At various times, at-large elections, racially gerrymandered districting schemes that unnecessarily fragment or unnecessarily concentrate minority group voters, laws that prohibit single-shot voting, discriminatory annexations or deannexations, and the abolition of elected or appointed offices or the changing of the means of selection have been used to dilute minority voting strength. These practices are not necessarily dilutive, but when they are combined with other social and historical circumstances, they may create an unequal opportunity for minority groups or white voters to elect their preferred candidates.

The determination of whether a jurisdiction is engaging in minority vote dilution requires an examination of the "totality of circumstances." The circumstances that courts examine include racial bloc voting; a history of discrimination; depressed minority socioeconomic status; a paucity of elected minority officials; the use of racial campaign appeals; the existence of formal or informal "slating" groups, which are groups of candidates who band together or who are endorsed as a group by other organizations; and the employment of devices that enhance the possibility for discrimination, such as numbered positions.

Although much of the voting rights legislation was designed to vindicate the suffrage rights of blacks, other groups have also used the law to attempt to enhance their own political power. For example, American Indians used litigation pursuant to modern voting rights legislation in such attempts. Indians have the same right to vote as all other citizens, and election districts in which they vote must be apportioned under the one person, one vote principle. All three nonblack minority groups—Hispanics, Asian Americans, and American Indians—are recognized as language minority groups under the VRA, and election administrators must take that into account in affected jurisdictions.

A common remedy applied when vote dilution is found or when legislators are reapportioning or redistricting following the census is to draw districts in which a majority of the residents are nonwhite—"majority minority" districts. Both the creation of such districts and the shape of some of them are matters of continuing controversy. A series of U.S. Supreme Court decisions about the appropriateness of considering race in the drawing of congressional districts, raised in the context of a number of oddly shaped districts, has apparently limited the drawing of majority minority districts. The first such case heard by the Court, *Shaw v. Reno* (1993), focused on a congressional district drawn in North Carolina in response to Justice Department pressure to give effect to potential minority voting strength in certain parts of the state. The plan that was adopted created a district in the north central part of the state that linked two urban black population concentrations with a 160-mile-long "bridge," at times no wider than the I–85 right-of-way. The Court subjected this arrangement to strict scrutiny and ultimately struck down the majority black district as an example of racial gerrymandering (*Shaw v. Hunt* 1996). Specifically, the Court found that when districts' shapes are "bizarre"— that is, when they are inexplicable on grounds other than race—strict scrutiny by the Court is required. Building on and clarifying this decision, the Court struck down districting plans in Georgia (*Miller v. Johnson* 1995) for three majority black congressional districts and in Texas (*Bush v. Vera* 1996) for two majority black districts and one majority Latino district, requiring that congressional districts in both states be redrawn. More recently, in February 1997, federal district courts declared the majority black Third District in Virginia and the majority Latino 12th District in New York unconstitutional. These rulings meant that in the 2001 round of redistricting, following the Census of 2000, the crafting of new majority minority districts was severely constrained.

The issue is important because of what majority minority districts mean relative to the ability of blacks and Latinos to be elected to office. There is substantial evidence that racism persists in American society, that voting is still racially polarized, and that racial appeal tactics are still used in political campaigns (Grofman, Handley, and Niemi 1992; Davidson and Grofman 1994; Reeves 1997). Nevertheless, controversy surrounds the creation of majority minority districts because some believe that the VRA has become an affirmative action tool to get minorities elected, thereby making representation an entitlement; that racism among whites has decreased; and that racially polarized voting is no longer a problem (Thernstrom 1987). From the latter viewpoint, if minorities are not elected in white majority districts, it is for reasons other than racial ones, and therefore the drawing of districts to maximize minority electoral prospects is unnecessary (Reeves 1997).

Such controversy is part of the ongoing struggle over whether and, if so, how to merge the reality of racial minorities' political status with the rhetoric of American democracy, and its resolution will have a tremendous impact on the strategies chosen by minority political activists. At its heart, this controversy centers on the notion of representation and what it means. The structure of our electoral process, and of who wins and loses in the process, affects who will raise the questions and what positions will be taken.

Lani Guinier, Harvard University law professor and President Clinton's failed nominee for assistant attorney general for civil rights in 1993, has ideas on representation and power that are not as outlandish as her opponents and the media portrayed them to be (Guinier 1994). Her questioning of whether it is fair in a majoritarian system for a majority—50 percent plus one—in any given election to hold 100 percent of the power is gaining currency. What about the other 50 percent minus one? Should they, because they are in the minority, be excluded from the governing body? It should be understood that whereas Guinier is concerned with the electoral representation of racial minorities, in her view minority refers not only to racial minorities but to gender minorities and to Republican or Democrat minorities as well. She also questions whether concentrating racial minorities in majority minority districts is the best approach to rectifying the exclusion of such minorities from the political process. One of her solutions to this imbalance is the concept of cumulative voting.

Cumulative voting, a technique used until recently by the state of Illinois in its legislative races, is a mechanism that benefits numerical minorities, whether they are blacks, Latinos, Asians, Indians, women, Democrats, or Republicans. The concept is simple. At present, if there are seven seats on the city council, each voter votes for one individual in each of seven contests. In essence, each voter has seven votes but can vote for only one candidate in each contest. Under cumulative voting, each voter has seven votes and can assign them however he or she wants. The voter can give five votes to one candidate and one each to two others or can give all seven votes to one candidate. In this manner, numerical minorities could give all of their votes to a particular candidate, thus increasing their chances of electing members of their own group. Cumulative voting systems have allowed the Sisseton Sioux Indians in South Dakota to elect a representative to the local school board and in Chilton County, Alabama, allowed blacks to elect a black to the County Council along with two white Republicans who, until the implementation of cumulative voting, had never been able to overcome the Democratic registration and voting majorities. In 1994, a federal judge ordered the institution of a cumulative voting system in Worcester County on Maryland's eastern shore in an effort to overcome the inability of blacks to elect members to the Board of County Commissioners. In May 2000, as a result of the settlement of a voting rights law suit, cumulative voting was used in Amarillo, Texas, to elect members of the school board. Despite constituting a significant portion of the city's population, blacks and Latinos had not been elected to the school board in more than two decades. Under cumulative voting, both a black and a Latino were elected to the seven-member school board. More than 100 jurisdictions have adopted alternative voting systems with cumulative voting being among the most preferred.

Although cumulative voting is often mentioned in relation to the four groups that are the subject of this book, it would also benefit whites who are increasingly becoming numerical minorities in many urban centers. Clearly, a serious yet highly charged discussion of the concepts of majority and the access of numerical minorities will take place in the future.

Conclusion

Political success has not been attained without struggle. Civil rights movements have been necessary for each group openly to challenge the system in which it was not only at a disadvantage but in which the rules were structured to keep it that way. One of the goals of each of these movements has been to achieve the right to vote, which it hopes it can use as a tool for winning political victories and protecting the fruits of those victories. The Voting Rights Act, as amended, has provided some protection for each of the groups. We now address the way members of these groups have been able to play a role in the U.S. political system.

3

....

America's Racial Minorities in the Contemporary Political System: Actors

Two black garbage truck drivers are awarded $2.6
million by a majority white federal jury as damages for
repeatedly being called "porch monkeys" and other
racial epithets by a white boss and having their
complaints brushed off by the boss's supervisor as
"harmless."

—Fairfax County, Virginia, December 2004

JAMES MADISON, IN *FEDERALIST NO. 10*, envisioned the United States as a society in which conflict rather than consensus would predominate. The citizenry would be divided into many groups, parties, and factions that would compete for benefits they felt to be rightly theirs. For Madison, the chief cause of these divisions was economic in origin, but, as we well know, race has emerged as a major dividing factor in American society. Madison's concept of U.S. society is represented in political science by pluralist theory. **Pluralism**, the reigning paradigm in political science, states in part that if citizens participate in the political process by voting and other means, the political system will produce electoral and policy outcomes favored by the participants.

Yet many of pluralism's assumptions do not favor the participation of, or acknowledge the barriers to, participation in the political process by America's racial minorities. Pluralism assumes that many centers of power exist and that different groups have access to a variety of power centers; thus, if a group is blocked from one center of power, it will always have access to another. Therefore, although groups may differ in their levels or types of political resources—for example, population size versus financial means—on balance the government will play a neutral role, and the resource differential will be balanced through the competition process. Pluralism also assumes that every group has equal access to the political process and that not every group will win all of the time but will win or lose depending on the issue and on its ability to use political resources.

Despite its preeminence in political science, pluralism has numerous critics. Pluralism assumes that interests will become diversified across economic, social, and political issues, resulting in little need for racial and ethnic groups to organize around group-based issues. Race and ethnicity will thus be obscured as these other issues take precedence. Pluralism also states that once groups realize their subjective interests, they will become incorporated into the political system. Critics argue that these notions of interest diversification and incorporation dismiss the fact that racial minorities are treated as groups; no individual achievement improves the status of the individual or changes the position of the group (Pinder-hughes 1987:38).

Another criticism is that pluralism has a class bias; upper-income individuals are better situated to compete for political outcomes. Despite pluralism's contention that political resources are counterbalanced, with one group's financial resources being neutralized by another group's population base, pluralism tilts political outcomes in favor of those with economic and political resources. As E. E. Schattschneider (1960:34) observes, "The flaw in the pluralist heaven is that the heavenly chorus sings with a strong upper-class accent."

There is a great deal of conflict in the scholarly literature over the utility of the pluralist framework in explaining the political behaviors of and outcomes for America's racial minorities. Nevertheless, African Americans, Latinos, American Indians, and Asian Americans are players—albeit often unequal players—in the U.S. political system. What we have not done is use any particular conceptual framework to approach the study of these groups. It may be impossible to use one particular framework to guide the analysis of all four groups, or a chosen framework may work better in guiding analysis of a particular group at one point in time rather than at another. Regardless of which framework one uses, it is important to remember that if one is to undertake serious, empirical study of racial and ethnic politics in the United States—an endeavor we highly recommend—one inevitably adopts some type of conceptual framework that affects what one studies, which in turn affects the conclusions one reaches about the status of and the prospects for the future evolution of these politics. Below we provide brief sketches of frameworks that have been used to study racial and ethnic politics or particular groups within the American context. We cannot do justice to these approaches in the confines of this book, but we provide at least a core reference for students wishing to explore any or all of them in greater depth.

- *The Moral Dilemma Framework*
  An approach mentioned at the very beginning of this book is the moral dilemma approach presented by Gunnar Myrdal (1944). To Myrdal, the basic problem in U.S. racial and ethnic relations was an alleged contradiction between commitment to a demo-

cratic creed and the presence of racial discrimination. One possible implication of this framework was that racial conflict would disappear when whites' attitudes changed, suggesting a strategy of persuasion rather than of confrontation.

- *The Power Relations Framework*
  Sociologist Hubert Blalock (1967) has argued that race relations in the United States can be characterized as power contests between dominant whites and subordinate minorities. If power is the product of multiplying "total resources and the degree to which these resources are mobilized" (Blalock 1967:110), then change will occur when minorities' resources are enhanced or are more effectively mobilized.

- *Two-Tiered Pluralist Framework*
  We introduced pluralism at the beginning of this chapter. Pluralism promises change through individual and collective participation in the existing political regime. As we noted when the concept was first discussed, there are problems with this framework. An innovative attempt to adapt the concept to fit the situation in which minorities find themselves is "two-tiered pluralism," devised by Rodney Hero (1992). Based on his analysis of the situation of Latinos in the U.S. political system, Hero describes "two-tiered pluralism" as a system "in which there is formal legal equality on the one hand, and . . . actual practice that undercuts equality for most members of minority groups" (1992:188–190). Thus, the pluralist solution to racial and ethnic conflict cannot work efficiently or effectively because there is only marginal inclusion of minority group members within the political system.

- *The Modernization/Developmental Framework*
  Advocates of this approach see racial and ethnic relations corresponding to specific levels of socioeconomic development and improving as greater socioeconomic development occurs. For example, Harry Holloway (1969) employed this approach in his study of blacks in southern politics.

- *The Internal Colonialism Framework*
  This final framework draws an analogy to the colonial experience
  in world history. In this instance the colonized people reside
  within the political and social system of the United States. As developed by Robert Blauner (1972), this framework emphasizes
  the political powerlessness, economic dependence, and decultur-
  ation of minority populations within the United States.

None of these frameworks has proven to be the one best way of examining racial and ethnic politics in the United States. However, a variety of
perspectives can be useful, and as you explore the topics and issues raised
in this volume more thoroughly, you may find one of these lenses helpful
in clarifying or magnifying your chosen focal point.

This chapter explores approaches to the second dilemma—what is to
be done—by examining ways in which racial and ethnic minorities participate in the political system. The aspects of political attitudes and participation addressed are: (1) **group identity** or cohesion—the extent of
feelings of solidarity with other members of the group—and perceptions
of discrimination; (2) **political ideology**, the underlying beliefs and attitudes of a group that shape its opinions and actions on political issues; (3)
partisan identification, the attachment to and intensity of feeling for a
particular political party; (4) **voting behavior**, the way people vote in elections and the forces that influence these votes; and (5) **interest group activities**, actions taken by organized groups seeking to influence public
officials and policies.

For each of the areas, when applicable, discussion is broken down along
gender lines so that differences in the attitudes and behaviors of women
and men within a group, as well as those between groups, are highlighted.
These distinctions are important for a variety of reasons. We often hear
about the political behavior and feelings of groups, but group feelings and
actions may vary in intensity or even in kind when broken down into responses by men versus women. The salience and importance of gender for
women in framing their political attitudes and behaviors may result in different attitudes and behaviors from those of men. Further, we cannot assume that gender issues will resonate similarly for all women. It is
reasonable to expect that the beliefs of black women may differ not only
from those of black men but also from those of Latinas, Indian women,
and Asian women. The same expectation holds true for various combina-

tions of women. Moreover, women from one racial or ethnic minority may have views similar to those of men in other ethnic or racial categories. As has been and will continue to be demonstrated throughout this book, race and its effects on the political system may be different for different racial groups.

The best data sources for identifying the political attitudes of blacks, Latinos, and Asians are the National Black Election Study, 1984–1988 (NBES); the National Black Politics Study, 1993 (NBPS); the National Black Election Study, 1996 (NBES96); the Joint Center for Political and Economic Studies 2004 National Opinion Poll (JCPES2004); the Latino National Political Survey, 1990 (LNPS); *The Washington Post*/Kaiser Family Foundation/Harvard University Survey Project, National Survey on Latinos in America, 1999; the Pew Foundation 2002 and 2004 Latino Surveys; and the Pilot Study of the National Asian American Political Survey, 2000 (PNAAPS). These sources are national probability samples of the appropriate populations and represent the most comprehensive basis to date for determining the political attitudes of these groups. Data on American Indian political attitudes are much more limited. To date, we have no national surveys exclusively devoted to this population. Thus, we must rely on the results from a small number of local surveys from various cities and areas around the country and aggregate the small number of American Indians in national surveys.

Group Identity and Perceptions of Discrimination

Actual or perceived **group cohesion** (group solidarity) has been identified in political science research as being strongly associated with increased levels of political participation among racial and ethnic minority groups in the United States (Olsen 1970; Verba and Nie 1972). The more individuals identify with other members of a group, the more they are likely to participate in politics and to coalesce around candidates and policy issues they perceive as being beneficial to the group. One of the measures of group cohesion among racial and ethnic minorities is the degree of perceived discrimination against both the individual and one's group. Another measure of group cohesion is the degree of closeness an individual feels to other people in the group with respect to ideas and feelings about issues.

According to the 1984 NBES, 90 percent of blacks surveyed believed discrimination was still a problem for African Americans, with 68 percent

TABLE 3.1   Proportion of Blacks Perceiving That They Share a Common Fate with Other Blacks

	1984 (%)[a]	1988 (%)[a]	1993 (%)[b]	1996 (%)[c]
Yes	73.5 (796)[d]	77.4 (339)	77.9 (904)	83 (954)
No	26.5 (287)	22.6 (99)	22.1 (256)	17 (196)
Total	100 (1083)	100 (438)	100 (1160)	100 (1150)

[a] Preelection sample, 1984 and 1988 National Black Election Studies.
[b] 1993 National Black Politics Study.
[c] 1996 National Black Election Study, Preelection sample.
[d] Figures in parentheses represent the number of respondents.

Source: Authors' computations from the 1984 and 1988 National Black Election Studies, 1993 National Black Politics Study, and 1996 National Black Election Study.

believing strongly that racial discrimination was still a problem (Gurin, Hatchett, and Jackson 1989:75–81). Additionally, as reported in another source, a majority of blacks indicated that they had experienced discrimination in education, housing, employment, and wages (Sigelman and Welch 1991). The same pattern was evident in the 1988 NBES data (Tate 1993).

Regarding closeness, 93 percent of the black respondents in the 1984 NBES data reported being close to other blacks in terms of feelings and ideas (Gurin, Hatchett, and Jackson 1989:75–81), and a majority felt that what happens to the group affects them personally. As Table 3.1 exhibits, fully three-fourths of blacks surveyed in the 1984 and 1988 NBES (Tate 1993:25), the 1993 NBPS, and the NBES96 felt that what happens to black people will shape their lives.

The level of cohesiveness among Latinos, as measured on these dimensions, is very different from the pattern found among African Americans. The LNPS found that regardless of national origin, the majority of Latinos believed they had not personally been discriminated against because of their ethnicity. Mexicans were more likely than Cubans to report instances of discrimination. Yet when queried about their perceptions of discrimination, overwhelming majorities of Mexican Americans and Puerto Ricans perceived a lot or some discrimination against their ethnic origin group; additionally, both groups were also inclined to perceive a lot or some discrimination against the other group and against Cubans. Cubans were the least likely to perceive discrimination against Mexican Americans and Puerto Ricans, although a majority still perceived such discrimination. Less than a majority of Cubans perceived a lot or some discrimina-

TABLE 3.2   Perception of Discrimination Against African Americans and
Asians by Latino National Origin Groups

	Mexican (%)	Puerto Rican (%)	Cuban (%)
Degree of discrimination against African Americans			
A lot	43.6 (383)[a]	57.5 (336)	29.9 (93)
Some	39.9 (350)	28.4 (166)	35.0 (109)
A little	12.9 (113)	9.0 (52)	14.3 (44)
None	3.6 (32)	5.1 (30)	20.9 (65)
Total	100 (877)	100 (584)	100 (312)
Degree of discrimination against Asians			
A lot	15.5 (134)	14.0 (81)	4.6 (14)
Some	43.9 (379)	37.9 (219)	35.2 (109)
A little	26.9 (232)	30.1 (174)	23.9 (74)
None	13.5 (119)	18.1 (104)	36.3 (112)
Total	100 (864)	100 (577)	100 (308)

[a] Figures in parentheses represent the number of respondents.

Source: Rodolfo O. de la Garza et al., 1992, *Latino Voices: Mexican, Puerto Rican, and Cuban Perspectives on American Politics* (Boulder: Westview Press), Tables 7.8 and 7.9, p. 93.

tion against their own group; in fact, fully one-third of the Cuban respondents said they perceived no discrimination against Cubans (de la Garza et al. 1992:91–96).

This finding may reflect the geographic concentration and political power of Cubans in Dade County, Florida. Cubans clearly evidence a different pattern of perceptions than do Mexican Americans and Puerto Ricans. This may partially result from the fact that "Mexicans, Puerto Ricans, and Cubans have little interaction with each other; most do not recognize that they have much in common culturally, and they do not profess strong affection for each other" (de la Garza et al. 1992:14).

As seen in Table 3.2, when Hispanics were questioned about their perception of discrimination against African Americans and Asian Americans, some interesting patterns emerged. Clear majorities of Mexican Americans and Puerto Ricans perceived that discrimination is a problem for African Americans and Asian Americans. Yet one-fifth of Cubans believed discrimination against blacks is nonexistent in the United States, and one-third indicated that discrimination does not exist against Asian Americans.

Data from the Pilot Study of the National Asian American Political Survey found that about one-third, 36 percent, of all Asian respondents reported that they have been discriminated against, with Korean and Japanese Americans, 42 and 40 percent respectively, reporting the highest level of discrimination, and Vietnamese Americans reporting the lowest amount of discrimination, 13 percent. Close to two-fifths, 39 percent, of all Asian respondents feel that they are discriminated against less than blacks and Latinos, while about one-third, 31 percent, believe that Asians are discriminated against as much as are blacks and Latinos. Earlier analysis of data collected in 1984 in California found that perceptions of discrimination among Asian Americans have a generational dimension. Second-generation Asian Americans are far more likely than are first-generation individuals to perceive discrimination (Cain and Kieweit 1986). This might explain why Vietnamese Americans, among the most recent immigrants to the United States, perceive considerably less discrimination than do other, more long established Asian American groups.

Only about 15 percent of Asian Americans in the PNAAPS identified themselves using the pan-ethnic identification of Asian American, while 64 percent identified themselves using their ethnic group, for example, Japanese American or Korean American. Yet, despite the lack of a pan-ethnic identity, almost half, 49 percent, of Asian Americans believe that what happens to other groups of Asians in the United States affects what happens to them. Moreover, a similar proportion, 50 percent, feels that people of Asian decent in the United States share cultural similarities. Despite the identification with one's own ethnic group, it is clear that at least half of Asian Americans feel a connection with other Asian Americans. Whether this connection will translate into Asian American political cohesion is still an open question. We simply do not know at this point. But, given the research that suggests that second-generation Asians have stronger feelings about discrimination and other issues than do first-generation Asians, it is possible that Asians will develop a stronger sense of their racial and political identity in the future.

High levels of group cohesion may translate into increased levels of political participation, especially registering to vote and actually voting, by racial minority groups. Blacks have higher levels of group cohesion and share more of a common destiny than do Latinos and Asians. As we will see later in this chapter in the section "Voting Behavior," lower levels of voter registration and actual voting among Asians and Latinos may be partly explained by the lack of group cohesion, although other factors also contribute to this outcome.

Political Ideology

In popular culture and the news media, racial minorities are often described as ideologically and politically "liberal" on a conservative-to-liberal continuum. Yet those who study black and Latino political attitudes argue that it is inappropriate to use the standard political ideology labels of liberal, moderate, and conservative, which were developed from national studies that contained few nonwhites, and apply them to the black and Latino populations. This simple application of labels misses the complexity and variability of attitudes within the various racial communities. Moreover, the application of the labels implies that there is an agreed-upon definition of their meaning and that individuals who identify themselves by these labels are able to define what they mean (Hero 1992; Smith and Seltzer 1992; Tate 1993).

Are we safe in saying that if an individual or a predominant portion of a group believes the federal government should take a more active role in reducing unemployment, providing services for the poor, and improving the socioeconomic position of blacks and other racial minorities, that individual or group is liberal? By the same token, are we safe in saying that if an individual or the majority of a group supports prayer in public schools, the individual or group is conservative? Based on popular notions of liberal and conservative, the answer would be "yes" to both questions. Yet we commonly find such responses within African American public opinion, which raises doubts about the assignment of stereotypic labels such as liberal and conservative.

Contrary to popular wisdom, as Table 3.3 shows, blacks are spread across the ideological spectrum, with only an approximately ten-percentage-point gap between the number of blacks self-identifying as some degree of liberal and those identifying as some degree of conservative in the 1984 and 1988 NBES data, and an approximately four-percentage-point gaps between the same categories in the 1993 NBPS and the 1996 NBES data. Of particular note are the two-fifths, 41.1 percent, of blacks who identify themselves as moderates in the 1996 NBES data. But the meaning behind these labels is unclear. When asked to define what they meant by liberal or conservative when identifying themselves as such, some respondents were unable to do

TABLE 3.3   Black Ideological Identification

Ideology	1984 (%)[a]	1988 (%)[a]	1993 (%)[b]	1996 (%)[c]
Strongly liberal	21.8 (154)[d]	18.5 (63)	23.9 (241)	18.4 (181)
Not very strongly liberal	12.9 (91)	18.0 (61)	11.9 (121)	13.5 (133)
Slightly liberal	16.5 (116)	18.0 (61)	—[e]	—
Moderate/leaning liberal	—	—	15.4 (155)	—
Moderate	7.0 (49)	1.8 (6)	2.4 (24)	41.1 (406)
Moderate/leaning conservative	—	—	22.7 (219)	—
Slightly conservative	16.6 (117)	22.1 (75)	—	—
Not very strongly conservative	11.3 (80)	10.2 (35)	9.3 (94)	11.5 (113)
Strongly conservative	13.9 (98)	11.4 (39)	15.4 (155)	15.5 (153)
Total[f]	100 (705)	100 (340)	100 (1009)	100 (986)

[a] Postelection sample, 1984 and 1988 National Black Election Studies.
[b] 1993–1994 National Black Politics Study.
[c] 1996 National Black Election Study, preelection sample.
[d] Figures in parentheses represent the number of respondents.
[e] Differences in response categories between National Black Election Studies and National Black Politics Study.
[f] Totals may not sum to 100 due to rounding.
Source: Authors' computations from the 1984 and 1988 National Black Election Studies, 1993–1994 National Black Politics Study, and 1996 National Black Election Study.

so. Moreover, higher-income blacks were no more likely than lower-income blacks to identify themselves as conservatives, but older blacks were far more likely than younger blacks to identify themselves as liberal. Regardless of self-identified ideological labels, blacks' policy preferences are generally fairly liberal across a variety of issues, but, with the exception of capital punishment, they are relatively conservative on a range of social issues (Tate 1993:31–32, 38).

The meanings of the terms liberal and conservative do not resonate well with Latinos or accurately reflect the attitudes of various Latino groups (Hero 1992). Table 3.4 displays the range of ideological orientations among Latinos. In both the 1989/1990 LPNS and the 1999 *Washington Post* data, Mexican Americans are almost equally likely to describe themselves as some degree of liberal, as moderate, and as some variant of conservative. Puerto Ricans in the 1999 data were more liberal and moderate and less conservative than they reported in the 1990 data. In fact, there was a drop of slightly more than 14 percentage points in the portion of Puerto Ricans who considered themselves some form of conservative during the interval. A similar shift appears to have occurred among

TABLE 3.4 Latino Ideological Identification

Ideology	Mexican (%) 1989/90[a]	1999[b]	Puerto Rican (%) 1989/90	1999	Cuban (%) 1989/90	1999	Central Amer.[c] (%) 1999	Dominican (%) 1999	Salvadoran (%) 1999	Other (%) 1999
Very liberal	4.9 (42)[d]	—	7.0 (40)	—	3.7 (16)	—	—	—	—	—
Liberal	11.6 (100)	26.25 (204)	12.3 (71)	34.55 (104)	13.0 (40)	34.03 (98)	29.80 (118)	28.72 (27)	25.97 (40)	33.62 (77)
Slightly liberal	12.1 (104)	—	9.2 (53)	—	6.3 (19)	—	—	—	—	—
Moderate	35.4 (305)	38.48 (299)	24.7 (142)	32.89 (99)	22.5 (69)	36.81 (106)	38.38 (152)	36.17 (34)	31.17 (48)	35.37 (81)
Slightly conservative	14.8 (128)	—	16.3 (93)	—	14.3 (44)	—	—	—	—	—
Conservative	15.4 (133)	35.26 (274)	22.7 (130)	32.56 (98)	34.2 (106)	29.17 (84)	31.82 (126)	29.17 (84)	42.86 (66)	31.0 (71)
Very Conservative	5.8 (50)	—	7.8 (45)	—	5.2 (18)	—	—	—	—	—
Total	100 (863)	100 (777)	100 (574)	100 (301)	100 (439)	100 (288)	100 (396)	100 (94)	100 (154)	100 (229)

[a] Latino National Political Survey.

[b] The Washington Post/Kaiser Family Foundation/Harvard University Survey Project, National Survey on Latinos in America, 1999.

[c] Central Americans, Dominicans, Salvadorans, and Other Latinos were not surveyed in the 1989–1990 Latino National Political Survey.

[d] Figures in parentheses represent the number of respondents.

Sources: Latino National Political Survey, Rodolfo O. de la Garza et al. 1992. Latino Voices: Mexican, Puerto Rican, and Cuban Perspectives on American Politics (Boulder: Westview Press), p. 84; The Washington Post/Kaiser Family Foundation/Harvard University Survey Project, National Survey on Latinos in America, 1999.

Cubans in the decade between the data collection points. Cubans are far more likely to identify themselves as liberal or moderate than conservative. This is a major reversal from the earlier period when Cubans were more likely to self-describe as some degree of conservative than as liberal or moderate. Regardless of their self-identified ideological label, large majorities of all three groups support what could be characterized as core elements of a liberal domestic agenda (de la Garza et al. 1992).

The 1999 *Washington Post* data provides information on the ideological orientations of other subgroups of Latinos that were not surveyed in the earlier LPNS survey. Salvadorans appear to be more conservative than moderate or liberal whereas Central Americans and Dominicans identify more as moderates. Almost equal percentages of Central Americans and Dominicans identify themselves as liberal or as conservative. Among the catchall category "Other Latinos," almost equal percentages identify as liberal, moderate, and conservative.

The recent collection of the Pilot Study of the National Asian American Political Survey data finally provides us with information on the ideological orientations of Asian Americans. Prior to these data, we had to rely on local survey results that did not break down the Asian population into specific ethnic groups to infer their ideological orientations. The 1984 Cain and Kiewiet survey of political attitudes of California's three principal minority groups—blacks, Latinos, and Asian Americans—found that Asians generally support a liberal domestic agenda: increased support for welfare programs, support of the equal rights amendment, and support of a ban on handguns. Moreover, they are far more likely than are blacks and Latinos in California to take a pro-choice position. Data from the PNAAPS, reported in Table 3.5, indicates that Japanese Americans are just as likely to identify as some form of liberal (34 percent) as they are to identify themselves as moderates or middle of the road (37 percent). About one-quarter (24 percent) identify themselves as some form of conservative. Chinese Americans are more likely to identify themselves as moderates (42 percent), with slightly less than one-third (30 percent) identifying as some form of liberal. Interestingly, 15 percent of Chinese Americans either do not identify with the labels of liberal or conservative or do not attach those labels to their political views. Koreans appear to be almost evenly distributed across the ideological spectrum. About one-third of Koreans identify as either some form of liberal (33 percent) or some form of conservative (31 percent), with slightly less than a third (28

TABLE 3.5   Asian American Ideological Identification

Ideology	Japanese (%)	Chinese (%)	Korean (%)	Filipino (%)	All[a] (%)
Very liberal	9	4	4	8	8
Somewhat liberal	25	26	29	32	28
Middle of the Road	37	42	28	18	32
Somewhat conservative	20	11	27	29	18
Very conservative	4	2	4	5	4
Not Sure	4	15	8	6	10
Total[b]	99	100	100	98	100

[a] Included are also responses for Vietnamese, and South East Asians, which are not reported here.
[b] Totals do not sum to 100 because those who refused to answer have been excluded.
Source: Pilot Study of the National Asian American Political Survey. The PNAAPS is the first multicity, multiethnic, and multilingual survey of Asian Americans. A total of 1,218 adults of the top six Asian ethnic origin groups residing in the nation's five major population hubs of Asians were surveyed by phone between Nov. 16, 2000, and Jan. 28, 2001. The survey was sponsored by a grant from the National Science Foundation (SES 9973435) and supplemented by a community grant from KCSI-TV of Los Angeles. Pei-te Lien is principal investigator.

percent) identifying as moderates. Filipino's are slightly more liberal than the other groups, with two-fifths (40 percent) classifying themselves as some form of liberal. They also had the smallest proportion of moderates (18 percent), and about one-third identifying as some form of conservative (34 percent).

Unfortunately, data on the ideological leanings of American Indians are rare. We identified only two studies. One study (Ritt 1979) concludes that Indians are ideologically moderate, but this conclusion is based on only 151 American Indian respondents to a national survey. The other study (Hoffman 1998), based on a slightly larger sample, found that Indians more likely identify themselves as moderate or conservative rather than liberal. In the absence of large numbers of American Indians in national probability samples and in an effort to move us further along on identifying ideological orientations of American Indians, we combined all Native American respondents in the American National Election Studies 1990 to 2002 cumulative data into a single file. This resulted in a sample of approximately 300 American Indians. Table 3.6 shows that, of those individuals who responded to the question, slightly more than two-fifths (42.67 percent) identified as some form of conservative, whereas a little less than one-third identified as moderate. About a quarter (25.78 percent) identified as some form of liberal. These results appear to contradict somewhat

TABLE 3.6   American Indian Ideological Identification

Ideological Identification	1990–2002 (%)
Extremely liberal	2.22 (5)[a]
Liberal	12.89 (29)
Slightly liberal	10.67 (24)
Moderate	31.56 (71)
Slightly conservative	17.78 (40)
Conservative	18.67 (42)
Extremely conservative	6.22 (14)
Total[b]	100 (n=225)

Note: 115 respondents did not answer the question.
[a] Figures in parentheses represent the number of respondents.
[b] Total does not add to 100 due to rounding.
Source: American National Election Studies Cumulative Data File (1948–2002). All respondents who identified as Native American in the 1990–2002 American National Election Studies were combined into a single file in order to obtain a sufficient sample size to identify partisan identification. These data do not allow for the tribal affiliation of the respondents.

the earlier findings of Ritt and Hoffman. Nevertheless, the small samples in Ritt's, Hoffman's, and our analyses suggest that we must be circumspect in discussing this group's ideology.

This section has revealed the complexity and range of the ideological identifications of blacks, Latinos, Asians, and, to a lesser extent, Indians. This range of orientations has implications for one strategy of the second dilemma—it makes the formation of interminority group coalitions more difficult. As Chapter 5 discusses, ideology is one of the bases on which interracial coalitions are formed. Shared racial minority group status in the United States does not mean that all minority groups occupy the same end of the ideological spectrum. Blacks, Latinos, and Asians are dispersed all along the ideological continuum, but the meanings of the terms liberal, moderate, and conservative for these groups differ from the popular culture definition of the terms.

Partisan Identification

As each presidential election nears, the media point to the heavily Democratic orientation and voting within the African American community. Many assume that because blacks vote heavily Democratic, all racial minority groups do likewise. Despite the acknowledgment of this orientation among African American voters, the media never ask the reasons for the orientation and how it came about. The Republican Party, in attempting to appeal to black voters, conveniently ignores the history of the relationship between blacks and the party dating from the party's inception in 1856. Most students of American politics and the public at large believe it was the policies of the Democratic Party rather than the pressure from the Republican Party that resulted in the present configuration of black partisan identification. Moreover, the media never explore the issues of the strength of blacks' commitment to the Democratic Party and whether other racial minority groups have different points of view.

Blacks

Although space does not allow a recitation of the complex history of the relationship between blacks and the political parties in the United States, a little of that history must be reviewed before we can place the current identification of African Americans with the Democratic Party in perspective. From the Republican Party's inception in 1856 around the issue of the abolition of slavery, blacks were heavily involved in it. Before the end of Reconstruction, 16 blacks were elected to Congress, all as Republicans. Blacks were actively involved in the party organization, with John R. Lynch, a state legislator from Mississippi, serving as temporary chair of the 1884 Republican Convention. At the 1892 Republican Convention, 13 percent of the delegates were black (Gurin, Hatchett, and Jackson 1989).

After the compromise of 1877, in which Rutherford B. Hayes promised to remove federal troops from the South and to allow the former Confederate states to deal with the "Negro problem" in their own way if he were elected president, the Democratic Party became the party of white supremacy, and the Republican Party became the party of blacks. In attempts to rebuild the Republican Party in the South, successive Republican presidents pursued a strategy aimed at drawing more southern whites into the party while at the same time pushing out or alienating black Republicans. The conflicts between what became known as the **Lily White Republicans** and the **Black and Tan Republicans**—the anti- and pro-civil rights wings of the party, respectively—continued until the 1956 election. Between 1877 and the complete shift of blacks to the Democratic Party in the 1964 elections, numerous pejorative acts and perfidious behaviors toward black Republicans by white

Republicans at the national, state, and local levels resulted in the change of blacks' allegiance.

It was not just the push of the Republican Party but also the pull of the Democratic Party that resulted in a shift of allegiance by blacks. The neglect and hostility of Republican administrations led some prominent blacks, including W. E. B. DuBois, to support Woodrow Wilson in the 1912 presidential election. However, Wilson's subsequent segregation of the federal government and the city of Washington, D.C., and his limited attention to black concerns resulted in blacks returning to the Republican Party in subsequent elections. The perception that Herbert Hoover was pursuing an overtly racist strategy in his administration policies and his explicit overtures to Lily White Republicans, coupled with the Depression and the election of Franklin D. Roosevelt in 1932, set the stage for the beginning of the black party realignment.

Although the implementation of many of Roosevelt's New Deal policies was tinged with racial discrimination, and many blacks were still uncertain about Roosevelt's commitment to addressing issues of concern to blacks, many blacks were persuaded enough to vote Democratic in large numbers. Roosevelt's informal formation of a group of black government advisers, commonly referred to as the Kitchen Cabinet—which included such prominent individuals as Robert C. Weaver, Ralph J. Bunche, Mary McLeod Bethune, and Rayford W. Logan, among others—was a first for any presidential administration.[1] Moreover, the visibility of Roosevelt's wife, Eleanor, on issues of importance to the broader black community raised blacks' confidence in Roosevelt's commitment to them. Thus, by Roosevelt's 1944 reelection, blacks voted overwhelmingly Democratic and provided the margin of victory in seven states: Pennsylvania, Maryland, Michigan, Missouri, New York, Illinois, and New Jersey (Gurin, Hatchett, and Jackson 1989:36).

After Roosevelt's death, however, Harry Truman found black loyalty to the Democratic Party was tied to Franklin Roosevelt and realized that he could not automatically count on black votes in the 1948 election. Both Truman and the Republican candidate, Thomas Dewey, knew they would need black votes in the major urban areas to win. Dewey, as governor of New York, had a very good record on issues of concern to blacks. Prior to the 1948 election, Truman had made his civil rights recommendations, based on a report from a commission he had established, to Congress. In addition, a civil rights plank was inserted into the Democratic platform at the 1948 Democratic Convention, which resulted in the walkout of southern Democrats—led by then-Governor Strom Thurmond—and in the formation of the Dixiecrats. The controversy surrounding Truman and his civil rights initiatives led many to assume that Dewey would win the election; however, Truman was victorious.

In the 1952 election, in protest of the influence of the Dixiecrats and the connection between the Dixiecrats and the Democratic Party in the South, many southern blacks voted for Dwight Eisenhower. Eisenhower's appointment of Earl Warren as chief justice of the Supreme Court and the subsequent ruling on *Brown v. Board of Education of Topeka* in 1954 led many blacks to credit Eisenhower with the victory.[2] An estimated 38 percent of the black vote went to Eisenhower in the 1956 election (Gurin, Hatchett, and Jackson 1989). During his second term, however, Eisenhower's administration was viewed as less committed to civil rights and equality, as was evidenced by Eisenhower's reluctance to implement the 1957 Civil Rights Act and to take a strong stand to enforce school desegregation in Little Rock. This reluctance on the part of the Republican administration played to the Democrats' advantage in the 1960 presidential election contest between John F. Kennedy and Richard M. Nixon, although both parties actively campaigned for the black vote. The black vote shifted in large numbers to the Democrats in that election primarily because Kennedy's telephone call to Coretta Scott King to express his concern over the jailing of her husband Martin Luther King Jr. in Georgia got through before Nixon's call. The shift observed in 1960 solidified in 1964 when the Republicans nominated Arizona Senator Barry Goldwater as their presidential candidate. Goldwater's extreme conservative positions and his opposition to civil rights legislation alienated many blacks who previously had supported the Republican Party. Black voters have remained solidly Democratic since 1964.

In the 1984 NBES data, 83.5 percent of blacks surveyed considered themselves Democrats, yet the degree of partisanship varied. As Table 3.7 demonstrates, slightly less than half of blacks reported themselves as strong Democrats; in 1988, considerably more blacks identified themselves as such. The percentage of blacks identifying themselves as strong Democrats decreased to slightly less than half in the 1993 NBPS data and the NBES96. In 2004, 63 percent of blacks identified as Democrats, almost a quarter (23 percent) as independents, and 10 percent as Republicans. Both the 1984 and 1988 NBES data suggest a gender split within the black electorate—black women were more likely to identify strongly with the

TABLE 3.7   Black Partisan Identification

Partisan Identification	1984 (%)[a]	1988 (%)[a]	1993[b] (%)	1996[c] (%)	2004[d] (%)
Democrat	—[e]	—	—	—	63
Strong Democrat	45.8 (521)[f]	57.0 (260)	49.5 (597)	49.8 (583)	—
Weak Democrat	23.5 (267)	21.5 (98)	20.7 (249)	20.1 (236)	—
Independent/ leaning toward Democrat	14.2 (162)	10.3 (47)	12.4 (149)	—	—
Independent	4.8 (55)	2.9 (13)	6.5 (78)	20.4 (239)	23
Independent/ leaning toward Republican	—[g]	—	3.3 (40)	—	—
Republican—all strengths	7.8 (88)	6.3 (29)	3.7 (45)	4.0 (47)	—
Republican	—	—	—	—	10
Other/apolitical	3.8 (44)	2.0 (9)	3.9 (47)	5.7 (67)	—
Don't know	—	—	—	—	4
Total	100 (1,137)	100 (456)	100 (1205)	100 (1172)	100 (850)

[a] Preelection sample, 1984 and 1988 National Black Election Studies.
[b] 1993–94 National Black Politics Study.
[c] 1996 National Black Election Study, preelection sample.
[d] Joint Center for Political and Economic Studies, 2004 National Opinion Poll.
[e] Response categories were Democrat, Independent, and Republican; no measurement of strength.
[f] Figures in parentheses represent the number of respondents.
[g] Differences in response categories between National Black Election Studies and National Black Politics Study.

Source: Authors' computations from the 1984 and 1988 National Black Election Studies, 1993–1994 National Black Politics Study, and 1996 National Black Election Study; data from Table E, Joint Center for Political and Economic Studies, 2004 National Opinion Poll.

Democratic Party than were black men; the latter were more likely to be weak or independent Democratic supporters, political independents, or Republicans (Tate 1993:64). The 1993 NBPS data suggest that the gender split may have dissipated—black men now appear just as likely as black women to identify strongly with the Democratic Party. Yet the 1996 data indicate that the gender split had returned, with black women far more likely to identify with the Democratic Party than were black men. In 2004, the JCPES2004 data suggest, based on responses to potential presidential vote choice, the gender gap had disappeared again, with almost equal proportions of black women (69 percent) and black men (68 percent) indicating a preference for the Democratic candidate.

There also appears to be a generational split emerging that is the obverse of previous observed black generational differences. In past studies, older blacks tended to be more strongly Democratic than were younger blacks. Yet, the 2004 JCPES data suggests that young blacks (ages 18–25) are more Democratic (71 percent) than older blacks, where only 55 percent of those ages 51–64 and 66 percent of those over age 65 identified as Democrats. It also appears that whatever shift might have occurred toward the Republican Party within black Americans is from this older cohort. In 2002, JCPES data indicated only 5 percent of blacks 51 to 64 years of age and 7 percent of blacks over 65 years of age identified as Republicans. In 2004, however, the proportions had jumped to 15 and 12 percent, respectively. The other age cohorts' identification with the Republican Party remained either the same or declined.

Latinos

The history of Latinos and the two political parties is not as well documented as that of African Americans. Overall, Latinos tend to lean Democratic in their partisan identification, but they do not equal blacks in their strength of identification with the Democratic Party. As data in Table 3.8 demonstrate, in the 1990 LPNS data, two-thirds of Mexican Americans indicated that they were Democrats of varying strengths. In 1999, however, only two-fifths (41.58 percent) identified as Democrats, but close to two-fifths (38.21 percent) identified themselves as independents. This is a substantial increase from the 11 percent that identified as independents in the LPNS data a decade earlier. Interestingly, the proportion of Mexican Americans that identify as Republicans remained relatively constant over the interval. Thus, the loss for the Democrats was not a gain for the Republicans but indicates a greater willingness on the part of Mexican Americans to remain unattached either political party. Given Puerto Ricans' tendency to self-identify across the ideological spectrum, popular wisdom would predict a more Republican identification among those that identify as conservative. Once again, the data run counter to conventional wisdom. Nearly three-fourths of Puerto Ricans in 1990 and close to two-thirds in 1999 identified themselves as Democrats of varying strengths.

Cubans departed significantly from this pattern. In 1990, more than two-thirds of Cubans identified themselves as Republicans. In fact, more Cubans identified themselves as strong Republicans than the proportion of

TABLE 3.8 Latino Partisan Identification

Partisan Identification	Mexican (%) 1989/90[a]	Mexican (%) 1999[b]	Puerto Rican (%) 1989/90	Puerto Rican (%) 1999	Cuban (%) 1989/90	Cuban (%) 1999	Central Amer.[c] (%) 1999	Dominican (%) 1999	Salvadoran (%) 1999	Other (%) 1999
Democrat[d]	—	41.58 (284)	—	60.0 (165)	—	34.30 (95)	48.22 (176)	66.67 (58)	45.39 (64)	46.0 (92)
Strong Democrat	31.0[e] (252)	—	37.2 (205)	—	14.4 (45)	—	—	—	—	—
Not strong Democrat	28.6 (232)	—	26.4 (145)	—	5.1 (16)	—	—	—	—	—
Closer to Democrat	7.2 (59)	—	7.4 (40)	—	6.0 (18)	—	—	—	—	—
Independent/other	11.5 (94)	—	11.5 (63)	—	5.7 (18)	—	—	—	—	—
Independent (only)	—	38.21 (261)	—	24.0 (66)	—	25.63 (71)	40.0 (146)	22.99 (20)	39.01 (55)	29.50 (59)
Republican	—	20.20 (138)	—	16.0 (44)	—	40.07 (111)	11.78 (43)	10.34 (9)	15.60 (22)	24.50 (49)
Closer to Republican	5.5 (45)	—	3.6 (20)	—	4.8 (15)	—	—	—	—	—
Not strong Republican	11.6 (94)	—	7.2 (40)	—	16.2 (50)	—	—	—	—	—
Strong Republican	4.4 (36)	—	6.7 (37)	—	47.8 (147)	—	—	—	—	—
Total	100 (811)	100 (683)	100 (550)	100 (275)	100 (309)	100 (277)	100 (365)	100 (87)	100 (141)	100 (200)

[a] Latino National Political Survey.

[b] The *Washington Post*/Kaiser Family Foundation/Harvard University Survey Project, National Survey on Latinos in America, 1999.

[c] Central Americans, Dominicans, Salvadorans, and Other Latinos were not surveyed in the 1989–1990 Latino National Political Survey.

[d] Response categories were Democrat, Independent and Republican.

[e] Figures in parentheses represent the number of respondents.

Source: Rodolfo O. de la Garza et al. 1992. *Latino Voices: Mexican, Puerto Rican, and Cuban Perspectives on American Politics* (Boulder: Westview Press): 127.

Protestors demonstrate outside six-year-old Elián Gonzalez's Miami, Florida, home, Friday, April 7, 2000, in an effort to keep him in the United States. (AP Photo: Amy E. Conn)

Mexicans and Puerto Ricans who identified as strong Democrats. Once again, however, we must caution that Cuban identification with the Republican Party stems more from foreign policy concerns, particularly U.S. relations with Cuba, than from concern with social policy issues. The LNPS demonstrates that the majority of Cubans favor increased government spending on health, crime, drug control, education, the environment, child

TABLE 3.9   Asian American Partisan Identification

	Japanese (%)	Chinese (%)	Korean (%)	Filipino (%)	All[a] (%)
No, do not think in those terms	18	33	8	13	20
Republican	9	8	21	20	14
Democrat	40	32	43	40	36
Independent	20	3	12	14	13
Not Sure	11	23	15	10	16
Total[b]	98	99	99	97	99

[a] Included are also responses for Vietnamese and South East Asians, which are not reported here.
[b] Totals do not sum to 100 because those who refused to answer have been excluded.

Source: Pilot Study of the National Asian American Political Survey. The PNAAPS is the first multicity, multiethnic, and multilingual survey of Asian Americans. A total of 1,218 adults of the top six Asian ethnic origin groups residing in the nation's five major population hubs of Asians were surveyed by phone between Nov. 16, 2000, and Jan. 28, 2001. The survey was sponsored by a grant from the National Science Foundation (SES 9973435) and supplemented by a community grant from KCSI-TV of Los Angeles. Pei-te Lien is principal investigator.

services, and bilingual education. In essence, a majority of Cubans support what could be characterized as core elements of a liberal domestic agenda, even though they are more likely to self-identify as conservative (de la Garza et al. 1992:14). Yet by 1999, Cuban identification with the Republican Party had dropped to around two-fifths (40.07 percent), whereas the proportion of independents and Democrats had increased. Data on the newer Latino groups also suggest a preference for the Democrats, especially among Dominicans (66.67 percent), or for remaining independent of both political parties. The increasing proportion of Latino independents indicates that these voters are susceptible to appeals from both political parties.

Little research exists on the political behaviors, attitudes, and experiences of Latinas (women), but the few extant studies suggest some subtle gender differences within the Latino groups. On partisan identification, one study that used national exit poll data for the 1980, 1984, and 1988 presidential elections found Latinas to be more liberal and more Democratic than Latinos (Welch and Sigelman 1992).

Asians

Until recently, research had indicated that in the aggregate, Asian Americans appeared to be more Republican than Democratic, with Chinese

Asian American supporters of Republican presidential candidate Texas Governor George W. Bush greet him at the Asian Market Garden in Westminster, California, September 13, 2000. [Framed photo is former President George H. W. Bush, Governor Bush's father.] (AP Photo: M. Spencer Green)

Americans being more strongly Republican than other groups (Cain and Kiewiet 1986; Stokes 1988; Cain, Kiewiet, and Uhlaner 1991). However, partisan attachment was weak, and either party could benefit from Asian American support.

Data from the recent PNAAPS presented in Table 3.9 suggests that a shift appears to have occurred, with all Asian groups more likely to identify with the Democratic Party than with the Republican Party. Although early re-search indicated that Chinese Americans leaned Republican, these data do not confirm that early finding. Only 8 percent of Chinese Americans in the sample identify as Republicans. About one-fifth of Koreans and Filipinos identify as Republicans, but two-fifths identify as Democrats. What is inter-esting about these data is the significant number of all Asians who indicate that they do not think in partisan terms and the significant number that identify as political independents. About one-third of Chinese Americans say that they do not think of themselves in partisan terms, and about one-fifth of Japanese Americans identify as political independents. Also, signifi-cant numbers indicated that they were not sure. These findings appear to be consistent with the observation that a high proportion of Asian Ameri-cans consider themselves political independents rather than members of either political party. Asian Americans as a whole are more likely than ei-ther blacks or Latinos to be political independents.

American Indians

Few studies exist of the political behavior of American Indians in non-tribal elections. The existing studies indicate that Indian peoples are not strongly tied to either political party but tend to lean toward the Demo-crats, although significant differences in party affiliation are found across tribes. For example, over time the Navajos have shifted from Republican to Democratic and, during the Reagan years, slightly back to the Republi-cans in national elections, yet they remain fiercely Democratic in Arizona state politics. Since the 1956 presidential election, the Papagos have con-sistently voted Democratic (Ritt 1979; McCool 1982). An examination of the partisan preferences of American Indian voters in the Upper Midwest (Wisconsin, Minnesota, and North and South Dakota) in elections from 1982 through 1992 reveals a strong preference for Democrats (Doherty 1994). Hoffman (1998) also found that American Indians were more likely to be Democrats or Independents than Republicans. Personnel from the

TABLE 3.10   American Indian Partisan Identification

Partisan Identification	1990–2002 (%)
Strong Democrat	14.33 (51)[a]
Weak Democrat	17.98 (64)
Independent leaning Democrat	16.85 (60)
Independent	11.24 (40)
Independent Leaning Republican	13.76 (49)
Weak Republican	14.61 (52)
Strong Republican	11.24 (40)
Total	100 (n=356)

[a] Figures in parentheses represent the number of respondents.

Source: American National Election Studies Cumulative Data File (1948–2002). All respondents who identified as Native American in the 1990–2002 American National Election Studies were combined into a single file in order to obtain a sufficient sample size to identify partisan identification. These data do not allow for the tribal affiliation of the respondents.

Democratic National Committee credited Indian voters with providing the margin of victory for the Clinton-Gore ticket in Arizona in the 1996 presidential election (Michel 1998).

We turn again to the American Indian respondents in the combined American National Election Studies data in an effort to provide more information on American Indian partisan identification. Table 3.10 shows that slightly less than half (49.16 percent) of American Indians identify as either Democrats or lean Democratic, whereas slightly less than two-fifths (39.4 percent) identify as either Republican or lean Republican. Approximately one-tenth, 11.24 percent, of the sample identify as independents.

One of the factors that has determined Indian party affiliations at the national level has been an administration's stance on Indian issues. During Richard Nixon's administration, many Indians, such as the Navajos, voted Republican because Nixon was viewed as having a strong stance regarding American Indian policy. But they shifted to Jimmy Carter during his years in office because he was also viewed as being "good for Indians." President Clinton enjoyed strong American Indian support because of his policies and his outreach to American Indian tribes and their leaders. These limited data suggest that categorizing American Indians as either primarily Democrats or Republicans is impossible without taking into account reservation compared with nonreservation Indians and a party's stance on federal Indian policy.

Voting Behavior

Prior to the Voting Rights Act, only 6.7 percent of blacks in Mississippi were registered to vote; by 1967, 59.8 percent of voting-age blacks were registered. It is estimated that in the seven states originally covered by the act, black registration increased from 29.3 percent in March 1965 to 56.6 percent in 1971–1972. Moreover, "the Justice Department estimated that in the five years after passage, almost as many blacks registered in Alabama, Mississippi, Georgia, Louisiana, North Carolina, and South Carolina as in the entire century before 1965" (Davidson 1992:21). Table 3.11 shows the 2002 registration and voting figures for the 44 U.S. states with the highest proportions of blacks and Latinos in their electorates. Because "most American national elections are won by 5 percent or less," blacks and Latinos have the potential to be a significant force in determining the outcome of these elections (Williams 1987:101). Moreover, in some states the ability of blacks, Latinos, Asians, and American Indians to decide electoral outcomes is very strong.

In 2002, approximately 210 million Americans were eligible to vote. Non-Latino African Americans accounted for 10.59 percent of the total voting-age population and Latinos for 7.41 percent of that population. Non-Latino Asian constituted 2.86 percent of the total voting-age population. The Census Bureau did not report data for American Indians, Aleuts, and Eskimos for the 2002 election.

In 1968, the gap between black and white voter registration rates was 9.2 percentage points; this had narrowed to only 3.3 percentage points in 1984 (Williams 1987). Yet as Table 3.12 demonstrates, by 2002, the gap had widened again to 6.7 percentage points—69.4 percent of non-Latino white voting-age citizens were registered to vote compared with 62.7 percent of non-Latino blacks. The gap between non-Latino white and Latino and non-Latino Asian voter registration rates was considerably wider, with the difference of 16.9 percentage points between non-Latino whites and Latinos and 20.2 percentage points between non-Latino whites and non-Latino Asians. Stated differently, only 52.5 percent of voting-age Latino citizens and 49.2 percent of non-Latino Asian citizens who were of voting age were registered to vote. What explains the increase in the gap between white and black voters, and why are the numbers of Latinos and Asian Americans registered to vote at levels significantly below those of blacks and whites?

TABLE 3.11 Registration and Voting by Race for 44 States with Highest Black and Latino Proportions of the Electorate, 2002

	% of Total Electorate (Citizens Only)			% of Voting-Age Citizens Registered			% of Registered Who Voted		
	Non-Latino Black	Latino	Non-Latino White	Non-Latino Black	Latino	Non-Latino White	Non-Latino Black	Latino	Non-Latino White
Mississippi	31.7	1.2	66.6	69.1	34.8	72.1	59.2	50.0	61.9
Louisiana	29.5	3.5	65.6	75.1	59.4	75.6	64.1	60.3	69.0
Georgia	29.2	1.9	67.6	63.9	50.0	65.3	63.1	62.5	65.8
Maryland	26.0	2.5	67.4	63.2	47.7	67.3	72.7	64.3	78.9
South Carolina	24.2	2.1	73.2	68.8	44.3	68.2	71.0	66.7	68.0
Alabama	24.1	0.5	74.7	67.5	58.8	74.2	64.1	0.0	69.1
Virginia	20.8	1.8	73.3	49.3	36.8	66.7	57.3	43.8	59.4
North Carolina	20.4	1.5	74.7	59.3	39.3	66.2	72.4	66.7	69.0
Delaware	18.2	3.0	76.6	58.8	52.9	71.6	61.7	55.6	66.8
Arkansas	15.0	2.3	81.0	63.5	52.3	64.4	71.0	65.2	73.6
New York	13.4	10.5	71.6	61.4	51.7	67.0	66.7	54.9	67.3
Illinois	13.3	6.2	77.9	69.4	56.5	66.3	74.1	57.2	69.9
Tennessee	13.2	0.9	84.3	56.1	37.1	65.2	73.8	46.2	73.7
Texas	12.9	27.6	56.3	67.7	56.2	70.2	68.2	48.8	65.0
Michigan	12.8	2.3	82.3	66.1	65.3	72.9	68.9	51.4	70.3
Florida	12.5	13.9	72.1	59.9	59.7	66.6	69.6	69.9	74.2
Ohio	11.6	1.3	86.1	61.0	40.7	66.0	66.2	63.0	66.8
New Jersey	11.1	9.6	75.8	59.8	44.7	65.9	68.5	62.5	65.9
Missouri	11.1	1.0	86.7	74.8	52.5	72.8	70.1	57.1	72.9
Connecticut	8.8	7.3	82.3	65.6	56.0	70.2	56.2	51.0	70.2
Oklahoma	8.8	2.8	78.4	57.4	55.1	70.6	66.9	76.3	73.3
Pennsylvania	8.5	2.6	87.7	60.3	45.8	63.8	71.7	60.6	68.1
Indiana	7.4	1.5	90.5	54.0	42.3	62.6	74.5	46.7	65.4

(continues)

TABLE 3.11 (continued)

	% of Total Electorate (Citizens Only)			% of Voting-Age Citizens Registered			% of Registered Who Voted		
	Non-Latino Black	Latino	Non-Latino White	Non-Latino Black	Latino	Non-Latino White	Non-Latino Black	Latino	Non-Latino White
Kentucky	7.2	0.4	91.5	53.7	58.3	68.8	65.5	71.4	68.0
California	7.1	20.2	60.5	55.9	50.8	64.0	68.4	59.8	73.1
Kansas	7.0	5.5	85.0	45.9	42.1	69.8	74.2	55.6	73.4
Nevada	6.3	13.1	74.8	50.0	36.3	60.9	69.8	64.6	77.1
Massachusetts	5.3	4.0	88.4	72.0	41.1	70.1	78.2	62.2	73.4
Wisconsin	4.2	2.8	90.8	57.6	45.1	70.7	71.6	39.2	71.2
Colorado	3.9	12.2	81.3	61.4	50.8	68.9	70.0	64.1	76.4
Rhode Island	3.9	4.5	89.4	48.3	48.5	67.9	57.1	75.0	75.6
Nebraska	3.7	3.4	91.4	61.4	40.0	72.4	51.9	56.3	66.2
New Mexico	2.8	39.2	47.2	71.4	56.7	62.3	72.0	71.2	78.5
Washington	2.7	3.2	87.8	64.0	47.0	71.6	67.6	54.0	73.2
Arizona	2.7	16.2	75.9	56.7	48.7	60.2	76.5	59.8	75.2
Minnesota	2.5	1.3	94.1	44.4	66.7	79.5	87.5	78.1	84.9
Alaska	2.4	3.6	74.9	40.0	73.3	74.6	75.0	72.7	77.6
West Virginia	2.4	0.6	96.4	45.5	62.5	60.7	66.7	60.0	61.1
Iowa	2.1	2.3	94.5	68.2	34.0	72.5	53.3	75.0	70.8
Oregon	1.8	3.3	89.9	66.7	59.3	70.4	93.3	43.8	80.9
Hawaii	1.4	2.9	24.1	36.4	30.4	59.2	100.0	85.7	84.2
Utah	0.9	4.8	91.3	53.8	44.9	65.4	100.0	35.5	69.7
Wyoming	0.8	4.9	91.6	NA	55.6	66.7	NA	70.0	83.6
Idaho	0.2	3.9	93.9	100.0	38.9	63.1	50.0	57.1	75.3

NA—Base in data sample was too small to make an estimate.

Source: U.S. Census Bureau, Current Population Survey, November 2002 (July 28, 2004), "Table 4a. Reported Voting and Registration of the Total Voting-Age Population, by Sex, Race and Hispanic Origin, for States: November 2002," http://www.census.gov/population/www/socdemo/voting/p20-552.html.

TABLE 3.12 Registration and Voting by Race, National Sample Citizens Only: White, Black, Latino, and Asian, 2002

Race	% of VAP[a]	% Citizens	% of Citizens Registered	% of Citizens Reported Voting	% of Registered Voting
Non-Latino White	69.94	98	69.4	49.1	70.7
Non-Latino Black	10.59	95	62.7	42.7	68.1
Latino[b]	7.41	62	52.5	30.4	57.9
Asian/Pacific Islander	2.86	62	49.2	31.2	63.4

[a] VAP=Voting-Age Population (population 18 years and older).
[b] Latinos may be of any race.
Source: U.S. Census Bureau, Current Population Survey, November 2002 (July 28, 2004), "Table 2. Reported Voting and Registration, by Race, Hispanic Origin, Sex, and Age, for the United States: November 2002," http://www.census.gov/population/www/socdemo/voting/p20-552.html.

Since 1964, black registration rates have followed general national trends, going up in the 1960s, down in the 1970s, and up again in the 1980s (Williams 1987). The 1990s have exhibited a mixed pattern. Drops in black registration rates from the rates in 1984 and 1988 seem to parallel similar drops in white registration from the rates for the 1984 to 1988 time period. Although white registration in 1992, at 70.1 percent, was higher than the 67.9 percent registration rate in 1988, by 1994, the rate had dropped again significantly, to 64.6 percent, but had climbed again to 69.3 percent in 1998. Black registration rates fluctuated much like that of whites. Jesse Jackson's 1984 presidential campaign and the resultant voter registration drives apparently increased voter registration, but Jackson's 1988 run, although more successful in terms of primary outcomes, may not have had the same effect on national black registration efforts (Tate 1993). In 1992, black registration stood at 63.9 percent, dropping to 58.5 percent in 1994, rebounding to 63.7 percent in 1998, and remaining relatively stable in 2002, at 62.7 percent.

Latinos and non-Latino Asians have considerably lower registration rates than do non-Latino African Americans. Latino registration rates have also dropped since 1984 when they stood at 40.1 percent of the voting-age population, declining to 35.5 percent in 1988, 35.1 percent in 1992, and 31.3 percent in 1994. Recent data that look only at voting-age citizens, rather than the entire voting-age population that includes non-citizen Latinos, provides a much different portrait of Latino registration rates (see Table 3.12). Using the voting-age population in 1994, only 31.3

percent of Latinos were registered. Yet in 2002, using Latino citizen voting-age population, 52.5 percent were registered to vote. Although this number is lower than black and white registration rates, it is significantly higher than the 1994 rate. Latinos are disproportionately younger, poorer, and less educated than the general population, which may suggest that the labyrinth of laws and administrative procedures that exist may have a greater suppressive effect on Latino registration than the 9 percent effect estimated for the population in general (Calvo and Rosenstone 1989; Hero 1992). Other reasons for lower registration might include difficulty with the English language (Calvo and Rosenstone 1989; Meier and Stewart 1991), and difficulty in understanding U.S. politics and the U.S. political system (Vigil 1987:43). Because 1992 was the first year the Census Bureau included Asian Americans in the survey, we can observe changes only from 1992 to 2002. Again, the early data included all voting-age Asians regardless of citizenship, and those data indicated that the percentage of Asian Americans registered to vote declined from 31.2 percent in 1992 to 28.7 percent in 1994. Examining data for Asian citizens of voting age in 1998 and 2002 presents a picture of a substantial increase in voter registration over the figures for all Asians regardless of citizenship status; 49.1 percent of Asian voting-age citizens were registered to vote in 1998, and as Table 3.12 indicates, a similar percentage, 49.2 percent, were registered to vote in 2002. Yet the numbers are still below registration rates of other groups.

Again, American Indian voting and registration data were not reported by the Census Bureau for 2002. But 1998 data from the Census Bureau for American Indians suggest a continuation of the pattern identified in the 1994 data. In 1994, 55.5 percent of the American Indian population of voting age was registered to vote, and in 1998, 58 percent of voting-age American Indian citizens were registered to vote. American Indian voter registration rates almost parallel the levels of blacks, but they are slightly lower.

Although 62.7 percent of the black voting-age citizen population was registered to vote in 2002, 68.1 percent of those blacks who were registered to vote reported voting in the 2002 congressional elections (see Table 3.12). This represents only a 2.6-percentage-point gap between black and white voting rates among registered voters in 2002. Voter turnout rates are always lower in midterm congressional elections, elections held two years after the last presidential elections. The national voter turnout rate for the 2002 congressional elections was 48.1 percent, calculated on the total voting-age population in the United States without regard to citizenship status. This is down from the already low voter turnout rate of 59.5 percent for the 2002 presidential election. The voting levels for Latinos and Asians were once again substantially lower than those for African Americans. Only 30.4 percent of voting-age Latino citizens and 31.2 percent of voting-age Asian citizens actually voted. This represents a gap between Latino and white and Asian and white voting rates of 18.7 percentage points and 17.9 percentage points, respectively. The differences between black and Latino and black and Asian rates were 12.3 percentage points and 11.5 percentage points, respectively. Looking at the behavior of registered voters presents a slightly better yet still deficit picture of Latino and Asian voting. Of those Latino and Asian citizens who were registered to vote, 52.5 and 49.2 percent, respectively, slightly more than a majority (57.9 percent) of Latinos and close to two-thirds of Asians registered to vote actually voted. These numbers are still less than those for non-Latino whites and non-Latino blacks. Again, using the 1998 data, American Indian voting levels are close to those of Asian Americans in 2002, with 61 percent of American Indians registered to vote having voted in the 1998 congressional elections. This level is far above the limited data available on earlier American Indian voting that suggest that for the six elections from 1982 through 1992, turnout averaged approximately 40 percent. Clearly, in 1998, American Indian voter turnout was higher than that for Latinos, but lower than that for non-Latino whites, non-Latino blacks, and Asian Americans.

Of particular interest are the differences in registration and voting rates between men and women in the three groups—non-Latino blacks, Latinos, and non-Latino Asians—shown in Table 3.13. In 2002, black women and Latina women had higher registration rates than did black men and Latino men. When we compare black women and Latinas, both groups that held a registration advantage maintained that advantage in voting—a higher percentage of black and Latina women voted than did black and Latino men. When examining the voting rates for registered voters that reported voting, however, only black women continued to maintain their advantage over black men. Although the Census Bureau did not report data for 1998 for American Indian men and women separately, 1994 data indicated that American Indian women had higher registration and higher voting rates than did American Indian men.

TABLE 3.13   Registration and Voting by Race and Sex, National Sample
Citizens Only: Black, Latino, and Asian, 2002

| Category | Non-Latino Black | | Latino | | Non-Latino Asian | |
	Male	Female	Male	Female	Male	Female
% VAP[a]	9.6	11.4	7.5	7.3	2.3	2.9
% VAP Registered	57.9	66.5	49.8	55.1	50.5	48.0
%VAP Reported Voting	38.5	46.0	29.3	31.5	32.9	29.6
% Registered Voting	66.5	69.2	58.8	57.1	65.2	61.6

[a]VAP = Voting-Age Population (population over 18 years old).

Source: U.S. Census Bureau, Current Population Survey, November 2002 (July 28, 2004), "Table 2. Reported Voting and Registration, by Race, Hispanic Origin, Sex, and Age, for the United States: November 2002," http://www.census.gov/population/www/socdemo/voting/p20-552.html.

The reasons for higher levels of registration and voting among black women than among black men may stem from the higher levels of education and the labor force distribution of black women in more white-collar and fewer blue-collar jobs than is true for the black male labor force, although black women have higher turnout rates than black men within the same occupation, income, education, and employment status group. Survey data on group consciousness reveal that another possible reason for the differences may be that black women perceive discrimination on the basis of both race and gender. This dual consciousness, therefore, may foster participation of black women to a greater degree than racial consciousness alone stimulates that of black men (Williams 1987). The same argument could be made for the higher levels of registration and participation of Latinas and Asian women, although no survey data are available to support this contention.

Given the high levels of immigrants within the broader Latino and Asian populations, one question that is often raised is whether these immigrant populations, once naturalized, will register and vote in similar or higher numbers than the native-born populations. It is assumed that given the increasing size of the Latino population in particular, Latino political strength will increase substantially as soon as these new immigrants become naturalized citizens. Although we are unable to answer this question definitely, the data presented in Table 3.14 may be sugges-

TABLE 3.14   1996, 2000, and 2004 Presidential Election Results by Race, Gender, and Party Affiliation

	1996			2000			2004		
	Clinton	Dole	Perot	Gore	Bush	Nader	Kerry	Bush	Nader
Total Vote (%)	49	41	8	48	48	2	48	51	1
Whites	43	46	9	42	54	3	41	58	0
Blacks	84	12	4	90	8	1	88	11	0
Latinos	72	21	6	67	31	2	53	44	2
Asians	43	48	8	54	41	4	56	44	*
Black Men	78	15	5	85	12	1	*a	*	*
Black Women	89	8	2	94	6	0	*	*	*
Black Democrats	93	4	2	97	2	0	*	*	*
Black Republicans	39	54	5	*	*	*	*	*	*
Black Independents	69	18	10	74	22	2	*	*	*

[a] Edison/Mitofsky exit polling did not provide information on detailed categories of the black sample in 2004.

Source: Voter News Service exit polling, 1996 and 2000, *New York Times*. Edison/Mitofsky exit polling, 2004, CNN.

tive of future trends. In each instance—black, Asian and Pacific Islander, and Latino—naturalized citizens are registered to vote in proportions lower than the native-born population, and larger proportions of the naturalized citizens are not registered to vote. When we look at voting behavior in the 2002 elections, native-born blacks voted in higher proportions than did naturalized blacks, 42.4 percent to 40.2 percent. The same appears to be the case for native-born Asians who voted in a larger proportions than did naturalized Asians—32.3 percent to 30.5 percent. The only reversal in this pattern appears to be among Latinos, where naturalized Latinos voted in greater proportions than did native-born Latinos—33.4 percent to 29.5 percent. Data from the 2000 election also reveal a similar pattern—naturalized Latinos reported voting in greater proportions than did native-born Latinos—49.6 percent and 43.6 percent, respectively. Although two election cycles are not sufficient to settle the question of increased Latino political strength from newly naturalized citizens, we should note that although the rates are higher among naturalized Latinos than among native-born Latinos, the numbers are not especially high.

The 1996 Elections

The 1996 presidential election saw President Bill Clinton reelected with stronger Latino support than in 1992 (72 percent in 1996 versus 61 percent in 1992), solid black support (84 percent in 1996 and 83 percent in 1992), and substantially increased Asian American support (43 percent in 1996 and 31 percent in 1992) (see Table 3.14). Overall, voter turnout in 1996 was substantially lower than that in 1992 (95.8 million as compared to 104.4 million)—in fact, 1996 is estimated to be the lowest level of voter participation since 1924 (Bositis 1996). (Figures from the U.S. Bureau of the Census on the 1996 presidential election say the turnout rate was 54.2 percent overall, 56 percent for whites, 50.6 percent for blacks, and 26.7 percent for Latinos.) Although voter turnout was down overall, absolute black voter turnout increased from 1992 to 1996. Whereas in 1992 blacks had cast 8 percent (8.35 million votes) of all ballots, in 1996 that proportion increased to 10 percent (9.58 million votes). Black women had outvoted black men in 1992; in 1996, black men and women voted in equal numbers. Yet the equality of turnout rates actually represents a decline of more than 400,000 in the total number of black female voters and an increase of 1.6 million black male voters from 1992 to 1996 (Bositis 1996). Even though both black women and men overwhelmingly voted for Clinton, a larger proportion of black women voted for him than did black men—89 percent and 78 percent, respectively. Interestingly, 39 percent of black Republicans and 69 percent of black independents voted for Clinton as well.

As with black voters, Latino voter turnout increased substantially from 1992 to 1996—from 3 percent (3.13 million) to 5 percent (4.8 million) of all votes cast (Bositis 1996). Aside from voting overwhelmingly for Clinton and in increasing numbers, Latinos voted overwhelmingly Democratic in congressional races—73 percent to 27 percent. This was a significant increase over the 1994 congressional elections when Latinos favored Democrats 61 percent to 39 percent (DeSipio and de la Garza 1997).

Asian American voter turnout in 1996 remained at 1 percent (1 million) of all votes cast, the same level as in 1992. Nationally, Asian Americans almost split their votes between Clinton and Dole, and of the three racial minority groups, they gave the largest proportion of their vote (8 percent) to Ross Perot, the presidential candidate of the Reform Party. An exit poll in Los Angeles and Orange counties found that 53.2 percent of Asian Americans voted for Bill Clinton, and 40.8 percent and 3.9 percent voted for Bob Dole and Ross Perot, respectively (UCLA Asian American Studies Center 1996a). An election-day exit poll of Asian American voters in New York City found that despite low voter turnout nationally and citywide, Asian American turnout was extremely high, with approximately 18 percent of those polled indicating that they were first-time voters who became naturalized citizens within the past two years. In New York City, 71 percent of Asian Americans supported Clinton, 21 percent supported Bob Dole, and 2 percent voted for Ross Perot. Among first-time Asian American voters, an even higher percentage (79 percent) voted for President Clinton (Asian American Legal Defense and Educational Fund 1996). On the west coast, Asian American turnout (61 percent) in San Francisco County in November 1996 was higher than the city-level turnout (59 percent).

The overall percentage of the total presidential vote in 1996 represented by black (10 percent), Latino (5 percent), and Asian (1 percent) voters gives the impression that the votes of these groups were inconsequential on a national level, but the votes of these groups were key to Clinton victories in several states. Conversely, Senator Bob Dole's loss of these populations in those same races made his difficult race for the White House even more so. For example, Arizona had not voted Democratic in a presidential election since 1948. Florida also had not voted Democratic in a presidential election since 1976. However, in 1996 both of these states fell in Bill Clinton's column. The reason was the Latino vote. The Republican Party's anti-immigrant stance—its continual blaming of immigrants for U.S. problems and its threat to withdraw benefits from legal immigrants—renewed the historical memories of many Latino Americans. Latinos began to recall how during the Depression, Mexican Americans in the southwestern states had been blamed for poor economic conditions there, rounded up, put on trains, and shipped to Mexico. Their citizenship did not matter; what mattered was their Mexican origin. The Republican Party, which did not understand this history, failed to realize that its rhetoric would galvanize Latino communities and bring them to the polls, especially in Arizona, Florida, and California.

For instance, in California, 656,000 Latinos registered to vote between 1992 and 1996, a 47.3 percent increase (Decker 1997). Thus, whereas Latinos had represented 7 percent of all Californians voting in the 1992 presidential election, in 1996 they were 10 percent. California also has experienced a tremendous surge in the number of Latinos becoming naturalized U.S. citizens. An estimated 83 percent of new Latino citizens registered to vote for the 1996 election (NALEO 1996). Approximately 75 percent of all registered Latinos voted in the city of Los Angeles, and 70 percent voted in the state of California. This is dramatically higher than the overall state estimate of 65.5 percent total voter turnout (Decker 1997). This increased Latino voter turnout resulted in the largest number of Latinos elected to office in California's history—5 Latinos to the U.S. Congress, 4 to the state senate, and 14 to the state assembly. The Southwest Voter Registration and Education Project and the Tomás Rivera Political Institute attribute the increased naturalization, voter registration, and voter turnout directly to the anti-immigrant positions of California's Republican Governor Pete Wilson; to Proposition 187, a measure seeking to deny benefits to illegal aliens, which was passed in 1994 but was not implemented due to court challenges; and Proposition 209, on the ballot in 1996, which was aimed at curtailing state affirmative action programs.

In Arizona, the number of Latinos registered to vote increased from 169,000 in 1994 to 236,000 in 1996. Exit polls showed that Latinos voted for Clinton by a more than 10–1 margin, a margin that put Arizona in Bill Clinton's column (McDonnell and Ramos 1996).

Florida is a particularly interesting case because Cuban Americans traditionally have voted Republican. Nevertheless, Republicans failed to recognize that of all the Latino groups, none is more concerned with immigration than the Cuban American community in Florida. The Republicans' anti-immigrant rhetoric and Dole's alienation of large blocks of Cuban Americans resulted in the Cuban American vote splitting evenly between Clinton and Dole, thus giving Florida's electoral votes to Clinton. Clinton's share of the Cuban American vote in 1996 was twice his share in 1992 (McDonnell and Ramos 1996). Florida is also a state in which Latino voter registration increased substantially—from 383,000 in 1994 to 566,000 in 1996 (Southwest Voter Research Institute 1997).

A stunning example of the power of the Latino vote was the defeat of ultraconservative Congressman Bob Dornan by Loretta Sanchez in California's 46th Congressional District. Over time, the 46th District has changed demographically, and its population is now 50 percent Latino, 12 percent Asian, 2 percent black, and 18 percent other races. Yet Dornan continued to be one of the most anti-immigrant representatives in Congress, either arrogantly or naively ignoring the demographic shifts in his district. His district responded in kind and voted him out of office. Sanchez won by 984 votes, and Dornan (unsuccessfully) challenged the election outcome in Congress.

The Louisiana senate contest in which Democrat Mary Landrieu beat Republican Louis "Woody" Jenkins turned on the black vote. Landrieu knew early that to win she needed a large black turnout in Orleans Parish (New Orleans). To get that turnout, she was going to have to mend fences with black voters. In the 1995 gubernatorial race, Landrieu, who ran in the Democratic primary, ran campaign ads against the eventual Democratic nominee, Congressman Cleo Fields, implying that Fields could not win because he was black. When Fields ended up in the runoff against the eventual winner, Republican Mike Foster, Landrieu refused to endorse him. Fields withheld his endorsement of Landrieu until she apologized to Louisiana blacks for her behavior. Landrieu eventually received endorsements from Fields and from other prominent black leaders in Louisiana, such as New Orleans Mayor Marc Morial. On November 5, Landrieu and Jenkins were running about even in some of the parishes, with Jenkins outpolling Landrieu in many others. However, when Orleans parish's vote came in with 143,006 for Landrieu and 42,653 for Jenkins, Landrieu was able to defeat Jenkins by a margin of 5,788 votes. Jenkins, like Dornan, unsuccessfully challenged Landrieu's victory in the U.S. Senate.

The 1998 Congressional Elections

Midterm elections—elections held in years between presidential elections—are characterized historically by low voter turnout, with the party holding the White House losing seats in Congress. The 1998 midterm elections, however, occurred against the backdrop of pending impeachment hearings against President Clinton and the assumption that the president's problems would affect the outcome. The pundits warned that Democrats were demoralized and would not go to the polls, while the Republicans would increase their majority in the Senate and the House of Representatives. The results of the elections were surprisingly different from the projections and resulted in the disarray of the Republicans.

The real story of the November 3, 1998, elections is the important role racial minorities played in the outcome in various congressional and state elections. Overall, national voter turnout was only 36.1 percent. Nonetheless, black voters increased their share of the electorate from 6 percent in

1994, the last midterm election, to 11 percent in 1998. Latino participation levels were 6 percent of the 1998 electorate, an increase from 3 percent in 1994. The votes of racial minorities made the difference in many races around the country, highlighting the importance of these groups to the U.S. electoral process. Even though suffering some losses, minority candidates also made gains in national and state elective offices.

The U.S. Senate in the 106th Congress had no black senators. Carol Moseley-Braun of Illinois, the first black Democratic member and the first black female member of the U.S. Senate, lost her bid for reelection. Moseley-Braun, first elected in 1992, made a number of personal ethical missteps during her six years in office and allowed her opponent, Republican Peter Fitzgerald, to make her ethical lapses the central issue of the campaign. Despite an apology and momentum in the last week of the election, Moseley-Braun lost 47 percent to Fitzgerald's 51 percent. The two other racial minority senators were reelected readily. Overcoming concern that his switch from the Democratic to the Republican Party would hurt his reelection bid, Ben Nighthorse Campbell of Colorado was reelected easily, 62 percent to 35 percent over his Democratic opponent, Dottie Lamm. Campbell did face opposition in the Republican primary, but was never behind in the polls during the general election. In Hawaii, Democrat Daniel Inouye of Hawaii was reelected by an overwhelming 79 percent of the vote.

In the House of Representatives, Louis Stokes, Democrat of Ohio, retired and was replaced by Stephanie Tubbs-Jones, a black female Democrat. All of the other black incumbents were reelected. Melvin Watt of the 12th District of North Carolina was initially considered vulnerable because his district had been redrawn as a result of Supreme Court's decision in *Shaw v. Hunt* (1996) that reduced the percentage of blacks in the district. However, the district remains Democratic-leaning, and Watt had no serious opposition.

Two Latino representatives—Esteban Torres of California and Henry Gonzalez of Texas—retired but were replaced by two Latinos, Grace Napolitano for Torres in California and Charlie Gonzalez for Henry Gonzalez in Texas. All of the other Latino incumbents were reelected. In the California House district, in a rematch between Representative Loretta Sanchez and Robert Dornan, Sanchez won reelection decisively, 56 percent to 39 percent of the vote.

Jay Kim, the Republican Korean American representative from California, lost his seat in the Republican primary. Nevertheless, the number of

Asian Americans in the 107th Congress remained the same due to the election of Democrat David Wu in the 2nd District of Oregon. Wu is a Chinese American lawyer who was a former Oregon state representative.

The votes of racial minorities were crucial in several Senate and House elections around the country. In California, racial minorities were key to the reelection of Democratic Senator Barbara Boxer in her race against Republican Matt Fong, the Chinese American California state treasurer. The race was considered a toss-up during the summer of 1998, with Fong having pulled even with Boxer in the polls. Moreover, in the Republican primary, he drew a majority of Asian American votes, meaning that Asian Democrats crossed over to vote for Fong. Fong, however, made a series of missteps late in the campaign. For example, when it was revealed that he contributed $50,000 of unspent campaign funds from a previous election to a conservative group characterized by the newspapers as extremist, his standing in the polls dropped. For her part, Boxer successfully painted Fong as too conservative for California. In the general election, Fong pulled 50 percent of the white vote to Boxer's 46 percent, but Boxer received 85 percent of the black, 72 percent of the Latino, and 54 percent of the Asian American vote, giving her a 53 percent to 43 percent victory over Fong. (It should be noted that the exit poll conducted by the *Los Angeles Times* had Fong receiving 51 percent of the Asian American vote to 48 percent for Boxer.)

The votes of blacks, Latinos, and Asians were also important in the election of Democrat Gray Davis to the California governor's office. Latinos were still angry at the Republican Party and the former Republican governor, Pete Wilson, for the anti-immigrant rhetoric during Wilson's reelection campaign in 1994 and the 1996 presidential elections, as well as the recent passage of Proposition 227 aimed at ending bilingual education. Added to this anger was the presence of Cruz Bustamante, former speaker of the assembly, as the Democratic candidate for lieutenant governor. The push and pull of these factors combined to increase Latino voter turnout, a vote that went against Dan Lungren, the Republican attorney general running as the Republican gubernatorial candidate. Davis beat Lungren 58 percent to 39 percent and pulled 76 percent of the black, 71 percent of the Latino, and 65 percent of the Asian vote.

Blacks, Latinos, and Asians increased their electoral participation in California in 1998 from their proportion in 1994. In 1994, blacks were 5 percent of the electorate, Latinos 8 percent, and Asians 4 percent, but in

1998 blacks were 13 percent, Latinos 13 percent, and Asians 8 percent of California voters. This increased turnout resulted in significant Latino gains in elective office in California. In addition to the election of Cruz Bustamante as lieutenant governor, three Latinos—all Republicans—were elected to the State Assembly, while an additional three Latino Democrats were elected to the State Senate. The Republicans in the assembly elected Rod Pacheco as their new leader, moving Latinos into the top two positions in the assembly, the speaker and the minority leader.

In New Mexico, although Democrat Martin Chavez lost the gubernatorial race against incumbent Republican governor Gary Johnson 54 percent to 46 percent, Latino votes were crucial in the defeat of incumbent Republican Bill Redmond by Democrat Tom Udall in New Mexico's 3rd Congressional District. Redmond had won Bill Richardson's old congressional seat in a three-way special election in 1997. Redmond, in an attempt to attract Mexican American voters, sponsored the Guadalupe Hildalgo Treaty Land Claims Act, a bill that would create a commission to assess northern New Mexico families' claims to lands unfairly lost in the aftermath of the Mexican War. This move succeeded in gaining Redmond endorsements of several Latino Democrats, but Udall, with strong Latino support, defeated Redmond 53 percent to 43 percent. Three Latinos and one American Indian/Latino won statewide offices: Patricia Madrid (D), American Indian and Latino, was elected attorney general; Domingo Martinez (D) was elected state auditor; Rebecca Vigil-Giron (D) was elected secretary of state; and incumbent Michael Montoya (D) was reelected state treasurer. In addition to victories in Nevada, Colorado, and Arizona, Latinos picked up three seats in the Massachusetts House of Representatives and gained their first state legislators in Michigan and Wisconsin. In Colorado, Democrat Ken Salazar was elected attorney general, and in Texas former Secretary of State Tony Garza, a Republican, was elected railroad commissioner. Clearly, in 1998, Latino votes counted.

In South Carolina, black votes were the key margin of victory for the reelection of U.S. Senator Ernest Hollings and for the upset of the incumbent governor, David Beasley, and in North Carolina in the upset of the incumbent senator, Lauch Faircloth. In South Carolina, blacks were 25 percent of the voters who went to polls. Senator Ernest Hollings received only 39 percent of the white vote to 59 percent for his challenger, Bob Inglis. However, Hollings received 91 percent of the black vote, giving him a 52 percent to 46 percent victory. Clearly, without a high black turnout or overwhelming support from black South Carolinians, Hollings would have lost his seat. The same factors accounted for the upset loss of the incumbent South Carolina governor Beasley. He received 58 percent of the white vote, but black South Carolinians voted overwhelmingly for the Democrat, Jim Hodges, giving him a 53 percent to 45 percent victory. In North Carolina, losing senator Lauch Faircloth received 57 percent of the white vote, but blacks were 20 percent of the voters and gave the Democrat, John Edwards, 91 percent of their votes, resulting in a 51 percent to 47 percent victory over Faircloth.

The same pattern was evident in Georgia and Alabama. In Georgia, blacks, who were 29 percent of the voters, gave Democrat Roy Barnes the governor's office. Barnes's opponent, Republican Guy Millner, received 58 percent of the white vote to Barnes's 37 percent, but Barnes received 90 percent of the large black vote, providing him the margin he needed to defeat Millner, 53 percent to 44 percent. Blacks in Alabama helped Democrat Donald Siegelman defeat incumbent Republican Governor Forrest "Fob" James Jr. James received a slim majority of the white vote, 51 percent to 48 percent for Siegelman. Blacks were 19 percent of the voters and gave 95 percent of their vote to Siegelman, resulting in Siegelman's 58 percent to 42 percent margin of victory.

In Maryland, Parris Glendening, the Democratic incumbent, also owes his reelection to black Marylanders. Glendening had alienated several prominent black elected officials at the beginning of his tenure and alienated black voters during the campaign by distancing himself from President Clinton. Glendening realized quickly that he needed black voters to defeat his challenger, Ellen Sauerbrey, in a rematch of 1994, and he actively sought to mend fences. He asked the White House to help broker a truce with the black elected officials and asked President Clinton to come to Maryland on his behalf, both of which were done. Black voter turnout was high, with blacks representing 21 percent of the voters. Sauerbrey received 54 percent of the white vote, but Glendening received 90 percent of the black vote, providing him with 56 percent to Sauerbrey's 44 percent. Clearly, in these as well as other congressional and state races, black votes mattered.

Blacks were also successful in several statewide races below the governor's office. In Georgia, Democrat Thurbert Baker was elected attorney general, and Michael Thurmon was elected labor commissioner, the first blacks to hold statewide elective office in Georgia. Vikki Buckley, the black

Republican Colorado secretary of state, was reelected (but died soon after of a heart attack); Democrat H. Carl McCall was reelected comptroller of New York; and Republican Ken Blackwell, Ohio state treasurer, was elected secretary of state.

Of particular note are the election results from the gubernatorial races in Texas and Florida and the senate races in Missouri and Ohio. Although racial minorities were rejecting Republican candidates in other parts of the country, George W. Bush in Texas and Jeb Bush in Florida aggressively courted minority voters. Governor George W. Bush, who speaks Spanish and used it extensively during the campaign, actively campaigned in Latino and black communities, eventually gaining the endorsement of the normally Democratic black minister's group, the Baptist Ministers Association of Houston and Vicinity. Bush's outreach to blacks and Latinos, an overwhelmingly Democratic population in Texas, resulted in his receiving an incredible 27 percent of the black vote and 49 percent of the Latino vote. In Florida, Jeb Bush capitalized on a major schism in the Florida Democratic Party and received the endorsement of several prominent Democratic black elected officials, most notably State Representative Willie Logan. Logan had been elected by the Democrats as the head of the party and "speaker-in-waiting" if the Democrats gained a majority again in the Florida House. After a year, a group of white Democrats organized and ousted Logan, an act that threw the party into disarray amid charges of racism. Black Democrats threatened to abandon the Florida party and support the Republican Bush. Bush aggressively courted black voters and received 14 percent of the black vote in the general election, a significant number.

In Missouri, Senator Christopher S. "Kit" Bond pulled 34 percent of the black vote. Blacks were so upset with the Democratic candidate, Missouri's Attorney General Jeremiah "Jay" Nixon, over his proposal to end state aid for school desegregation that many actively worked to defeat him. In Ohio, former Cleveland Republican mayor and current governor George V. Voinovich won 29 percent of the black vote in the election for the open U.S. Senate seat vacated by retiring Senator John Glenn.

For Asian Americans, in addition to the election of David Wu to the House of Representatives, Democrat Benjamin Cayetano was reelected governor of Hawaii, and Democrat Maize Hirono was elected lieutenant governor. Democrat Mae Yih was elected to the Oregon State Senate; Paul Shin, a Democrat, was elected to the Washington State Senate; three Asian

Democrats—Kip Tokuda, Velma Veloria, and Sharon Tomiko Santos—were elected to the Washington State House of Representatives; and Democrats Mike Honda and George Nakano were elected to the California State Assembly. Despite the successes of Asian Americans in Washington State legislative races, Asian American Governor Gary Locke, along with major state-based corporations Microsoft, Boeing, and Starbucks, lost the battle to defeat Initiative 200, aimed at ending affirmative action in state government. Modeled after California's Proposition 209 and pushed by conservative black California businessman Ward Connerly, the measure passed 58 percent to 42 percent, was challenged in court, and was upheld as constitutional. Washington State is 90 percent white, and affirmative action was not an issue until Connerly is targeting other predominantly white states in an effort to gain national momentum for his anti-affirmative action campaign but has met with little success thus far.

The 1998 midterm elections illustrated the growing power and influence of black, Latino, and Asian voters. As the demographics of the United States continue to change, the importance of racial minorities to outcomes in the political process will continue to grow.

The 2000 Elections

The 2000 presidential election was the closest and most contentious in recent memory. The outcome of the race between Vice President Al Gore and Texas Governor George W. Bush turned on the outcome of the popular vote in Florida that would determine which candidate would receive the states' 25 electoral votes, giving one candidate the 270 required electoral votes. On election eve, fewer than 1,700 votes out of 6 million votes cast separated Bush and Gore, with Bush holding the advantage. The less than one-percent difference triggered an automatic recount under Florida law. At the end of the automatic recount and the counting of absentee ballots, Bush led by 535 votes. Both parties filed a number of suits in state and federal courts, and Bush filed an appeal with the U.S. Supreme Court. After 36 days of differing court decisions that favored Bush at one moment and Gore at another, the U.S. Supreme Court, in a 5–4 decision, stopped the full statewide recount ordered by the Florida Supreme Court, effectively giving the election to Governor Bush. Although Bush won the electoral vote and thus the presidency, he lost the popular vote to Gore by 500,000 votes.

The controversy surrounding the election and its aftermath still res-onates among some racial minorities. A Gallup Poll collected in December 2000 found that almost seven in ten blacks (68 percent) said that they felt "cheated" after the election, compared to 55 percent of white Democrats. Moreover, one-half of blacks, 50 percent, felt that Bush stole the election. This feeling of injustice among blacks is related to the fact that a substan-tial majority of blacks, 64 percent, felt that fraud was involved in Florida's voting procedures. Additionally, blacks across the country, 68 percent, felt that black voters in Florida were less likely to have their votes counted fairly in that state than were white voters. The negative perception of the election system on the part of blacks extended beyond Florida, with 76 percent of blacks saying that the election system in the United States is dis-criminatory (Gallup 2000).

Even before the problems with the vote count in Florida, questions of possible violations of voting rights arose in various locations around the state. The weekend before the election, many black Floridians received calls saying that the caller was with the National Association for the Ad-vancement of Colored People (NAACP) and urged them to vote for George W. Bush. The NAACP, which was involved in a massive nationwide get-out-the-vote campaign, is a nonpartisan, nonprofit organization and does not officially endorse candidates. Similar calls were reported in Vir-ginia and Michigan.

Roadblocks were set up within a few hundred yards of voting places in predominantly black communities in Volusia County where police asked black males to get out of their cars and show identification. In Hillsbor-ough County, a disproportionate number of black voters were turned away from polls. Also in that county, sheriff's deputies checking voter identifications turned people away by saying that the race indicated on the voter identification did not match the race of the person standing in front of them. Clearly, the determination of the race of the people was based on the visual subjective judgment of the sheriff's deputies. Other blacks claimed that they were told that polling places had run out of ballots and that the polls were closed (Bayles 2000). Even though these examples are from Florida, similar complaints of interference with the right of blacks to vote were registered from black voters around the country, for example, in Durham, North Carolina.

Other complaints from Florida concerned the high number of votes of minority citizens that were not counted. Ballot errors were very high in a number of Florida black precincts. In Miami-Dade County, about 2.7 percent of ballots were discounted because of over-voting, voting for more than one candidate for president. But in about two dozen innercity neighborhoods, between 8 and 11 percent of ballots were invalidated (Robles and Dougherty 2000). At least fifty Miami-Dade precincts, including Liberty City, Goulds, Overtown, and part of Coconut Grove, had rates of 7 percent or higher. One hundred of the county's 617 precincts had over-vote rates of 5 percent or higher (Robles and Dougherty 2000). A precinct-by-precinct analysis of Florida counties by *The Washington Post* found that heavily Democratic and African American neighborhoods lost many more presidential votes than other areas because of outmoded voting machinery and rampant confusion about ballots. In fact, the analysis identified a racial component to Florida's election process—counties with high proportions of black voters were more likely to have outmoded voting machinery than were counties with predominately white populations (Mintz and Keating 2000).

Table 3.14 presents trends in racial minority voting in presidential elections from 1996 to 2004. The results from 1996 have been discussed, but some important changes in 2000 need to be highlighted. First, Bush took a majority of the white vote, 54 percent to 42 percent for Gore. What kept the race at a 48 percent tie were the votes of racial minorities. Blacks supported Gore in higher proportions, 90 percent, than they did Bill Clinton in 1996. In fact, Bush received a smaller proportion of black votes, 8 percent, than did Bob Dole in 1996, 12 percent. Exit poll data from Texas indicate that even though Bush pulled 27 percent of the black vote in Texas in his reelection bid for governor in 1998, for his presidential bid in 2000, only 5 percent of black Texans voted for him. Ninety-one percent of black Texans voted for Gore (CNN 2000). After two years in his second term as governor, Bush lost considerable support among black Texans.

As in 1996, a majority of Latinos, 67 percent, supported the Democratic presidential candidate, Al Gore. Although this represents a drop from Clinton's 72 percent in 1996, it is higher than Clinton's initial 61 percent of Latino votes in 1992. Even though he did not receive a majority of the Latino votes, Bush pulled more Latino votes, 31 percent, than did Bob Dole, 21 percent, in 1996, and the elder George Bush, 25 percent, in 1992. Of interest is the Latino vote in Texas. In 1998, when Bush ran for reelection for governor, 49 percent of Latino Texans voted for him. That percentage dropped to 43 percent in the 2000 presidential election (CNN

2000). Although the drop in support is not close to the drop in black support, Bush did lose some Latino support in the two years since his gubernatorial reelection.

Of tremendous interest is that, for the first time, a majority of Asian Americans voted for the Democratic presidential candidate, Al Gore. This is a reversal from the 1992 pattern where a majority of Asian Americans, 55 percent, voted for the Republican candidate, the elder President George Bush. This new voting pattern is consistent with the Asian partisan identification data presented earlier—Asians on a whole are becoming more Democratic in their voting patterns.

Despite black anger and bitterness over the outcome of the presidential election, if there was a winner in the 2000 election, it was minority voters, especially black voters. In many ways, this is a similar story to that of the 1998 midterm elections. Massive voter registration and get-out-the-vote drives across the country made a significant difference in black voter turnout. In Florida, the black share of the vote grew from 10 percent in 1996 to 15 percent of the vote in 2000 (Bositis 2000). This increased black voter turnout helped lift Democrat Bill Nelson over Republican Bill McCollum in the U.S. Senate race. McCollum, a former House of Representative's manager during the impeachment of President Bill Clinton, took the majority of the white and Latino vote, 53 percent in each case, but Nelson's 88 percent share of the increased black turnout gave him his margin of victory, 51 percent to 46 percent. Even the presence of Willie Logan, a Democratic black state senator who experienced problems with the state Democratic Party in 1998, running as an independent in the senate race did not pull substantial black votes from Nelson; only 4 percent of black voters cast a ballot for Logan.

In Missouri, the black share of voters on Election Day climbed from 5 percent in 1996 to 12 percent in 2000 (Bositis 2000). This significant increase in black voter turnout contributed directly to the defeat of Senator John Ashcroft. If you remember, Ashcroft's Democratic opponent, Governor Mel Carnahan, died in a plane crash several weeks before the election. State law prevented substitution of another candidate, so Carnahan's name remained on the ballot. The Democratic governor of Missouri stated that if voters "elected" Mel Carnahan, he would appoint his widow, Jean, to the senate seat. Black Missourians were furious with Ashcroft's torpedoing, in what was perceived to be an underhanded and unethical manner, the nomination of Ronnie White, a black Missouri Supreme

Court justice, to a position on the federal bench. As they did with their opposition to Democratic Attorney General Jay Nixon in his senate race in 1998, blacks conducted massive voter registration and voter turnout drives that resulted in the substantial increase in black voting on election day. Despite Ashcroft's carrying the majority of the white vote, 53 percent to 46 percent for Mel Carnahan, black Missourians gave the deceased Carnahan 82 percent of their votes, which gave Carnahan a 51 percent to 47 percent victory over Ashcroft (CNN 2000).

Black and Latino voters were critical to the victory of Jon Corzine in the New Jersey senate race. Blacks were 11 percent of those who turned out to vote on election day, and Latinos were 5 percent. Republican Bob Franks took the majority of the white vote, 52 percent to 44 percent, but Corzine's 88 percent to 12 percent margin among blacks and 63 to 35 percent margin among Latinos gave Corzine a 51 percent to 47 percent victory.

At the state level, Latinos in California continued to make significant strides politically. Latinos were 14 percent of those who turned out to vote on election day, with blacks and Asians making up 7 percent and 6 percent, respectively. In other words, 27 percent of California voters were racial minorities. Latinos increased their number of representatives in the State Assembly by four, bringing their total to 20—16 Democrats and 4 Republicans. They maintained their eight seats in the State Senate. In other states with sizable Latino populations, Latinos picked up two additional seats in New Mexico and one additional seat each in Arizona and Colorado. In states with smaller Latino populations, Latinos won state house seats in Rhode Island, bringing the total to two, and in New Hampshire, the first Latino pick up of a state legislative seat (NALEO 2000b).

Asian Americans also elected four members to the California Assembly, a record high. In January 2001, the assembly members formed the first Asian Pacific Islander Legislative Caucus (APILC) in California history. Democrat Mike Honda, who in 1998 was elected to the California State Assembly, was elected to the U.S. Congress, bringing the number of Asian Americans in the House of Representatives, excluding nonvoting delegates, to four. This trend in increased Latino and Asian American representation at the state level will continue as the demographics in California and other parts of the country continue to favor increased Latino political influence. According to the 2000 census, Latinos now comprise about one-third of the California population, with Asians representing 12 percent and blacks 6 percent.

The 2004 Elections

George W. Bush was elected president in 2000 while losing the popular vote, so the 2004 race was bound to be hotly contested. A majority of white voters had supported Bush in 2000; a majority of nonwhite voters supported his opponent, Al Gore. Furthermore, Gallup (2000) reported that almost 70 percent of blacks felt "cheated" after the 2000 election, one-half felt that Bush stole the election, and more than three-quarters said that the U.S. election system is discriminatory. With that background, it is not surprising that the 2004 election produced a massive mobilization effort, especially among racial and ethnic minorities, for the contest between Democratic Senator John F. Kerry (D–Mass.) and George W. Bush.

While nonwhites increased their proportion of all voters, President Bush was able to achieve a decisive reelection by increasing his margin of victory among white voters, particularly among white women. Thus, white female voters, in this election, at least, narrowed the "gender gap" between Democrats and Republicans, which had been occasioned by males moving toward the Republican Party over time (Kaufmann and Petrocik 1999).

If, as DeSipio and de la Garza (2002:398) assert, "with each presidential election, the media and the punditocracy discover Latinos anew," 2004 took this phenomenon to new heights. Spurred perhaps by the census reports of Latinos becoming the nation's "largest minority" earlier than anticipated and by President Bush's self-proclaimed success at making inroads into this traditional Democratic constituency, speculation about the Latino vote was the rage during the campaign—and after. The post-election speculation was fueled by election-day exit polls that reported the Latino vote for Bush to be as high as 44 percent. This figure is higher than any preelection poll showed and is suspect. These polls showed broad support for Kerry across a range of demographic categories, with only non-Catholic Latinos favoring Bush (Leal et al. 2005:43–44). Leal and his colleagues (2005:48) conclude that 39 percent is a more likely figure of the level of Latino support for Bush, which would be similar to the support garnered by Ronald Reagan in 1984. They conclude that whatever the accurate figure is that it "may represent not the beginning of a Latino realignment but the electoral ceiling for Republican presidential candidates with appealing personalities" (Leal at al. 2005:48).

The same exit polls that may have overreported Latino voting for Bush attributed only 11 percent of the black two-party vote to the GOP incumbent. This represented a 3-percentage-point increase over the 8 percent of blacks who voted for Bush in 2000. The 2004 percentage is similar to the partisan margins observed in previous presidential elections, with the exception of 2000. One difference in 2004 was Bush's ability, through his faith-based initiative—a policy to send federal funds to church-based social service programs—to bring a small number of conservative black clergy actively to support him in the 2004 election. The influence of this small group of clergy helped Bush in two 2004 battleground states—Florida and Ohio. In Florida, Bush's percentage of the black vote increased from 6 percent in 2000 to 13 percent in 2004, and in Ohio, his percentage increased from 7 percent to 16 percent. Despite the increase in the Republican share of the black vote in a couple of states, the real story about black voters in the 2004 presidential election is the increase in turnout. Blacks turned out at such a rate that they came close to approximating their proportion in the population in the electorate.

If Asian Americans made news in 2000 by, for the first time, supporting the Democratic presidential candidate with a majority of their votes, the 2004 exit poll results suggest the beginning of a trend. These polls suggest that John Kerry collected at least 58 percent of the Asian American vote. Exit polls focusing on Asian Americans in eight states, conducted by the Asian American Legal Defense and Educational Fund, and conducted in 23 languages or dialects, found a record turnout among Asian American voters, with Bush collecting not quite one-fourth of their votes. A *Los Angeles Times* poll estimated that slightly more than one-third of Asian Americans voted for the winning Bush.

American Indians, according to the National Congress of American Indians, turned out in record numbers. Most notably, the number of Indian peoples voting in Minnesota is estimated to have doubled over previous levels. From the limited information available, American Indians appear to have continued their recent historical preference for the Democratic presidential candidate.

Racial minorities also made significant gains in national elective offices in 2004. The U.S. Senate now has a record number of racial minorities as members of its body. Illinois returned a black Democrat, Barack Obama, to the Senate. Obama, who is the second black Illinois has sent to the Senate in the past 15 years, is the only black currently in the U.S. Senate. In addition to Obama, two Latino senators were elected. Ken Salazar, the Democratic Attorney General of Colorado, became the only Mexican American in the Senate where the last Mexican American to serve in that body was the late Joseph Montoya of New Mexico, who was defeated in 1976. Florida also elected the first Cuban American to the U.S. Senate, Republican Mel Martinez. Obama, Salazar, and Martinez joined Senators Daniel Inouye and Daniel Akaka of Hawaii for a total of five nonwhite senators. This is the largest number of nonwhites to serve in the Senate at the same time since Reconstruction.

Racial minorities also increased their numbers in the House of Representatives, with blacks picking up three new seats, one each in Wisconsin, Texas, and Missouri, and Latinos picking up one in Colorado.

After the 2000 election fiasco in Florida, Congress passed the Help America Vote Act of 2002 (HAVA), whose purpose is to reform aspects of the voting process and increase voter education and turnout. It provides money for states to replace outdated voting machines; mandates provisional ballots, a process that allows people who believe they are registered to vote but do not appear on voter rolls to cast a ballot—which is reviewed and checked later—be available in all states; reforms voter registration procedures; and provides better access to voting for the disabled and better training for poll workers. The act also created a new federal registration form to make it easier for new voters to register. The provisions of the act are to be phased in, with all provisions being implemented by 2006. Despite the aims of HAVA, many Florida residents voted on the same machines in 2004 that caused so many problems in 2000. The Associated Press estimated that three-quarters of U.S. voters in 2004 would vote on the same machines in use in 2000.

Whereas Florida was the hot spot in 2000, Ohio was at the center of the 2004 elections, with the outcome of the election hinging on its 20 electoral votes. John Kerry did not concede Ohio until the day after the election, but that did not quell the complaints and concerns about Ohio's voting process. Prior to the election, Secretary of State Kenneth Blackwell, a black Republican, who was also co-chair of the state Bush-Cheney campaign, made several decisions that appeared to be aimed at helping George Bush win the state. For example, voter registration drives were in full force in Ohio, and more Democrats were being registered than Republicans when Blackwell instructed county board of elections, only a few weeks before the deadline for registration, to reject registrations on paper less than 80-

pound weight—the type used for covers of paperback books and post-cards, rather than the 20- to 24-pound stock in everyday use. He said his concern was with registrations being mangled in the mail, but his directive applied to all registration forms, even those mailed in envelopes or delivered by hand to election boards (*New York Times* 2004). The criticism that arose was so fierce that Blackwell had to back off, but it was impossible to know how many people had their registrations rejected before the directive was lifted (*New York Times* 2004). He also directed that voters who had requested absentee ballots but had not received them could not vote by provisional ballot, stating that the ruling was necessary to prevent double voting. Blackwell was sued in federal court, and the court ordered Blackwell to advise election officials that they had to issue provisional ballots to all who appeared at a polling place and claimed to be eligible to vote (Liptak 2004). He also decided to interpret strictly a state law on provisional ballots by ruling that voters must cast provisional ballots not merely in the county in which they lived but in the exact precinct where their name would have appeared on the registration list. This meant that in cities such as Cleveland and Cincinnati, which are Democratic strongholds and where election officials had accepted provisional ballots cast in the wrong precinct previously, many provisional ballots would be disqualified (Powell and Slevin 2004).

Electoral problems on Election Day kept thousands of Ohio voters from voting. Bipartisan estimates say that in Columbus 5,000 to 15,000 voters left the polls in frustration without voting because of long lines due to election officials allocating too few voting machines for urban precincts. Voters in Cincinnati and Toledo and on college campuses stood in line for as long as ten hours, many leaving without voting, because there were too few voting machines to handle the increased number of voters (Powell and Slevin 2004). In Cleveland, poorly trained poll workers gave voters faulty instructions that led to the disqualification of thousands of provisional ballots and misdirected hundreds of others to third-party candidates. And in Youngstown, 25 electronic machines transferred an unknown number of votes for Senator Kerry to Bush (Powell and Slevin 2004). In one precinct, Bush received 4,258 votes to Kerry's 260 votes, even though only 638 people voted in the precinct (*The Columbus Dispatch* 2005). Another area of contention was the 96,000 ballots that registered no vote for president, 77,000 of which were cast on punch-card voting machines. The problem was most pronounced in minority precincts. An analysis by *The New York Times* of zip codes in Cleveland, which is approximately 85 percent black, found that 1 in 31 ballots registered no vote for president, more than twice the rate of predominately white zip codes, where 1 in 75 registered no vote for president (Dao, Fessenden and Zeller 2004).

Meanwhile, Blackwell has declared himself a candidate for governor in 2006. Shortly after the election, he sent out a fundraising letter touting his ability to deliver the state of Ohio votes to George Bush and soliciting campaign contributions. His letter also directly solicited corporate contributions, which is illegal. He claimed the solicitation of corporate checks was "an oversight and that criticism of his partisan activities for Bush is 'misdirected,'" (Niquette 2005). He refused to attend a congressional hearing in Washington, D.C., called by Ohio Republican Bob Ney, author of the Help America Vote Act, held to explore problems that occurred in the 2004 election, even though he was in Washington to attend at board meeting and a ceremony to honor the unveiling of the Ronald Reagan postage stamp (Torry 2005). Ney then brought the hearings to Ohio in March 2005, thereby forcing Blackwell to testify, who defended his handling of the 2004 elections (Provance 2005). He also repeatedly interrupted questions from two black female Democratic members of Congress, Ohio Representative Stephanie Tubbs Jones and California Representative Juanita Millender-McDonald. At one point in an exchange with Tubbs Jones, she told him to "haul butt" if he would not answer her questions (Smyth 2005). We will see if Ohio voters elect Blackwell governor in 2006.

Interest Group Activities

As we mentioned at the beginning of this chapter, one of the principal components of pluralist theory is competition between interest groups. Although this theory presents some problems for the study of racial minority group politics, interest groups that focus on issues of importance to blacks, Latinos, Asians, and American Indians have been essential to the progress made toward the incorporation of these groups into the American political system. There are far more groups than we have space to cover; therefore, we will highlight several of the major groups—particularly those that have used litigation as a tactic—along with those that are the best known for each of the groups under consideration.

Racial and ethnic minority groups have frequently turned to the courts in an attempt to improve their positions because victories in the courts are more likely to be determined by an appeal to what is right than merely to what is politically popular. For African Americans—and, indeed, as a model for all other racial and ethnic groups—the **NAACP Legal Defense and Educational Fund** (LDF), founded in 1939 by a group of attorneys dedicated to affirming and expanding the rights of blacks, has been the pathbreaking group. The LDF's strategy was to "secure decisions, rulings, and public opinion on the broad principle instead of being devoted to mere miscellaneous cases" (founder Charles Houston, quoted in Vose 1959:23). The LDF, using test cases and class action suits, became known as the group through which to attack segregation. Its most famous victory came in *Brown v. Board of Education of Topeka* (1954 and 1955; this case is discussed further in Chapter 4), which overturned *Plessy v. Ferguson* (1896), the case that had established the separate but equal doctrine.

The LDF and its litigation approach to removing the barriers to full participation in the political process by blacks have served as a model for Latinos. With the guidance of LDF attorneys and funding from the Ford Foundation, the Mexican American Legal Defense and Education Fund (MALDEF) was established in 1968. MALDEF functions for Mexican Americans in much the same way the LDF has historically functioned for African Americans. In 1972, the Puerto Rican Legal Defense and Education Fund (PRLDEF) was created in New York City to play a similar role for Puerto Ricans.

Additionally, as is characteristic of the diversity that exists within the Asian American community, there are various lawyers' interest groups— the Asian Law Caucus, based in San Francisco; the Asian American Legal Defense and Educational Fund in New York; and the Asian Pacific American Legal Center, based in Los Angeles—loosely united under the aegis of the National Asian Pacific American Legal Consortium. The Asian Pacific American Legal Consortium was incorporated in 1991. It coordinates litigation on civil rights issues important to the Asian American community. It educates the public, files amicus curiae briefs, and provides legal counsel on a host of issues including hate crimes, immigration, affirmative action, language rights, and census methods. Additionally, through its Community Partners Network, it disseminates successful strategies that Asian American communities around the country can use to achieve policy objectives (National Asian Pacific American Legal Consortium n.d.).

The Native American Rights Fund (NARF), located in Boulder, Colorado, was founded in 1970 with the help of the Ford Foundation. It was the first national program to provide legal aid to Indians. Although NARF was officially organized in 1970, it actually began as an outgrowth of California Rural Legal Assistance (CRLA). It soon became clear that Indians had unique legal problems that required special expertise; thus, the Indian Services Division of CRLA was organized. The division became a separate organization, California Indian Legal Services (CILS), in 1968, and CILS received a grant from the Ford Foundation in 1970 with which to establish NARF (James 1973). Most of NARF's attorneys and staff are Indians, although non-Indians are present in a number of positions, and its board of directors is composed of Indian leaders from across the country.

NARF has five priority areas: (1) the preservation of tribal existence; (2) the protection of tribal natural resources; (3) the promotion of human rights; (4) the accountability of governments to Native Americans; and (5) the development of Indian law (Native American Rights Fund 1993). NARF has been involved in a number of legal cases challenging barriers to Indian rights and political participation and challenging states and the federal government to honor treaties with Indian nations and peoples. NARF has either filed or submitted amicus curiae briefs in numerous cases and has been successful in more than two hundred cases.

NARF's litigation on behalf of the Catawba Tribe of South Carolina (*Catawba Indian Tribe of South Carolina v. United States* 1993) was settled when President Clinton signed Public Law No. 103–116, the Catawba Indian Land Claim Settlement Act of 1993. In another action, NARF won a suit against the Bureau of Indian Affairs on behalf of the Cheyenne-Arapaho Tribes of Oklahoma (*Cheyenne-Arapaho Tribes of Oklahoma v. United States* 1992) for failing to protect Indian interests in the pricing of minerals removed from Indian lands. NARF has also protected voting rights of Indians in several states, including South Dakota, New York, and Alaska.

In the area of nonlitigation-oriented interest groups, there is a plethora of African American interest groups, the longest lasting of which are the NAACP, founded in 1909 and the parent of the LDF; the National Urban League, founded in 1910; and the Southern Christian Leadership Conference (SCLC), organized in 1957. Others, such as the Student Nonviolent Coordinating Committee and the Congress of Racial Equality, were extremely important during the civil rights movement of the 1960s but are either diminished in their activity or are moribund today.

Some of the more prominent Latino interest groups are the **League of United Latin American Citizens (LULAC)**, a group of vocal, middle-class

Mexican American citizens formed in 1929 in south Texas, and the National Council of La Raza (NCLR). LULAC was established to fight discrimination against Mexican Americans in Texas. From its inception through the 1960s, LULAC was actively engaged in protest and litigation for equal and civil rights for Mexican Americans. It has grown from a small organization in several south Texas cities to a national organization "with active councils in twenty-eight states, a national headquarters in Washington, D.C., and a professional staff" (Márquez 1989:355–356).

NCLR, previously the Southwest Council of La Raza (founded in 1968), was initially oriented toward community organization and mobilization, but over the years it has developed into an umbrella organization for numerous local Latino organizations. It has voter education and registration programs and a research office that conducts studies and disseminates information on issues of concern to the broader Latino community. NCLR has recently focused its efforts on economic development and small-business investment (Hero 1992:77).

Asian American and American Indian interest groups have also been active. The Japanese American Citizens League (JACL), founded in 1930, is the best-established and largest national Asian American organization. JACL was instrumental in bringing the issue of reparations for Japanese interned during World War II to the political agenda and, in 1988, in pushing Congress to pass legislation providing for an apology and a payment of $20,000 to each of the survivors of the internment camps. When President Reagan signed the legislation, he admitted that the United States had committed "a grave wrong" (Takaki 1993:401).

Chinese Americans formed the Chinese American Citizens' Alliance (then known as the Native Sons of the Golden State) in 1895 in California. Still going strong after more than a hundred years, the Alliance works to increase Asian American representation on college campuses, to increase voter registration in the Asian American community, and to ensure that Asian Americans have opportunities to learn English (Hong 1995). The Organization of Chinese Americans was founded in 1973 to promote Chinese American participation in local and national affairs and to ensure the equal and fair treatment of Chinese Americans. Its policy concerns include addressing and preventing hate crimes through prosecution and legislation (Organization of Chinese Americans 1997). The 1992 riots in Los Angeles precipitated the founding in 1994 of the National Association of Korean Americans. Its goals are to protect the civil rights of Korean Americans, to build bridges of understanding between Korean Americans and other racial groups, to promote Korean culture, and to promote the unification of North and South Korea (National Association of Korean Americans n.d.). Leadership Education for Asian Pacifics (LEAP) was founded in 1982 by members of various Asian American ethnic groups. Its goal is to increase Asian American participation in leadership positions throughout the country and to ensure the equitable treatment of Asian Americans. To achieve this goal, LEAP has sponsored four initiatives: the Leadership Management Institute, the Asian American Public Policy Institute, the Community Development Institute, and Community Forums (Leadership Education for Asian Pacifics 1996).

Other Asian American interest groups include the National Association for Asian and Pacific American Education, founded in 1977. Its primary objective is to give a voice to the needs of Asian American students. It advances Asian American educational needs and concerns, argues for the inclusion of Asian American history in school curricula, and lobbies for bilingual education and special educational opportunities for Asian Americans and for greater inclusion of Asian American students as subjects of educational research (National Association for Asian and Pacific American Education n.d.). The Asian Pacific American Labor Alliance is an Asian AFL-CIO–affiliate founded in 1992 to organize Asian American workers and to enable them to address their concerns. It primarily seeks to eliminate barriers to promotion and unfair labor practices aimed at Asian Americans, but its policy initiatives toward these goals are varied. It has lobbied for reparations for Japanese Americans interned during World War II, for the prosecution of hate crimes directed at Asians and other minorities, for health care and fair wages, against employer discrimination, and for equal economic rights for women (Asian Pacific American Labor Alliance n.d.).

Indians organize along tribal lines when action involves members of one tribe in pursuit of tribal goals. But when the issue is of concern to more than one tribe, Indians organize along pan-tribal lines. Therefore, because many American Indian tribes enjoy some level of autonomy, they can and do act as interest groups. Many have lobbied the government and have brought cases to the federal courts, seeking to vindicate rights. Moreover, tribes hold the primary responsibility for Indian community development. There are also formal government agencies, such as the BIA and the National Council on Indian Opportunity (created by Lyndon Johnson), which are designed to look after the interest of Indians but do not usually follow through on their mandates. Over the decades, there has been sustained and increasingly vocal opposition to the BIA by both reservation Indians and urban Indians (Nagel 1982).

An example of a pan-tribal organization is the Alaska Federation of Natives, formed in 1966, which successfully filed land claims against the state amounting to 360 million acres, or a little more than the state's entire land area. Other pan-tribal Indian interest groups include the National Indian Youth Council (founded in 1961), the National Tribal Chairman's Association (circa 1960), the National Congress of American Indians (1944)—the largest intertribal interest group in the country, the Institute for the Development of Indian Law (1971), and the Native American Rights Fund (1970).

Conclusion

James Madison's assumption that conflict would prevail over consensus has proven to be well founded. Blacks, Latinos, Asians, and American Indians share some similar political attitudes and participation dimensions, but they differ dramatically on others. Clearly, racial minorities do not all think alike. This chapter also highlights the fact that in the political game, each of the racial and ethnic minorities has been at a disadvantage, despite its efforts to be active in the polity. Still, some successes are noted. In Chapter 4 we explore the way these groups have been treated by the political system, a revisiting of the first dilemma.

4

....

America's Racial Minorities and the Policymaking Process

Three white 18-year-old men were sentenced for firebombing a Mexican American family's home in July 2003. One received a sentence of one and a third to four years in prison, the second was sentenced to 420 hours of community service, and the third was sentenced to 500 hours of community service and five years probation.

—Farmingville, New York, July 13, 2004

PUBLIC POLICIES ARE WHAT GOVERNMENTS choose to do or not to do. These policies do not just happen; they are the outputs of the political process and of government institutions. Political scientists and public policy scholars speak of public policymaking as a process that consists of five interrelated stages—agenda setting, formulation, adoption, implementation, and evaluation.

Agenda setting is the process by which issues are identified and by which conflicts and concerns gain prominence and exposure so they are brought to the public arena for debate and possible government action (Cobb and Elder 1983). This stage occurs both within and outside of government institutions. **Formulation** is the stage at which policy issues are translated into actual proposals from which an alternative may be chosen for adoption, usually by a legislative body. Given the bargaining process that occurs in legislative bodies, political feasibility and ideological stances may become more important considerations than problem solving. Ideology may produce agreed-on policies that ultimately do not work (Lindblom 1980:39).

Policy **adoption** involves choosing between proposed alternatives to address the problem. In collective policymaking bodies such as legislatures and appellate courts, adoption requires building majority coalitions. After policy is adopted, it then moves to the **implementation** stage, the stage at which the policy is put into action. This activity is usually the domain of federal, state, or local government agencies. The implementation process is very fluid and is subject to numerous internal and external influences; therefore, the manner in which a policy is implemented or the shape the policy assumes may or may not resemble the intent of the individuals who formulated the policy. The final stage, **evaluation**, is the process of determining whether the policy had its intended effect and what unintended consequences, both positive and negative, may have occurred.

This chapter begins with a discussion of what is probably the most important stage of the public policymaking process for racial and ethnic minorities—agenda setting. Because historically minority group members

127

have been excluded from policymaking bodies, minorities' interests have often not been voiced. The chapter then details the contemporary situation in the major branches of government, highlighting the increased representation of members of racial and ethnic minority groups.

Next, a detailed explication of the effect of **federalism** on public policymaking is presented. Federalism, which involves the division of powers among the various layers of government—national, state, county, municipal—presents opportunities for access to the public policy process but barriers to effective, efficient policymaking. Although most people believe the action and power reside in national political activity and offices, the reality is that most of the decisions that affect the everyday lives of U.S. citizens are made on the state and local levels. Scholars who study state politics argue that states are "where the action is." These various levels of government require that, depending on the policy issue, racial minorities address their attention to a multiplicity of governmental units because a victory at one level can be undermined or overturned at another.

Finally, two specific policy areas, equal educational opportunity and **affirmative action** in employment, are discussed to give concrete examples of the linkages between structural aspects of American government and what the government has actually done in this important area. This discussion also provides important substantive information about the current issues and the current status of law and policy in these vital civil rights policy areas.

Agenda Setting

If an issue is never considered, it is impossible for the government to act upon it. Those who control the government agenda control the debate, the types of policies that are formulated, and the structure of the implementation process. The models of agenda setting are, in brief: (1) outside initiative; (2) mobilization; and (3) inside access. In the **outside initiative model**, groups outside of government push for their issues to be heard by the decisionmakers, usually through mass mobilization, such as demonstrations. The general issue is then translated into more specific demands and is expanded to include a broader number of groups, thus gaining attention as part of the public agenda.

In the **mobilization model**, issues are placed on the agenda by individuals either inside the government or with direct access to government, but the issues must be expanded to the public to gain its support. With the **inside access model,** items are placed on the agenda by individuals inside the government and are expanded only to those groups that place pressure on decisionmakers to move the problem forward. Issues are not expanded to the public, either because the policymakers do not require legitimation of the idea or do not want the public to know about it.

All of these models are based on pluralist theory, and the limited research on racial minorities and agenda setting has found that minorities have little access to or influence on the policy agenda-setting process (McClain 1993b). The only model minorities have thus far been successful in using in their attempts to influence the agenda has been the outside initiative model, of which the modern civil rights movement is a prime example.

Recent research suggests that the agenda-setting process is characterized by long periods of stability and of domination by privileged elites but may be subject to rapid change in political outcomes. Despite the disadvantage that outside groups have in getting access to the policy process, and the influence of policy monopolies on controlling the agenda, new issues do obtain a hearing through the extraordinary efforts of interested individuals and groups (Baumgartner and Jones 1993).

As is clear from this brief discussion of the policy process and agenda setting, individuals within the structures of government have tremendous influence on the policy outputs from those structures. It becomes necessary, therefore, for groups to have a significant presence in these institutions if they are to affect the policy process. The major national institutions of government—the office of the president, the Supreme Court, Congress, and the bureaucracy—play prominent roles in acting on or not acting on the issues that affect racial minorities. Furthermore, the fact that each of the national institutions is duplicated in some form at the state and local levels has often meant that racial minority groups' citizens have been caught between different levels of the federal system. Policies of both the U.S. and state governments have directly affected the ability of racial minorities to gain access to and participate in the political process.

Minority Representation

Since the passage of the Voting Rights Act (VRA) in 1965, there has been a significant increase in the number of black and Latino elected officials. As of January 2001, 9,101 African Americans hold office at all levels of government; of that number, 35.4 percent (3,200) are black females, a dramatic increase since 1970 when only 160 black women were in office. The number of black women elected to office is growing at a faster rate than that of black men, which has actually declined slightly (Joint Center for Political and Economic Studies 2001). Before the passage of the VRA, it was estimated that there were fewer than 500 black elected officials.

The VRA has also been important for the election of Latinos to national, state, and local offices. According to the National Association of Latino Elected and Appointed Officials, in 2004 there were 4,853 Latino elected officials, of which 29.4 percent (1,427) were female (NALEO 2004). In 2001, 565 Asian Americans held national, state, and local elected offices, whereas more than 1,000 held national, state, and local appointed offices (UCLA Asian American Studies Center 2001). American Indian elected officials, excluding tribal government officials, are more difficult to identify, but there are several visible officeholders, one of whom is former Colorado Republican Senator, Ben Nighthorse Campbell.

The Presidency

No member of a racial or an ethnic minority has ever held the office of president of the United States, the highest office in the political system. This fact is important because although the executive branch is only one of the three branches of government, the president has an extraordinary ability to shape public policy through executive powers, as well as from the "bully pulpit" of the office. Historically, presidents have used their executive powers and powers of persuasion both to include and to exclude racial minorities from the political process.

In 1830, President Andrew Jackson used his influence and authority to push his Indian Removal Bill through Congress. Jackson was successful in instituting a program of removing Indians from the southern states to provide land for expanded cotton production. Although a Supreme Court decision, *Worcester v. Georgia* (1832), ensured the sovereignty of the Cherokees, President Jackson refused to follow the decision and initiated what has been called the Trail of Tears. The Five Civilized Tribes—Cherokee, Chickasaw, Choctaw, Creek, and Seminole—were removed from the southeastern states and forced westward to Oklahoma, then the center of what was called Indian Territory.

Perched high on a pile of baggage and with a military policeman watching, a little Japanese boy is awaiting the return of his parents, April 6, 1942, in San Francisco, California. More than 650 citizens of Japanese ancestry were evacuated from their homes and sent to Santa Anita racetrack, now an assembly center for war relocation of alien and American-born Japanese civilians. (AP Photo)

In 1941, President Franklin Roosevelt issued Executive Order 8802, which banned discrimination in the defense industries and the federal government on the basis of race, creed, color, or national origin, after a threatened march on Washington by blacks to protest racial discrimination in the defense industry. The executive order also created a Committee on Fair Employment Practices. Yet in 1943, Roosevelt signed Executive Order 9066, which created zones in the United States in which the military had the power to exclude people. Under this order, more than 112,000 Japanese Americans who were residing in these zones were forcefully removed to "relocation" camps. Of note is the fact that German Americans and Italian Americans, whose ancestors also came from countries with which the United States was fighting in World War II, were not subjected to the same exclusion from these zones.

Lyndon B. Johnson used his knowledge of Congress and his political skill to persuade Congress to pass the Civil Rights Act of 1964 and the Voting Rights Act of 1965. More recently, President Bill Clinton invited representatives from the 545 federally recognized Indian tribes to meet at the White House to discuss Indian issues. (This number continually changes. As of 2001, the number of federally recognized entities—Indian nations, tribes, bands, organized communities, pueblos, and Alaskan Native villages and corporations—had risen to 561.) This was the first time since 1822 that Indians had been invited to meet officially with a U.S. president to discuss issues of concern to them. This high-profile visit indicated a shift in the U.S. government's approach to Indian affairs.

Presidential Appointments.   Presidents also send signals about their commitment to particular constituencies through the appointments they make. Four of President Clinton's initial cabinet officers during his first term were African American—Ronald Brown, secretary of commerce; Hazel O'Leary, secretary of energy; Jesse Brown, secretary for veteran's affairs; and Michael Espy, secretary of agriculture. (Although his was not officially a cabinet-level office, the director of the Office of Drug Policy, Lee Brown, was another African American whom President Clinton informally recognized as a cabinet-level official.) This was the largest number of blacks to serve in cabinet posts in any administration to date. President Clinton also had two Latinos as cabinet officers—Henry Cisneros, former mayor of San Antonio, Texas, served as secretary of housing and urban development; and Federico Peña, former mayor of Denver, Colorado, was secretary of transportation. As with African Americans, this is the largest number of Latinos ever to serve in the cabinet.

In his second term, President Clinton named three Latinos and four African Americans to serve in the cabinet or in cabinet-level positions. The Latino appointees were Transportation Secretary Federico Peña, who became secretary of energy, replacing Hazel O'Leary; New Mexico Congressman Bill Richardson, who became ambassador to the United Nations; and Aida Alvarez, director of the Small Business Administration. Peña resigned his post in mid–1998 and was replaced by Ambassador Bill

President Clinton walks with Sue Masten, president of the National Congress of American Indians, left, and Kelsey Begaye, president of the Navajo Nation, to a news conference where Clinton announces that $1.2 billion more will be pumped into federal Indian programs, Washington, D.C., February 25, 2000. (AP Photo: Joe Marquette)

Richardson. The African American appointees were Alexis Herman, secretary of labor; Rodney Slater, a Clinton friend and Arkansas highway secretary, who became secretary of transportation; Jesse Brown, who remained for a time as secretary of veterans' affairs, although he later resigned and was replaced by former Secretary of the Army Togo West; and Franklin Raines, director of the Office of Management and Budget, who resigned in April 1998. Clinton named the first Asian American, Norman Mineta, former congressman from California, to a cabinet position as secretary of commerce. Clinton also named Bill Lann Lee, a Chinese American lawyer from Los Angeles who has worked for the **NAACP Legal Defense Fund**, to the position of assistant attorney general for civil rights. Lee is the first Asian American to hold this important (although not cabinet-level) post. As with Clinton's earlier nominee to this post during his first term, Lani

Guinier, Lee was opposed by conservative Republicans, who refused him confirmation ostensibly because of his views on affirmative action and busing to achieve school integration. This Republican action outraged large segments of the Asian American electorate, who as discussed in Chapter 3 have the highest proportion of independent voters. This action made it more difficult for the Republicans to appeal to Asian American voters. President Clinton made Lee acting assistant attorney general for civil rights. He served until the end of Clinton's presidency.

Clinton's appointments to the lifetime positions on the federal courts have marked a "revolutionary" increase in minority group representation among a group of policymakers that prior to 1961 had included only one black male and one male who had a Mexican father (as well as two white females). During his first term, a majority of Clinton's appointments to the federal judiciary were white women and male and female racial minorities. He appointed 29 black men and 8 black women, increasing the black proportion of the federal judiciary from 5.4 (at the time of his election) to 8.5 percent. The Latino proportion increased from 4.0 to 4.4 percent with the appointment of twelve Latino men and two Latina women. Although Clinton appointed three Asian American men, Asian representation dipped slightly from 0.6 percent to 0.5 percent (Goldman and Slotnick 1997). He also appointed 50 white women to the federal judiciary and appointed the first American Indian federal judge, Billy Michael Burrage of Oklahoma (Goldman and Saranson 1994).

Although of a different political party, President George Bush's initial cabinet appointments were similar in racial and ethnic diversity to those of President Clinton. He appointed Colin Powell as the first black secretary of state; Rod Paige, a black former Houston superintendent, as secretary of education; Elaine Chao, an Asian American, as secretary of labor; Mel Martinez, a Cuban American from Florida, as secretary of housing and urban development; and Norman Mineta, Asian American Democrat who served as President Clinton's secretary of commerce, was retained by Bush in the cabinet as secretary of transportation. Although national security adviser is not a cabinet-level post, Bush appointed Condeleezza Rice as the first female and second black to serve in that capacity. Bush appears to be continuing the practice of diversity among his Cabinet members in his second term. Condoleezza Rice replaced Colin Powell as secretary of state, and Alberto Gonzales, former White House counsel, was confirmed as the first Latino attorney general of the United States. Elaine

Chao remains as secretary of labor, Norman Mineta was retained as secretary of transportation, and Alphonso Jackson replaced Mel Martinez as secretary of housing and urban development. Bush's record of judicial nominations is more mixed. Of his 200 judicial appointments, only 15 were African American—4 on circuit courts and 11 on district courts (Ruffin 2004). Despite this weak record, it should be noted that he appointed two blacks to the Fourth Circuit Court of Appeals that has jurisdiction over states with high black populations—Maryland, North Carolina, South Carolina, Virginia, and West Virgina. Roger Gregory of Virginia was originally nominated by President Clinton, but the Republican-controlled Senate refused to act on the nomination, and Allyson Duncan, a black Republican from North Carolina were both confirmed. Bush has done marginally better with Latino judges, with 17, excluding Territorial District Courts, being appointed.

Given the power of the president's office and the symbolism involved in running for the position, it was only a matter of time before a nonwhite candidate would make a serious attempt to gain the office. Indeed, in 1995, there was much talk and speculation about retired Joint Chiefs of Staff General Colin Powell as a possible Republican presidential candidate. In the end, however, Powell chose not to run. He also refused to be considered as a vice presidential candidate on the Republican ticket. We end our discussion of the presidency by examining the 1972 presidential campaign of Representative Shirley Chisholm, the 1984 and 1988 presidential candidacies of Jesse Jackson, and the 2004 campaigns of Carol Moseley-Braun and Al Sharpton. Chisholm's, Jackson's, Moseley-Braun's, and Sharpton's situations are part of the second dilemma—what do racial minorities do to gain access to the political system?

Shirley Chisholm's Presidential Campaign: 1972.   Most people think of Jesse Jackson's 1984 and 1988 presidential campaigns as the first by a "serious" black presidential contender, while we tend to forget Shirley Chisholm's run in 1972. Chisholm was serious about her bid and stayed in the race through the presidential primaries and into the Democratic convention.

The late member of Congress Shirley Chisholm ran for president in 1972 on a Democratic Party ticket. She entered the race after no woman or black chose to run for the nomination. Her goal was never to win, but rather to show it was possible for an African American woman to make a good standing in a presidential run.

This promotional photo provided by PBS Television shows Shirley Chisholm campaigning for president in 1972. Chisholm's losing campaign is the focus of the documentary *Chisholm 72: Unbought and Unbossed*. (AP Photo/PBS: Courtesy of Arlie Scott)

By building a coalition of African American and women voters, as well as concentrating her limited resources on more sympathetic states, she was able to make a good showing. Chisholm had a strong showing in Florida and Minnesota, despite the small number of blacks in both of these states, something she admits was "always so odd." It was the people in both of these states that raised $10,000 for her campaign and pushed her toward an actual run for the nomination. In fact, Chisholm became the first and only black woman to have her name placed into nomination at a national party convention. Despite receiving 430,000 votes before the convention even began, Chisholm's run for the nomination would ultimately fail.

Not all went well for Chisholm, however. She faced many obstacles in her bid for the presidential nomination. Many black males felt that her candidacy would divide the black voting block (Koplinski 2000). In fact, a number of black leaders claimed that, "A vote for Shirley Chisholm is a vote for George Wallace" (one of the frontrunner Democrats) (Koplinski 2000:100). Despite her attempt at coalition building, Chisholm faced criticism from the black community from those who felt that she was not representing the black point of view and was beholden to the women's rights movement. Ironically, many of the leading feminists would not endorse her either because they felt she never had a chance and did not want to lose the favor of the eventual nominee. Thus even though the strong base of her campaign was female and black voters, these groups at large were also unwilling to endorse what they perceived to be a doomed campaign, and so they threw their support to safer white male candidates. Nonetheless, she ran an impressive campaign considering her fairly late start and shoestring budget. In the end, she received 151 delegates on the first ballot of the roll-call vote.

Jesse Jackson's Presidential Campaigns: 1984 and 1988.   Blacks represent the largest single voting bloc within the Democratic Party, and by the early 1980s they were well integrated into the affairs of the party. Despite their integration and their placement on committees of the Democratic National Committee, many—including Jesse Jackson—questioned the level of influence blacks had within the party. There was also the emergent feeling among the black electorate that the Democratic Party was not seriously committed to furthering the advancement of blacks. This feeling, combined with the Reagan administration's negative policies and attitudes toward blacks and the perception that the Democratic Party had failed to oppose many of Reagan's initiatives, caused Jesse Jackson to seek the Democratic presidential nomination in 1984 (Tate 1993).

Jackson hoped to be the voice for those outside of the political system and to increase both his and, by inference, black influence on the policies and positions of the party. Jackson's 1984 candidacy was seen as a challenge to the Democratic Party and its leadership; it also represented a challenge and a problem to the black leadership establishment—that is, black elected officials and national civil rights leaders. His 1984 candidacy was opposed by most black elected officials—many of whom were already committed to other candidates at the point of Jackson's announcement—including most big-city black mayors and a majority of the **Congressional Black Caucus** (a group of black members of Congress who seek to exert influence and promote issues of interest to African Americans) as well as the leaders of the NAACP and the National Urban League. Jackson was also plagued by doubts regarding his ability to carry out a credible campaign, and there were fears that his candidacy would split the black vote and lead to the nomination of a conservative Democratic candidate (Smith 1990).

During the 1984 campaign, Jackson pushed a progressive agenda through the concept of a **Rainbow Coalition**—a joint effort of peoples of all colors—that he hoped might become the majority in the Democratic Party. This premise was based on the assumption that the black vote, which constituted 20 percent of the Democratic Party voter coalition, could be mobilized to form the base of the Rainbow Coalition and that enough nonblacks (whites, Latinos, Asians, and American Indians) would join in a coalition with blacks to form a multiethnic majority.

Jackson finished in third place, with 18 percent of the vote and 9 percent of the convention delegates, in the 1984 presidential primary and nominating process, and he received few concessions from the Democratic Party. All of his minority policy planks were defeated by the Walter Mondale forces at the national convention, and Mondale refused to meet or negotiate with Jackson until after the convention. "In 1984 Jackson's 'victories,' including his highly celebrated speech at the 1984 national convention, were largely symbolic" (Tate 1993:61).

Jackson's campaign for the presidency in 1988 contrasted sharply with the 1984 effort. Jackson gained the support of virtually the entire black leadership establishment: a majority of big-city black mayors, members of the Congressional Black Caucus, and leaders of the national civil rights organizations. "With the exception of Los Angeles Mayor Thomas Bradley and Atlanta's Andrew Young, who declared himself neutral (the latter ostensibly because of his role as convention city host); Detroit Mayor Coleman Young, who supported Mike Dukakis; and Missouri's Congressman Alan Wheat, who supported his home-state colleague, Richard Gephardt, it is difficult to think of a major national black leader that did not support Jackson's 1988 campaign" (Smith 1990).

In 1988 Jackson won the presidential primaries in the District of Columbia, Alabama, Georgia, Louisiana, Mississippi, and Virginia, and he won caucuses in Alaska, Delaware, Michigan, South Carolina, and Puerto Rico. By the time of the Democratic Convention, Jackson was second in a field of eight Democratic contenders; he garnered 29 percent of the primary vote compared to Dukakis's 43 percent and collected 1,105 delegates compared to Dukakis's 2,309 (Smith 1990:228). During the 1988 campaign, Jackson chose to focus on what political scientists call **valence issues**—

issues that have universal appeal, such as anticrime and antipoverty issues—and he is credited by Democrats as well as Republicans with being the campaign's most effective advocate on the issues of drug use and teens' personal responsibility regarding sex and pregnancy.

Jackson's two presidential campaigns were historic, and they marked a change in the public role blacks were ready to play in presidential politics. First, they demonstrated that black voters were prepared to support and mobilize behind one of their own, as evidenced by significantly increased black voter registration and participation in both 1984 and 1988. Second, despite the inability of Jackson's delegates to play a balance-of-power role in the choice of the party nominee in either 1984 or 1988, Jackson's two campaigns were successful in inserting progressive ideas and policy initiatives into the campaign debates on domestic and foreign policy issues—a perspective that may not have been articulated without his presence.

Carol Moseley-Braun and Al Sharpton: 2004.   In 2003, Moseley-Braun and Al Sharpton were two blacks among the nine Democrats running in the Democratic presidential primary. If Shirley Chisholm was a woman before her time, in 2003, former United States Senator Moseley-Braun marketed herself as a realistic candidate. Unlike Shirley Chisholm, who recognized the impossibility of her run for the presidency, Moseley-Braun stated "that Americans are prepared to think outside the box and elect a person who is female and African-American, a person who does not fit the mold that we have resorted to for the last 200 years" (Younge 2003:3). Although Moseley-Braun had little name recognition outside of the African American community, she represented an important demographic within the Democratic Party and the anti–Iraq War movement. She claimed to be "a budget hawk and a peace dove" (Younge 2003:1). With only 44 percent of African Americans in favor of the Iraq War and 51 percent of women in general, Moseley-Braun fulfilled a much-needed voice (Younge 2003). Although she lost her bid for reelection to the Senate in 1998, Moseley-Braun viewed her race for the Democratic nomination as a serious effort.

Al Sharpton was a Pentecostal minister, ordained at age 9, and is known more for his work as an activist than as a politician. He is founder and president of National Action Network and was a candidate for U.S. Senate in 1992 and 1994 and for mayor of New York City in 1997.

Moseley-Braun participated in only one presidential primary before she formally withdrew from the race on January 15, 2004. Sharpton, like

Chisholm, stayed in the race through the presidential primaries and did well at several contests; for example, he was second in his home state of New York, pulling 34 percent of the vote to John Kerry's 54 percent. Despite dropping out of the race early, Moseley-Braun raised $627,869 as of December 31, 2004, which does not include federal matching funds because her campaign failed to file for them. She also had expenses and debts totaling $885,267. Interestingly, Moseley-Braun raised more money than did Al Sharpton, who raised $611,757, which included $100,000 in federal matching funds. Moreover, Sharpton ended the race $556,550 in debt.

Congress

The U.S. Senate and the House of Representatives are the national legislative bodies. They are responsible not only for making laws but also for determining budget allocations to the entire federal government. Clearly, this body has significant influence over, and importance to, the issues of concern to racial minorities.

Levels of Representation.   In 1971, black members of the House of Representatives and the one black in the Senate formed the Congressional Black Caucus in an attempt to increase the influence of blacks in the House, as well as to provide research and information support for members. The 1992 elections—the first following the reapportionment and redistricting occasioned by the 1990 census—resulted in a substantial increase in the group's membership. Carol Moseley-Braun of Illinois was elected to the Senate, the first black woman (and the first black Democrat) to serve in that body. She was the first black in the Senate since the defeat of Edward Brooke, a Massachusetts Republican, in 1978. She lost her reelection bid in 1998. In 2004, Illinois elected a second black Democrat, Barack Obama, to the U.S. Senate. A former state senator, Obama, a Columbia undergraduate and Harvard-educated lawyer, received 70 percent of the statewide vote and won all but a handful of counties. In the 2004 elections, 40 blacks were elected to the House of Representatives—twelve of whom were women. In addition, two black female Democrats were elected as nonvoting delegates from the District of Columbia and the U.S. Virgin Islands. There are no black Republicans in the House of Representatives. Blacks now make up 9.2 percent of the House of Representatives, and women, excluding nonvoting delegates, are 30 percent of the black representatives (listed in Table 4.1). The potential influence of black representatives would be magnified if the House of Representatives were to return to Democratic control in the 2006 midterm elections. Several black members would be in line to chair major House committees—in particular, John Conyers of Michigan would chair the Judiciary Committee, and Charles Rangel of New York would chair the powerful Ways and Means Committee—based on the first year elected (see Table 4.1).

The effect of the Supreme Court's decisions with respect to minority majority districts was prominent in the 1996 congressional races, primarily due to the invalidation by the Supreme Court of the majority minority districts in Texas and Georgia. (North Carolina's districts also were invalidated, but the federal district court ruled that the state would not have to redraw the districts until the 1998 elections.) After Georgia redrew its lines, it went from three majority black districts to one—Representative John Lewis's 5th District. Representatives Cynthia McKinney's 11th District and Sanford Bishop's 2nd District were redrawn. McKinney decided that she would have a better chance for reelection if she moved from the 11th to the 4th District. At the same time, Steve Linder, the Republican incumbent in the 4th District, thought he would have a better shot at reelection from the new 11th District, so McKinney and Linder switched districts. McKinney ran as the incumbent in the 4th District, which is approximately one-third black. McKinney won the Democratic primary with 67 percent of the vote and ran against Republican John Mitnick in the general election. The campaign was tense and full of turmoil. Mitnick tried to link McKinney to Louis Farrakhan, whereas McKinney had to apologize for anti-Semitic comments made by her father. McKinney won the race with 57.8 percent to Mitnick's 42.2 percent.

Sanford Bishop's reelection race in the 2nd District, although competitive, was not as contentious as the McKinney-Mitnick contest. The redrawn 2nd District black voting-age population dropped from 52 percent to 35 percent. Bishop, a conservative, won the Democratic primary with 59 percent of the vote. His Republican opponent in the November election was Darrel Ealum. The race generated no fireworks, and Bishop won reelection with 53.8 percent to Ealum's 46.2 percent of the vote.

Corrine Brown of the 3rd Congressional District in Florida also ran in a reconfigured district (*Johnson et al. v. Mortham* 1995). Her old district had a black voting-age population of approximately 60 percent; the new district has approximately 40 percent. Brown had a spirited reelection contest

TABLE 4.1   Black Members of the 109th Congress, 2005–2007

Name	State	Party	First Elected
Senate			
Barack Obama	Illinois	Democrat	2004
House of Representatives			
John Conyers Jr.	Michigan	Democrat	1964
Charles B. Rangel	New York	Democrat	1970
Major R. Owens	New York	Democrat	1982
Edolphus Towns	New York	Democrat	1982
John Lewis	Georgia	Democrat	1986
Donald M. Payne	New Jersey	Democrat	1988
William J. Jefferson	Louisiana	Democrat	1990
Maxine Waters	California	Democrat	1990
Sanford D. Bishop Jr.	Georgia	Democrat	1992
Corrine Brown	Florida	Democrat	1992
James E. Clyburn	South Carolina	Democrat	1992
Alcee L. Hastings	Florida	Democrat	1992
Eddie Bernice Johnson	Texas	Democrat	1992
Bobby L. Rush	Illinois	Democrat	1992
Robert C. Scott	Virginia	Democrat	1992
Melvin L. Watt	North Carolina	Democrat	1992
Albert Russell Wynn	Maryland	Democrat	1992
Bennie G. Thompson	Mississippi	Democrat	1993
Chaka Fattah	Pennsylvania	Democrat	1994
Sheila Jackson-Lee	Texas	Democrat	1994
Jesse L. Jackson Jr.	Illinois	Democrat	1995
Julia Carson	Indiana	Democrat	1996
Elijah E. Cummings	Maryland	Democrat	1996
Danny K. Davis	Illinois	Democrat	1996
Harold E. Ford Jr.	Tennessee	Democrat	1996
Carolyn C. Kilpatrick	Michigan	Democrat	1996
Juanita Millender-McDonald	California	Democrat	1996
Barbara Lee	California	Democrat	1998
Gregory W. Meeks	New York	Democrat	1998
Stephanie Tubbs Jones	Ohio	Democrat	1998
William Lacy Clay III	Missouri	Democrat	2000
Diane Watson	California	Democrat	2001
Artur Davis	Alabama	Democrat	2002
Kendrick Meek	Florida	Democrat	2002
David Scott	Georgia	Democrat	2002
George K. Butterfield	North Carolina	Democrat	2004
Emanuel Cleaver	Missouri	Democrat	2004
Al Green	Texas	Democrat	2004
Cynthia McKinney	Georgia	Democrat	2004*
Gwen Moore	Wisconsin	Democrat	2004
Nonvoting Delegate in the House			
Eleanor Holmes Norton	District of Columbia	Democrat	1990
Donna M. Christian-Christensen	U.S. Virgin Islands	Democrat	1996

*Served in Congress from 1992 to 2002, elected again in 2004.
Source: Compiled by the authors.

in 1994 against black Republican Marc Little, with Brown winning 58 percent of the vote. In 1996, Brown faced another black Republican, James Preston Fields, and won handily with 61.4 percent of the vote.

All of Texas's congressional districts were redrawn in 1996 as a result of *Bush v. Vera*, forcing all congressional delegates into a primary election held on November 5. Those races in which one candidate did not receive a majority (50 percent plus one) of the votes went into a runoff election in December. The two majority black districts—the 18th, represented by Sheila Jackson Lee, and the 30th, represented by Eddie Bernice Johnson—were no longer majority black after the redistricting but retained a sizable black population base—45 percent and 44 percent respectively. Both Jackson Lee and Johnson won majorities on election day, with 77.1 and 54.6 percent of the vote, respectively, avoiding a runoff contest.

Another significant race in 1996 was the election of Julia M. Carson to the seat vacated by Representative Andy Jacobs in the 10th District in Indianapolis. The district is about 27 percent black and heavily Democratic, but Republicans have made gains over the years. (Jacobs won with approximately 53 percent in 1994, but his margin of victory has been declining in recent elections.) Carson ran against moderate Republican Virginia Blankenbaker, and going into November the race was a statistical dead heat. Nevertheless, Carson won with 52.6 percent—the same percentage won by Jacobs in 1994—to 45.1 percent for Blankenbaker.

We caution against drawing the conclusion from these races that blacks can win in majority white districts, particularly southern ones, for several reasons. First, although three blacks—McKinney, Bishop, and Brown—won in southern majority white districts, three other blacks lost in 1996 congressional contests in southern majority white districts (Bositis 1996). Second, the aforementioned winning black candidates had the advantages of incumbency and of running in primarily Democratic districts. (The most conservative of the new congressional districts was Bishop's. Bill Clinton won only 49 percent of the vote in Bishop's district, whereas Bishop himself pulled 54 percent of the vote there. By comparison, in the two other congressional districts, Clinton won handily, with percentages close to or exceeding those of the incumbents.) Third, although Jackson Lee's and Johnson's districts were no longer majority black, each contained a significant portion of Latinos (23 percent and 18 percent, respectively) making the districts still majority minority. Finally, with respect to Carson, she also ran in a heavily Democratic district where Bill Clinton

Senator-elect Barack
Obama, D–Ill., meets
with other newly elected
members of Congress
before the start of a
ceremony in the East
Room of the White
House, Monday, January
3, 2005, in Washington.
(AP Photo: Pablo
Martinez Monsivais)

outpolled Bob Dole, 54 percent to 37 percent. Since the initial contests in 1996, McKinney, Bishop, Brown, Jackson Lee, Johnson, and Carson were reelected handily in both 1998 and 2000, and all but Cynthia McKinney were reelected in 2002 and 2004. McKinney was defeated in 2002 by Denise Majette, a black Democrat, in the Democratic primary, but Majette stepped down to run for governor of Georgia in 2004, and McKinney was elected again from her old district.

Currently, two Latinos, both elected in 2004, serve in the U.S. Senate. Ken Salazar is a Mexican American Democrat from Colorado, and Mel Martinez is a Cuban American Republican from Florida. The number of Latinos in the House stood at 25 (listed in Table 4.2) after the 2004 elections. Seven of the 25 members are Latinas, and five are Republicans. Table 4.2 also shows the ethnic origin of the Hispanic members of Congress. Seventeen of the 25 are Mexican Americans, with 4 Cubans, 3 Puerto Ricans, and 1 of Portuguese ancestry. There is also a nonvoting delegate from Puerto Rico. There are two sets of siblings—Mario and Lincoln

TABLE 4.2   Latino Members of the 109th Congress, 2005–2007

Name	Ethnic Origin	State	Party	First Elected
Senate				
Mel Martinez	Cuban	Florida	Republican	2004
Ken Salazar	Mexican	Colorado	Democrat	2004
House of Representatives				
Solomon P. Ortiz	Mexican	Texas	Democrat	1982
Ileana Ros-Lehtinen	Cuban	Florida	Republican	1989
Jose E. Serrano	Puerto Rican	New York	Democrat	1990
Edward Pastor	Mexican	Arizona	Democrat	1991
Xavier Bacerra	Mexican	California	Democrat	1992
Henry Bonilla	Mexican	Texas	Republican	1992
Lincoln Diaz-Balart	Cuban	Florida	Republican	1992
Luis V. Gutierrez	Puerto Rican	Illinois	Democrat	1992
Robert Menendez	Cuban	New Jersey	Democrat	1992
Lucille Roybal-Allard	Mexican	California	Democrat	1992
Nydia M. Velazquez	Puerto Rican	New York	Democrat	1992
Ruben Hinojosa	Mexican	Texas	Democrat	1996
Silvestre Reyes	Mexican	Texas	Democrat	1996
Loretta Sanchez	Mexican	California	Democrat	1996
Charles A. Gonzalez	Mexican	Texas	Democrat	1998
Grace F. Napolitano	Mexican	California	Democrat	1998
Joe Baca	Mexican	California	Democrat	1999
Hilda Solis	Mexican	California	Democrat	2000
Dennis Cardoza	Mexican	Arizona	Democrat	2002
Henry Cuellar	Mexican	Texas	Democrat	2002
Mario Diaz-Balart Romero	Cuban	Florida	Republican	2002
Raul Grijalva	Mexican	Arizona	Democrat	2002
Devin Nunes	Portuguese	California	Republican	2002
Linda Sanchez	Mexican	California	Democrat	2002
John Salazar	Mexican	Colorado	Democrat	2004
Nonvoting Delegate in the House				
Robert Underwood	Chamorro	Guam	Democrat	1992
Luis Fortuno	Puerto Rican	Puerto Rico	New Progressive	2004

Source: Compiled by the authors.

Diaz-Balart, Republicans from Florida, and Loretta and Linda Sanchez, Democrats from California. John Salazar, Democrat from Colorado, was elected to the House of Representatives at the same time that his brother, Ken, was elected to the Senate in 2004. In 1977, Latino representatives established the Congressional Hispanic Caucus along lines similar to the Congressional Black Caucus (see glossary). Of the Latino members of the

TABLE 4.3   Asian-Pacific Island Members of the 109th Congress, 2005–2007

Name	Ethnic Origin	State	Party	First Elected
Senate				
Daniel Inouye	Japanese	Hawaii	Democrat	1962
Daniel K. Akaka	Native Hawaiian	Hawaii	Democrat	1990
House of Representatives				
David Wu	Chinese	Oregon	Democrat	1998
Mike Honda	Japanese	California	Democrat	2000
Bobby Jindal	South Asian	Louisiana	Republican	2004
Doris Matsui	Japanese	California	Democrat	2005
Nonvoting Delegate in the House				
Eni Faleomavaega	Samoan	American Samoa	Democrat	1988
Robert A. Underwood	Chamorro	Guam	Democrat	1992

Source: Compiled by the authors.

109th Congress, all 20 Democrats are members of the Caucus, whereas none of the Republicans are.

There is one Asian American senator, Daniel Inouye (D–Hawaii) and one native Hawaiian, Daniel Akaka (D), who is often counted as an Asian American legislator. There are four Asian American members of the House of Representatives—three Democrats and one Republican, plus two nonvoting Democratic delegates, one each from Guam and American Samoa (see list in Table 4.3). Representative Robert Matsui, the long-serving Japanese American Democrat from Sacramento, California, died in early January 2005. His wife, Doris, ran to fill his seat. She won a special election on March 8, 2005, receiving 72 percent of the overall vote and 88 percent of the vote among Democrats. In May 1994, the Congressional Asian Pacific American Caucus was formed. The late Representative Patsy T. Mink (D–Hawaii) was quoted as saying that the Caucus was formed because the Asian Pacific members of Congress have felt that "we have not been consulted on important steps taken by this [Clinton] administration and ones in the past" (*Washington Post* 1994:A10).

Although the number of all of the minorities in Congress is small, none is smaller than the number of American Indians serving—one, Republican Tom Cole (Chickasaw), elected to the House of Representatives from Oklahoma in 2002. (See Table 4.4 for a historical listing of American Indians who have served in the U.S. Senate and House of Representatives.)

TABLE 4.4   American Indians Who Have Served in the U.S. Senate and House of Representatives

Name	Tribe	State	Service Years
Senate			
Matthew Stanley Quay	Abenaki or Delaware	Pennsylvania	1887–1899, 1901–1904
Charles Curtis[a]	Kaw-Osage	Kansas	1907–1913, 1915–1929
Robert L. Owen	Cherokee	Oklahoma	1907–1925
Ben Nighthorse Campbell	Northern Cheyenne	Colorado	1992–2004
House of Representatives			
Charles Curtis	Kaw-Osage	Kansas	1893–1907
Charles D. Carter	Choctaw	Oklahoma	1907–1927
W. W. Hastings	Cherokee	Oklahoma	1915–1921, 1923–1935
William G. Stigler	Choctaw	Oklahoma	1944–1952
Benjamin Reifel	Rosebud Sioux	South Dakota	1961–1971
Ben Nighthorse Campbell	Northern Cheyenne	Colorado	1987–1992
Brad Cannon	Cherokee	Oklahoma	2000–2004
Tom Cole	Chickasaw	Oklahoma	2002–

[a]Curtis served as Herbert Hoover's Vice President, 1929–1933, and thus served as President of the Senate during that time.

Source: The information in this table was drawn from a table developed by Gerald Wilkinson, National Indian Youth Council, provided to the authors by the Office of Senator Ben Nighthorse Campbell, and data from the Congressional Research Service. This table is correct to the best of our knowledge. The Congressional Research Service indicates that the American Indian background of Quay is rumored but has not been verified.

The Supreme Court

The Supreme Court is often viewed as merely the final authority on constitutional issues, determining whether previous and current lower court judicial decisions, executive decisions, and legislative acts are constitutional. The Court, however, plays a much greater role because in many instances its decisions may establish new public policy. We can, therefore, view the Supreme Court as a participant in the policymaking process. For racial minority groups, the Supreme Court has been extremely important in their abilities to gain equal rights and constitutional protections. The

Court is a particularly important access point for racial and ethnic minorities because victories can be won by appealing to policymakers to do what is consistent with the Constitution rather than merely what the majority wants.

The Supreme Court has been especially important in establishing the legal framework within which racial minorities in the United States have had to exist. Although many of the most significant decisions—both favorable and unfavorable to minority litigants—have been made in cases involving African Americans, several decisions have also been made in cases brought by other groups. It should be understood that regardless of the minority group that brings the suit, the decision often has implications for the other groups as well.

Racial diversity on the Court has been and continues to be a significant political issue each time a seat becomes available. The first black to serve on the Court was Appeals Court judge, former U.S. solicitor general, and director/counsel of the NAACP-LDF Thurgood Marshall, who was nominated by President Johnson in 1967. Marshall's confirmation hearings were held up by southern senators, particularly Strom Thurmond of South Carolina, who adamantly opposed the appointment of a black to the Court. Marshall was a liberal member of the Court led by Chief Justice Earl Warren, which issued many of the decisions that opened up the political process for racial minorities.

Marshall retired from the Court in 1991, at which time President George Bush nominated the far-right black conservative Clarence Thomas to fill the vacancy. Thomas's nomination and the subsequent opposition by a sizable segment of black Americans highlight the fact that the race of a nominee does not ensure the support of other members of the racial group. Policy positions and attitudes may be even more important to racial minorities than similarities in color. Clarence Thomas's positions on a variety of issues—for example, equal protection, privacy rights, equal employment opportunity, and access to education—run counter to what many perceive to be the best interests of black America. Thus, whereas Anita Hill's accusations of sexual harassment and the televising of the second set of confirmation hearings drew attention to Thomas's nomination, many blacks, organized groups, and individuals testified in opposition to his nomination during the first set of hearings. Marshall and Thomas are the only two racial minorities to have served on the Court to date. (Two white females, Sandra Day O'Connor and Ruth Bader Ginsberg, currently serve on the Court.)

The Bureaucracy

Although the bureaucracy is technically part of the executive branch, any president quickly learns that he does not control it. People working within agencies cannot be strictly supervised; therefore even when the law is very specific, bureaucrats must necessarily exercise discretion. For example, within U.S. urban areas, the maximum speed limit is 55 miles per hour. Yet each of us has witnessed people breaking that law, and at times such transgressions are observed by law enforcement officers. If these local bureaucrats (police officers work within a bureaucracy and thus are bureaucrats) can affect the implementation of a specific policy such as speed limits, imagine the possibilities when they are charged with regulating in the public interest, detecting and prohibiting discrimination, or evaluating the work performance of subordinates—tasks assigned routinely to federal bureaucrats.

Because bureaucrats are appointed rather than elected, many people who are concerned about the representativeness of bodies such as Congress, or even with more visible nonelected bodies such as the Supreme Court, pay little attention to the composition of the bureaucracy. However, the representativeness of the bureaucracy can be important for a variety of reasons. First, such representativeness is a symbol of the openness of government. People may believe a government is legitimate if it employs people who are similar to them. Second, to the extent that people's attitudes are shaped by their socialization, a bureaucracy composed of a cross section of the nation's population will help to ensure that a full range of viewpoints will be articulated somewhere within the government. Third, to the extent that attitudes affect behavior, a more **representative bureaucracy**—one in which the demographic characteristics of the personnel mirror those of the population—may produce a more responsive bureaucracy. For example, there is evidence that black and Hispanic school children fare better when a greater number of black and Hispanic teachers, respectively, are present in their school systems (Meier, Stewart, and England 1989; Meier and Stewart 1991). Finally, citizens may be more willing to participate in government programs if the service providers are similar to them. For instance, there is evidence that HIV-infected patients, people desperately in need of bureaucratic services, clearly prefer to be served by people who share their race, gender, and sexual orientation (Thielemann and Stewart 1995).

TABLE 4.5   Representation of Racial/National Origin Groups in Federal Civilian Workforce and Civilian Labor Force, September 2003

	Federal Civilian Workforce (%)	Civilian Labor Force (%)
Blacks	17.6	10.4
Hispanics	7.0	13.1
Asian Americans	4.6	4.5
American Indians	2.0	0.6
Whites	68.7	71.4
TOTALS	99.9[a]	100.0

[a] Does not total to 100.

Source: U.S. Office of Personnel Management, 2003, *Annual Report to Congress on the Federal Equal Opportunity Recruitment Program* (Fiscal Year 2003) (Washington, D.C.: Employment Service, Office of Diversity), pp. 12.

Of course, the correspondence between the characteristics of the bureaucracy and those of the general population is not perfect. Studies from around the world, including the United States, consistently show that the middle class is overrepresented in the bureaucracy. This should not be surprising because members of the lower class generally lack the skills to perform bureaucratic tasks, and members of the upper class would not commonly engage in such activities. Further, these studies show that compared to other countries, on a variety of dimensions the United States has the world's most representative bureaucracy. To make another comparison, the federal bureaucracy much more closely mirrors the characteristics of the general population than does the "representative" legislative branch.

Beyond these generalizations, what specifically can be said about the representation of the nation's racial and ethnic minorities in the federal bureaucracy? Table 4.5 shows racial and ethnic group representation in federal civilian employment vis-à-vis that in the civilian labor force. Beyond the specifics, three points should be made. First, when compared to the general population proportions reported in Tables 2.1 and 2.2, blacks, American Indians, and, to a slight extent, Asian Americans are actually overrepresented in the federal bureaucracy. Second, the other groups fare poorly using the same standard. Third, blacks and American Indians are better represented among those employed in the public sector than among those who work in the private sector.

Even minority groups that are relatively well represented may not be distributed equitably within the federal bureaucracy. Table 4.6 shows the

TABLE 4.6   Distribution of Racial/National Origin Groups in Federal Civilian Workforce by Pay Grades, September 2003

Federal Pay Grade[a]	Total (%)	Blacks (%)	Hispanics (%)	Asian Americans (%)	American Indians (%)
1–4	5.1	5.4	4.0	4.3	8.5
5–8	31.6	34.6	30.7	20.7	33.3
9–12	34.0	32.4	37.8	35.6	31.2
13–15	15.6	14.0	14.1	25.4	11.1
SES/SL[b]	.4	.4	.4	.6	.4
Blue Collar	13.3	13.2	12.9	13.3	15.5
Totals	100.0	100.0	99.9[c]	99.9[c]	100.0

[a] Minimum-maximum salaries (2003) for each category are as follows:
1–4, $15,214–$27,234; 5–8, $23,442–$41,806; 9–12, $35,519–$66,961; 13–15, $61,251–$110,682; SES, $116,500–$134,000; SL, $102,168–134,000.
[b] Senior Executive Service and Senior Level.
[c] Totals do not equal 100.

Sources: U.S. Office of Personnel Management, 2003, *Annual Report to Congress on the Federal Equal Opportunity Recruitment Program* (Fiscal Year 2003) (Washington, D.C.: Employment Service, Office of Diversity), pp. 15–16, 21–22, 27–28, 33–34.

distribution of each minority racial and ethnic group across the federal pay grades. Blacks and American Indians are overrepresented at the lowest categories presented and underrepresented in the highest categories. In between, the pattern is mixed. At the next to the lowest categories, every group except Asian Americans is overrepresented. At the middle category, blacks and American Indians are notably underrepresented, Hispanics are almost perfectly represented, and Asian Americans are overrepresented. Just below the top, only Asian Americans are well represented.

In sum, it appears that the federal bureaucracy—despite its problems—is more open to minority employment than the private sector, which bodes well for an improvement in the way minorities are treated by the government. In addition, the trends appear to be positive for minorities moving into higher levels of the bureaucracy, which is one of the most viable avenues available for upward mobility. But we must remember that effective public policymaking also requires action in the states.

Federalism

A structural feature of American government that has had a major impact on racial and ethnic minorities is the division of powers between the national and state governments—federalism. Although the two levels share some powers—concurrent powers—it is in the areas in which the powers do not overlap that minorities have been most affected. Multiple levels of government create multiple access points, which are both good and bad. People who want change have ample opportunity to petition the government; so, too, do people who oppose change. The result is that the outcome of policy disputes depends as much on the locus of decisions—jurisdictional issues—as it does on the merits of policy proposals.

Much of the struggle over policies that affect racial and ethnic minorities in the United States hinges on the federal structure. As was seen in the earlier discussions of the Constitution and voting rights, the fact that policy decisions have been made in the states assured that those engaged in discrimination would be judging themselves. The Supreme Court, in a series of decisions, permitted this situation to exist. In the *Slaughterhouse Cases* (1873) the Court ruled that U.S. citizens had dual citizenship, national and local, and that the Fourteenth Amendment defended citizens' rights only against laws adopted by the national government and not against state governments' incursions. The decision in *United States v. Reese* (1876) interpreted the Fifteenth Amendment as allowing states to impose various criteria, including literacy tests, on prospective voters. In the *Civil Rights Cases* (1883) the Court voided the 1875 Civil Rights Act, ruling that the national government could not interfere with the private actions of individuals within states. And in *United States v. Harris* (1883) the Court struck down the Ku Klux Klan Act because it applied to the "private activities" of individuals. Taken together, these decisions allowed states to infringe on the civil rights of citizens, especially minority citizens.

It was not until the 1960s that states' rights arguments against minority civil rights were apparently overridden. Basing its authority on the commerce clause of the Constitution, the Civil Rights Act of 1964 asserted authority over what had previously been thought to be part of the "private" sector, access to "public" accommodations—buses, waiting rooms, restaurants, and hotels. Furthermore, as detailed later, increased reliance of local educational systems on federal funding gave the national government heretofore unknown leverage in achieving school desegregation in the states that had maintained de jure discrimination.

The post–1964 era was qualitatively different in terms of civil rights policy than the decades that preceded it. Richard Nixon represents an important break point because he showed that one could win the presidency by not being overtly racist but by allowing civil rights opponents to believe he agreed with them. The trend that started with Nixon reached its fruition with the Reagan and first Bush administrations, during which enforcement responsibilities were left to the states. Who are the state policymakers?

State Elective Office

At the state level, as of 2001, the largest numbers of black elected officials were found in ten states—Mississippi (892), Alabama (756), Louisiana (705), Illinois (624), Georgia (611), South Carolina (534), Arkansas (502), North Carolina (491), Texas (460), and Michigan (346) (Joint Center for Political Studies 2001). With the exception of Texas, Illinois, Arkansas, and Michigan, these states are covered, at least in part, by the Voting Rights Act. L. Douglas Wilder, whose term ended in January 1994, served as governor of Virginia, and the 1994 elections brought the total of blacks elected to statewide office to 18 (down from a high of 21), which includes the comptroller of New York state (a Democrat) and the late secretary of state of Colorado (a Republican). In addition to Governor Wilder, African Americans who have held or currently hold statewide offices include Merv Dymally, George Brown, and Joe Rogers, former lieutenant governors of California (Dymally) and Colorado (Brown and Rogers), and Michael Steele, the current lieutenant governor of Maryland; Roland Burris, former comptroller and state attorney general of Illinois; James Lewis, former treasurer of New Mexico; Ken Blackwell, former state treasurer of Ohio and current secretary of state; the late Vikki Buckley, secretary of state of Colorado; Denise Nappier, state treasurer of Connecticut; former state auditor of North Carolina Ralph H. Campbell Jr.; and state attorney general of New Jersey, Peter Harvey; Ed Brooke, former Republican senator from Massachusetts; Carol Moseley-Braun, former Democratic senator from Illinois; and current Democratic senator from Illinois, Barack Obama. Blackwell is and Buckley was a Republican.

Latinos also have had success in electing individuals to statewide offices. As of 2004, the largest numbers of Latino elected officials were found in nine states—Texas (2,075), California (1,035), New Mexico (664), Arizona (369), Colorado (149), Florida (112), New Jersey (102), Illinois (80), and New York (64). The state with the highest number of Latina elected officials is Arizona, where 36.3 percent (134) of the 369 Latino elected officials are female (National Association of Latino Elected Officials 2004).

Latinas have also played a very active role in New Mexico state politics. Two women who are especially worthy of note are Nina Otero Warren and Soledad Chacon. Warren began her career in politics in 1917 when she was appointed school superintendent of Santa Fe (Vigil 1996). She later went on to become chair of the Women's Division of the Republican State Committee for Women and ran for U.S. Congress, albeit unsuccessfully, in 1922. Also in 1922, Chacon ran for New Mexico secretary of state and won. She is most remembered for the fact that she served as acting governor in 1924, becoming the first Latina to serve in this capacity. Latinos have served as full-term, elected governors of New Mexico (Democrats Ezequiel Cabeza de Baca, 1917; Tony Anaya, 1983–1987; Jerry Apodaca, 1975–1979; Bill Richardson, 2003–; and Democrat-turned-Republican Octavian Ambrosio Larrazolo, 1919–1921), Arizona (Democrat Raul Castro, 1975–1977), and Florida (Republican Robert Martinez, 1987–1991); the former state attorney general in Texas, Dan Morales, was also Latino, as is the current attorney general in New Mexico, Patricia Madrid, and the current secretary of state of New Mexico, Rebecca Vigil-Giron. In addition, Latinos have begun to make inroads in the judicial branch in New Mexico. A majority of the justices of the state Supreme Court are Latino— Patricio Serna, Petra Jimenez Maes, and Edward Chavez. New Mexico is the only state in which Latino political representation is at least equal to the state's Latino population proportion (Brischetto 1996).

In the 2004 election, California elected 10 Latinos to the state senate and 19 to the state assembly, all but two Democrats. This is the largest number of Latinos in the state senate in California history, and one less than the high mark of 20 in the state assembly in 2000. In 1998, Cruz Bustamante, formerly the first Latino speaker of the assembly, was elected lieutenant governor, a position he still holds in 2004. Also in 1998, another Latino, Antonio Villaraigosa of Los Angeles, was elected speaker of the assembly following Bustamante in that position, and in the state senate, Democrat Richard Palanco was elected majority leader. The Republicans in the assembly elected Rod Pacheco as their new leader. Villaraigosa stepped down as speaker in 2000 and ran for mayor of Los Angeles in 2001. The current speaker of the assembly is also Latino, Fabian Nuñez, who took over from a black speaker, Herb Wesson.

Asian Pacific Americans have served as governor of Hawaii, lieutenant governors of Delaware and Hawaii, secretary of state and state treasurer in California, and in 54 state legislative seats in Hawaii. In a historic election

**Former Governor
Gary Locke,
State of Washington**

in 1996, Democrat Gary Locke, former King County executive and second-generation Washingtonian, was elected governor of Washington state, the first Asian American governor outside of Hawaii. Locke is also the first Chinese American governor. To date, Asian electoral successes have been regional rather than national (Nakanishi 1991). Locke's election is a major breakthrough in Asian electoral outcomes. Locke is a second-generation Chinese American: His grandfather came to the United States around the turn of the century and worked as a houseboy in Olympia, Washington. He returned to China at some point to marry but came back to the United States around 1930 when Locke's father was 13 years old. Locke's father served in the U.S. Army during World War II and later owned a restaurant and grocery store in Seattle. Locke, born in 1950, was one of five children growing up in a public housing project in Seattle. Through part-time jobs, financial aid, and scholarships, Locke received a BA from Yale University and a law degree from Boston University. He worked as a King County deputy prosecutor for several years and also worked for U.S. West. In 1982 he was elected to the Washington state house of representatives, and he served in that body for eleven years. In 1993, he was elected chief executive of King County, running for governor in 1996. Many consider Locke to be a liberal Democrat. Locke was re-elected handily to a second term in 2000, but he declined to run for a third term in 2004.

American Indian successes at the statewide level have been even rarer than those of Asians. Larry EchoHawk, a Democrat and a Pawnee Indian, has served in the Idaho state legislature and as attorney general but failed in his 1994 run for governor of that state. Bill Yellowtail, a Democrat and a Crow Indian, lost his bid in 1996 for Montana's only congressional seat. American Indians serve in the state legislatures of New Mexico (two in the house, two in the senate), Arizona (two and one, respectively), Oklahoma (two in the house), South Dakota (one in the house and one in the senate), Montana (six in the house and two in the senate), North Carolina (one in the house), North Dakota (one in the senate), Alaska (eight in the house and three in the senate), Colorado (one in the senate), Nevada (one in the house), Vermont (one in the senate), Washington (two in the house), and Wyoming (one in the house. The 2000 elections brought significant gains to American Indians in Montana. Six of seven Indians running for the state legislature were elected, representing five of the state's seven reservations. The Montana Democratic Party hired an Indian coordinator to help register and turn out Indian voters. It was successful and led to the increased gains for Montana's American Indians (NASA 2001). In 2004, Montana American Indians increased their electoral successes by reelecting those elected in 2000 and also by electing one additional member to the state senate and one additional to the state senate.

Table 4.7 shows the state distribution, tribal and party affiliations, and first year in office of American Indian and Alaskan Native state legislators. Although we lacked the data in Chapter 3 decisively to categorize American Indians as either Democrats or Republicans, such is not the case for those elected to state legislative offices, an overwhelming majority of whom are Democrats. The tribe with the largest number of representatives is the Navajo, but this may be a function of the fact that the Navajo nation is located in parts of four states, two of which are Arizona and New Mexico.

How does this representation work within the federal system to produce public policy? We now turn to two examples: equal opportunity in education and affirmative action in employment.

TABLE 4.7   American Indian and Alaskan Native State Legislators, 2005

State	Body	Name	Tribe	Party	First Year in Office
Alaska	House	Carl Moses	Aleut	Democrat	1965
		Richard Foster	Nome Esikimo	Democrat	1989
		Bill Williams	Tlingit	Republican	1993
		Beverly Masek	Athabascan	Republican	1994
		Reggie Joule	Inuit	Democrat	1996
		Albert Kookesh	Tlingit	Democrat	1996
		Carl Morgan	Yupik	Republican	1999
		Mary Slatter Kapsner	Yupik	Democrat	1999
	Senate	Lyman Hoffman	Yupik	Democrat	1990
		Georgianna Lincoln	Athabascan	Democrat	1992
		Donald Olson	Inupiat	Democrat	2001
Arizona	House	Sylvia Laughter	Navajo	Democrat	1999
		Jack C. Jackson	Navajo	Democrat	2003
	Senate	Albert Hale	Navajo	Democrat	2004
Colorado	Senate	Suzanne Williams	Comanche	Democrat	1997
Montana	House	Carol Juneau	Hidatsa Mandan	Democrat	1999
		Norma Bixby	No. Cheyenne	Democrat	2001
		Joey Jayne	Navajo	Democrat	2001
		Veronica Eastman	Crow	Democrat	2002
		Jonathan Windy Boy	Chippewa Cree	Democrat	2003
		Margaret Campbell	Assiniboine	Democrat	2004
	Senate	Frank Smith	Assiniboine	Democrat	1999
		Gerald Pease	Crow	Democrat	2001
New Mexico	House	James Madalena	Jemez Pueblo	Democrat	1985
		Ray Begaye	Navajo	Democrat	1999
	Senate	John Pinto	Navajo	Democrat	1977
		Leo Tsosie	Navajo	Democrat	1993
Nevada	House	John Oceguera	Walker River Paiute	Democrat	2001
North Carolina	House	Ronnie Sutton	Lumbee	Democrat	1991
North Dakota	Senate	Dennis Bercier	Turtle Mountain Chippewa	Democrat	1999
Okalahoma	House	Larry Adair	Cherokee	Democrat	1983
		Raymond McCarter	Chicksaw	Democrat	1997
		Chris Benge	Cherokee	Republican	1999
South Dakota	House	Paul Valandra	Rosebud Sioux	Democrat	2001
	Senate	Theresa Two Bulls	Oglala Sioux	Democrat	2004
Vermont	Senate	Julius Canns	Cherokee/ Tuscora	Republican	1992
Washington	House	Jeff Morris	Tsimshian	Democrat	1996
		John McCoy	Tulalip	Democrat	2002
Wyoming	House	W. Patrick Goggles	Northern Arapaho	Democrat	2004

Source: Compiled by the authors.

Equal Educational Opportunity

The struggle over equal educational opportunity provides a good example of the way the policymaking process within the federal system produces and thwarts policy change. Denial of such opportunity has been and continues to be a serious problem for members of the nation's racial and ethnic minority groups because it has important implications for one's chances for social mobility. The "American dream" of hard work being rewarded with higher income—which allows one access to better-quality housing, health care, and recreational opportunities—has always been, and is now even more, predicated on training or education. The way this works is not a mystery. Access to many jobs and to the professions, positions with greater responsibility and higher pay, is limited to those with higher levels of educational attainment. Unfortunately, education systems do not have a strong record of providing effective education for racial and ethnic minorities. Schools serve as "sorting machines" (Spring 1989), separating students into different categories based on a number of criteria— including race and ethnicity—and providing different groups of students with educations of different quality.

Blacks

When the U.S. Supreme Court accepted the "separate but equal" interpretation of the Equal Protection Clause of the Constitution (*Plessy v. Ferguson* 1896) and then soon made a decision that ignored the "but equal" part of the phrase in public education (*Cumming v. County Board of Education* 1899), racially segregated schools were legitimized. What followed was a long war, waged in courtrooms primarily by the legal arm of the NAACP, the NAACP Legal Defense and Educational Fund—the "Ink Fund"—in an attempt to overturn this momentous decision.

The Ink Fund, operating in an environment of uncertainty about how far courts were willing to go in reinterpreting the law and functioning with limited resources, adopted an incremental strategy. Litigation was seen as a means of minimizing costs while pursuing a benefit—education—that would improve the economic position of blacks, sometimes immediately and, at the least, in the long run. Litigation was also viewed as a way of testing and shaping public opinion that could facilitate policy change, of increasing the costs of maintaining segregation, and of mobilizing the black community. Any positive decision could be declared a victory in an attempt to assist in the mobilization effort (Tushnet 1987:2–14, 33–69).

Strategically, the Ink Fund focused on three types of cases—desegregation of public graduate and professional schools, salary equalization suits, and facility equalization suits. Attorneys won Supreme Court declarations that a black applicant to the University of Missouri Law School had the same right to an opportunity for legal education as whites within the state (*Missouri ex rel. Gaines v. Canada* 1938) and that the pay differential between black and white teachers in the Norfolk public school system violated even *Plessy* (*Alston v. School Board of Norfolk* 1940); in spite of these victories, separate but equal remained the law. The Ink Fund continued to use courts as alternatives to legislatures in the pursuit of policy change (Tushnet 1987:32–42, 59–81).

But the limited types of cases pursued by the Ink Fund meant that at some point the organization would have to change strategies. With case law in these areas having been developed as extensively as possible, unless the organization established and pursued new goals the basic problem—*Plessy*—would remain. Realization of this fact led to the adoption of a direct challenge to segregation that resulted in the Supreme Court's reversal of the *Plessy* decision in *Brown v. Board of Education of Topeka* (1954, 1955). In this case, the Court consolidated appeals from Kansas, South Carolina, and Virginia; accelerated an appeal from Delaware; and declared unanimously that separate schools, segregated by race, were "inherently unequal." The Ink Fund and the U.S. Supreme Court had combined to construct a new definition of equality and to make that new definition public policy (Tushnet 1987:142–161).

At that point, policymaking in the area of equal educational opportunity shifted from a focus on overturning a loathsome judicial precedent to implementing a favorable one. Initial euphoria led to overly optimistic predictions about the speed with which segregated school systems could be dismantled. Thurgood Marshall, the victorious attorney in the Brown case, thought it might take "up to five years" for segregation to be eradicated, but he was sure that by the "100th Anniversary of the Emancipation Proclamation [in 1963] . . . segregation in all its forms [will have been] eliminated" (quoted in Cruse 1987:25–26).

Reality, of course, was quite different. Encouraged by an implementation decree that called for desegregation with "all deliberate speed" and "at the earliest possible date," opponents of the Court's order expended massive amounts of energy deliberating and virtually no time moving quickly. Many could not envision a possible implementation date. Furthermore, the vast majority of deliberations focused on ways to evade the intent of the *Brown* decision rather than on ways to comply with that intent.

In the face of this resistance, implementation efforts were inconsistent. In federal district courts, the scenes of most of the desegregation battles, results varied. For example, whereas Judge Frank Johnson (Alabama) sought to implement Brown conscientiously, refusing to let the Court's "authority and dignity . . . be bent and swayed by . . . politically generated whirlwinds" (*In re Wallace* 1959:121), that same year Judge T. Whitfield Davidson (Texas) lectured black plaintiffs from the bench, saying that "the white man has a right to maintain his racial integrity and it can't be done so easily in integrated schools" (quoted in Peltason 1971:119). When the Fifth Circuit Court of Appeals, which heard most of the desegregation cases, remanded cases to these lower courts, the judges often found ways to further subvert the intent of *Brown*. By March 1961, for instance, district judges' opinions in the Dallas school desegregation case had already been reversed six times. Clearly, the appellate courts had difficulty establishing uniform standards at the trial court level.

Nor was support from the executive or legislative branches immediately forthcoming. President Eisenhower declared that he would not presume "that the judicial branch of government is incapable of implementing the Supreme Court's decision" (quoted in Peltason 1971:50); when he sent troops to Little Rock to help desegregate the schools there, his action was more unusual than it was typical. Presidential actions are generally explicable in terms of electoral rationality: "When presidential candidates faced an electoral imperative to seek blacks' votes, blacks finally began to gain allies in their struggle against a segregated second-class citizenship enforced by the laws of many states" (Robertson and Judd 1989:168).

Congress was even less supportive than the executive branch. Nearly all of the southern members, fearful of electoral repercussions if the *Brown* decision were implemented, signed the infamous **Southern Manifesto**, a declaration decrying the decision (Lewis 1965:39). Only when its typical inertia was outweighed by a combination of shifting public opinion—prompted at least in part by media coverage of the civil rights movement—the assassination of President Kennedy, the strong leadership of a southern-born President Lyndon Johnson, and an influx of new members swept into office in the 1964 elections, did Congress overcome its usual timidity and enact significant legislation (Sundquist 1968).

This legislation took the form of the 1964 Civil Rights Act (see Orfield 1969). With this legislation, some of the responsibility for desegregation efforts shifted to the bureaucracy, to what was then the Department of Health, Education, and Welfare (HEW), which provided the department with a little-noticed but powerful tool—the power to cut off federal funds to school districts that practiced discrimination. That power, in conjunction with increased federal funds flowing to local school districts following the passage of the Elementary and Secondary Education Act of 1965, gave HEW the leverage it needed to begin to make significant changes. The Office for Civil Rights (OCR), the agency within HEW charged with enforcement responsibilities, and the federal courts gradually tightened the ratchet on school districts so that by fall 1970, school districts in the South were more desegregated than those in any other part of the country. This massive change occurred because of bureaucratic and judicial pressure, and it happened in spite of President Nixon's electoral "southern" strategy (*Green v. New Kent County School Board* 1968; *Alexander v. Holmes* 1969; *United States v. Georgia* 1969; Panetta and Gall 1971).

In our federal system, because the national government does not actually operate an education system, the ultimate responsibility for providing equal educational opportunity lies with local school officials. For elected local officials the calculus in the desegregation process was similar to that for other elected officials. For example, elected school superintendents in Georgia resisted desegregation more vigorously than did their appointed counterparts for fear they would lose their positions (Rodgers and Bullock 1976:64–65).

Hispanics

In the Hispanic community, equal educational opportunity issues generally paralleled those of black Americans but were resolved much later. As relatively late arrivals in the United States, Puerto Ricans and Cubans were not the pathbreakers in Hispanic equal educational opportunity battles. That role was played by Mexican Americans.

Mexican Americans, although not subject to separate but equal laws in quite the same way as blacks, were routinely denied access to education or received only an inferior segregated education. "Mexican-only" schools, established by local school boards, were present in Texas at the advent of the twentieth century (Rangel and Alcala 1972). In California, segregated Mexican schools were established as soon as a locale had enough students to hold classes.

As the twentieth century progressed, the policy of limited education evolved into one of Americanization—of transforming Mexican Americans into "Americans." Although these assimilationist pressures came from the state level, local officials often took actions that were at odds with these forces. Compulsory school attendance laws were often ignored if Mexican American children were involved. These children were counted in the school census that was used to obtain funds from the state of Texas, but local school districts did not need to spend money on truant children. Even if Mexican American children did attend schools, funds were not apportioned on an even remotely equitable basis. The provision of unequal education was possible because most school districts established separate classes for Mexican Americans within Anglo-dominated schools. Such segregation was based on local school board policies rather than on constitutional or statutory grounds, as was the case with blacks (San Miguel 1987:33–37, 47–55).

In some areas that had few Mexican American students, segregating students was too expensive and awkward. Even in districts with officially segregated schools, segregation was not total (Wollenberg 1978:111–117). Integration might be allowed on the basis of "apparent prosperity, cleanliness, the aggressiveness of parents, and the quota of Mexican-Americans already in the mixed school" (Tuck 1946:185–186). Segregation was less common at the secondary school level because (1) the Americanization rationale no longer held (if students were to be Americanized, the process should have occurred in the elementary grades); (2) many school districts could not afford two secondary schools; and (3) the Mexican American dropout rate was so high that few Hispanic students stayed in school that long (Wollenberg 1978:117–118).

Even in the 1950s, many Mexican American students were offered a segregated education, either through separate schools or within formally desegregated schools. Postwar protests by Mexican Americans and the 1947 repeal of the California statute that made it legal to segregate an ethnic group had no impact on segregation (although Mexican Americans were not specifically mentioned in the code [Cooke 1971]; see *Romero v. Weakley* 1955:836). Intraschool segregation was taken to such lengths, for example, that Mexican American and Anglo junior high school graduates sometimes held ceremonies on separate days (Weinberg 1977:286).

For Hispanics, the litigation campaign challenging segregated schools was spearheaded by the League of United Latin American Citizens (LU-LAC). LULAC's initial challenge against segregation was a class action suit brought against the Del Rio, Texas, Independent School District, alleging that Mexican American students were being denied equal protection under the law as stated in the U.S. Constitution by being placed in segregated facilities (*Independent School District v. Salvatierra* 1930). For the first time in history "the courts were asked . . . to determine the constitutionality of the actions of a local school district with respect to the education of Mexican Americans" (San Miguel 1987:78). The court agreed that Mexican Americans could not be segregated simply because of their ethnicity but found that the school board was not engaged in this practice. The school board could continue to segregate Mexican Americans on the grounds of irregular attendance and, more important, language, which the court found permissible on educational grounds. Thus, its first foray into the courts was unsuccessful, and LULAC resolved to emphasize other tactics (San Miguel 1987:81).

Litigation was not used again until 1945, when LULAC came to the aid of several Mexican Americans who were challenging the segregation of Spanish-speaking pupils in Orange County, California. LULAC alleged denial of equal protection; a favorable ruling was obtained and upheld in the Circuit Court of Appeals (*Mendez v. Westminster School District* 1946, 1947). For the first time in history a federal court found segregation of Mexican Americans in public schools to be a violation of state law and a denial of the equal protection clause of the U.S. Constitution. This latter finding meant the decision was relevant to Mexican Americans elsewhere. Thus, the attorney general of Texas issued an opinion banning segregation of Mexican American students except for "language deficiencies and other individual needs and aptitudes demonstrated by examination or properly conducted tests . . . through the first three grades" (quoted in San Miguel 1987:120). The amount of actual change, however, varied. In Texas, with the absence of implementation guidelines, segregation continued. In California, many school systems desegregated, but de facto segregation in large urban areas led one observer to suggest that Mexican American students in California were more segregated in 1973 than they had been prior to *Mendez* in 1947 (Wollenberg 1978:132–134).

The legal battle shifted back to Texas in 1948. LULAC, in conjunction with a newly organized group of Hispanic World War II veterans, the American G.I. Forum, supported a lawsuit by several Mexican American parents charging officials in several central Texas school districts with unconstitutional segregation. The decision in this case, *Delgado et al. v. Bastrop Independent School District of Bastrop County et al.* (1948), enjoined local school officials from segregating Mexican American students. The decision in *Delgado* went beyond the one in *Mendez* to clarify that segregation of Mexican American students, even in the absence of articulated regulations or policies, was not permissible. The decision also held state school officials responsible for "condoning or aiding" the segregation of Mexican Americans. Unlike the aftermath of *Mendez*, implementation guidelines were issued by the state superintendent of public instruction,[1] but the results were much the same— massive noncompliance. When pressure from the Mexican American community convinced the state superintendent to withdraw the accreditation of the noncompliant Del Rio school district, the state legislature abolished that position and appointed another person to the newly created position of commissioner of education. It should be no surprise that the new commissioner was less than energetic about dismantling the dual schools for Mexican Americans and Anglos; in fact, his first decision was to reverse the disaccreditation of the Del Rio schools (San Miguel 1987:125–130).[2]

Throughout the 1950s—particularly after the *Brown* decision struck down segregation of blacks—cases were brought before the judiciary, occasionally resulting in a favorable decision or settlement. In *Hernandez v. Driscoll Consolidated Independent School District* (1957), the court found that Hispanics had been unconstitutionally assigned to separate classes on the basis of ancestry, but it allowed them to be assigned to such classes if they lacked English-language skills.[3] The actual dismantling of dual schools for Anglos and Mexican Americans was rare, and litigation was again temporarily abandoned as a tactic by Hispanic interest groups because of its perceived futility (Rangel and Alcala 1972:345).

Litigation was revived as a major tactic in support of equal educational opportunity for Mexican Americans with the formation of the **Mexican American Legal Defense and Education Fund (MALDEF)** in 1968 (O'Connor and Epstein 1984). MALDEF participated in litigation that covered a wide range of issues, but education was an important focus.

The type of education litigation most frequently undertaken sought to eliminate segregated schools. Segregation was a necessary focus for

MALDEF because OCR, the federal government's school desegregation enforcement agency, had originally treated Hispanics as whites for desegregation purposes; thus, they could remain segregated without arousing federal interest. In addition, local school districts could send both black and Hispanics students to the same schools to achieve some "desegregation," leaving other schools all Anglo (Rangel and Alcala 1972:365–372).

This policy changed formally in 1970 when Stanley Pottinger of OCR announced that the agency would henceforth be concerned with discrimination on the basis of national origin. As this applied to school districts, the memo stated: "Where inability to speak and understand the English language excludes national origin minority group children from effective participation in the educational program offered by a school district, the district must take affirmative steps to rectify the language deficiency in order to open its instructional program to these students" (quoted in Weinberg 1977:287).

A second weapon MALDEF needed in the fight against segregation was provided by the courts in *Cisneros v. Corpus Christi Independent School District* (1970). In this case, which was not filed by MALDEF, the plaintiffs asked the court to apply the principles of *Brown* to Mexican Americans. Such a finding would require that Mexican Americans be recognized by the courts as a separate class. The U.S. District court obliged, and for the first time in history Mexican Americans were declared to be an identifiable group within public school systems and were protected by the Fourteenth Amendment.

The thrill of victory was short-lived, however, because that same month the Fifth Circuit Court of Appeals handed down a decision in the Houston desegregation case that allowed local authorities to treat Mexican Americans as whites for desegregation purposes, leaving Anglos unaffected by the process (*Ross v. Eckels* 1970). Another decision allowed school officials in Miami to consider Cubans as whites for desegregation purposes (Orfield 1978:203). Thus, the task facing MALDEF was to obtain higher court acceptance of the *Cisneros* decision. In pursuit of this goal, MALDEF filed amicus curiae briefs in a number of Mexican American school desegregation cases pending before the Fifth Circuit. MALDEF's position was basically that "we want to know where we stand" (quoted in San Miguel 1987:180).

The Fifth Circuit, in appeals from Corpus Christi and Austin cases, found that Mexican Americans were an identifiable group and that they had been denied their constitutional rights in these instances (*Cisneros v.*

Corpus Christi Independent School District 1971; *U.S. v. Texas Education Agency* 1972). MALDEF obtained a victory, but the waters were still muddy. An intracircuit difference of opinion existed that had to be resolved.

The resolution came in *Keyes v. School District No. 1*, the Denver desegregation case decided in 1973. The decision in this case, which had been filed by blacks, required that the court take a position on the status of Mexican Americans. Denver had significant populations of blacks, Anglos, and Hispanics, so the court had either to lump Hispanics with Anglos or to recognize Hispanics as a separate group. The latter choice would have led to the conclusion that Hispanics also had been illegally segregated and would have required a plan to desegregate them as well. The U.S. Supreme Court decided that Mexican Americans were an identifiable minority group and that they were constitutionally entitled to recognition as such for desegregation purposes (*Keyes v. School District No. 1, Denver, Colorado* 1973). School officials in systems found to be unconstitutionally segregated could not treat Hispanics as whites for the purpose of desegregation. Subsequent decisions extended the logic of *Keyes* to Puerto Ricans in New York and Boston (*Hart v. Community School Board of Brooklyn District #2* 1974:733; *Morgan v. Hennigan* 1974:415).

The *Keyes* case did not spawn an abundance of Hispanic desegregation. Even though Hispanics as a whole were more segregated than blacks in the mid–1970s (National Institute of Education 1977; Orfield 1978:205–206), MALDEF turned its attention from desegregation to other methods of achieving equal educational opportunities. The remedy MALDEF stressed in its fight was **bilingual education**—the idea that non–English-speaking students should be taught in their native language or should be taught English. But the legal groundwork for movement in bilingual education was laid not by Hispanics but by Asians.

Asians

The situation of Asians in U.S. education systems has generally been one of discrimination. For example, the Supreme Court, in *Gong Lum v. Rice* (1927), upheld Mississippi's exclusion of Asian Americans from white schools. School segregation did not exist only to separate blacks from whites but to separate Asians from whites as well.

Given the population concentrations of Asians, their situation can best be exemplified by the history of Chinese Americans in San Francisco schools. As soon as there was a significant number of Chinese taxpayers in San Francisco, the Chinese community pressed local authorities to fund public education for their children. Only when the number of Chinese youths increased to one that could not be ignored did the local school board respond, and then it provided a segregated education. Even under these conditions, Americanization was remarkably successful. But obtaining access for Chinese children to the education system required a constant struggle with state and local legislative and education agencies from the mid–nineteenth century onward (Low 1982).

More dramatic than legislation or administrative action in its impact on policy was a case filed on behalf of Chinese students in San Francisco. In *Lau v. Nichols* (1974), the Supreme Court required that school districts "take affirmative steps to rectify the language deficiency [of national origin minority students] . . . to open [their] instructional program[s] to these students." The Court found that the failure of school districts to provide non–English-speaking students—in this case 2,800 Chinese students—with instruction they could understand denied them their right to an equal educational opportunity. The Court required that the school district take action but stopped short of mandating bilingual education.

American Indians

U.S. educational policy toward American Indians since the nineteenth century had been to create separate boarding schools, removing children from their home areas to see that they received a "proper" education. Although approximately 70 of these schools still exist, policy has changed considerably. In 1969, a Special Senate Subcommittee on Indian Education found that "national policies for educating American Indians are a failure of major proportions. They have not offered Indian children—either in years past or today—an educational opportunity anywhere near equal to that offered the great bulk of American children" (U.S. Senate 1969:163). Although nothing was done immediately to address this situation, the Indian Education Act of 1972 increased funding for Indian education, and the Indian Self-Determination and Education Assistance Act of 1975 and the Education Amendments Act of 1978 sought to promote "Indian control of Indian affairs in all matters relating to education" (25 U.S. Code § 2010). Today, approximately 80 percent of American Indian schoolchildren attend public schools in the communities in which they live.

American Indian children are also covered by the *Lau* decision. Rather than attempting to eliminate the use of tribal languages, in 17 states bilingual education programs are offered to American Indian children who only speak their tribal language. Even where full-fledged bilingual/bicultural programs have not been required, tutors have been provided for such children (*Guadalupe Organization, Inc. v. Tempe Elementary School District* 1978).

Continuing Issues

With the provision of equal educational opportunity left in the hands of the same local officials who had operated dual school systems, we should not be surprised that discrimination continues. Three issues—bilingual education, resegregation, and second-generation discrimination—demand attention.

Bilingual Education.   Even though bilingualism was given its impetus by litigation involving Chinese students, Hispanics are clearly the largest group of potential beneficiaries. The National Center for Education Statistics (1978) reports that 70 percent of the estimated 3.6 million children in the United States with limited English proficiency are Hispanic.

Problems with implementing bilingual education programs quickly became apparent. MALDEF's plan for a bilingual/bicultural educational program in a desegregated Denver school system was rejected as working at cross-purposes with desegregation: "Bilingual education . . . is not a *substitute* for desegregation" (*Keyes v. School District No. 1, Denver, Colorado* 1973:480; emphasis in the original). Although bilingual programs could be part of a remedy for unconstitutional segregation, the court did not believe they could be a remedy in and of themselves (Fernández and Guskin 1981:113). Thereafter, court decisions generally chose between desegregation—that is, dispersing students throughout a school system—and bilingual programs, which seemed to promote segregation based on language or national origin (for an example of the latter, see *Serna v. Portales Municipal Schools* 1974), although in some cases the court did adopt a bilingual education plan as part of a remedy for segregation (see *Bradley v. Milliken* 1975:1144).

Although MALDEF remained nominally committed to both desegregation and bilingualism (Orfield 1978:211–214), it emphasized the establishment of bilingual classes. Hispanic students boycotting East Los

Angeles high schools in 1968 asked for bilingual programs rather than desegregation (Wollenberg 1978:134–135). And when OCR struck at discrimination against Hispanics, bilingualism was often the preferred remedy, even if segregation remained (Orfield 1978:207).

The **Puerto Rican Legal Defense and Education Fund (PRLDEF)**, a relative latecomer to Hispanics' civil rights struggle, never argued for desegregation. Perhaps because language and culture are more salient for Puerto Ricans, and perhaps because Puerto Ricans are concentrated in urban areas where desegregation is impractical because of the scarcity of Anglos, bilingualism was the organization's primary goal from the beginning. PRLDEF sued or intervened in cases in New York City; New Jersey; Boston; Wilmington, Delaware; Buffalo; Philadelphia; and Waterbury, Connecticut. It negotiated an out-of-court settlement to establish the nation's largest bilingual education program in the New York City school system (Orfield 1978:211–217). The general thrust of legal intervention had become even more specific by the late 1970s. When Hispanic legal organizations took action, they usually intervened in cases at the remedy stage for or in defense of bilingual programs.

In the wake of *Lau*, OCR used its regulatory authority to require that school districts test non–English-speaking students and place them in bilingual education programs. Despite provisions designed to prevent the "existence of racially/ethnically identifiable classes" within such programs (Teitelbaum and Hiller 1977:160), segregation remains common. Segregated bilingual programs are prevalent because

1. Affected students normally attend schools that have considerable segregation.
2. Although OCR has brought heavy enforcement pressure on school systems to provide bilingualism, it has done virtually nothing about desegregation.
3. The regulations in the various programs are filled with loopholes that are so large they make a mockery of the policy statements about segregation. The regulations permit segregating groups defined by linguistic ability when local school officials say doing so is educationally necessary.

"In practice there has been almost routine segregation at the local level and no federal enforcement of integration policies" (Orfield 1978:220).

Resegregation. Blatant segregation remained the policy in some "desegregated" school systems—within classrooms (sometimes reinforced by room dividers), on buses, in lunchrooms, and in extracurricular activities (American Friends Service Committee et al. 1970). But these overt practices gradually stopped as a result of litigation or simply because of the inconvenience of maintaining such awkward policies.

However, more recent evidence suggests that resegregation is occurring. Southern schools were the most fully desegregated schools in the nation by fall 1970, and the level of integration remained fairly stable until 1988. But after that date, racial segregation began to increase once again. The segregation of Latino students is also on the rise. During the 1991–1992 school year, almost two-thirds (66 percent) of black students and almost three-fourths (73.4 percent) of Latino students attended predominantly minority schools. Slightly more than one-third of both groups (33.9 percent of blacks, 34 percent of Latinos) attended schools with a greater than 90 percent minority enrollment. Put another way, the typical black student attended a school with a 34.4 percent white enrollment; the typical Latino student attended a school with a 31.2 percent white enrollment (Orfield 1993).

Second-Generation Discrimination. Even if schools are desegregated, such desegregation is not necessarily synonymous with the provision of equal educational opportunity. The "quality of desegregation varies as much as [the] quantity" (Hochschild 1984:33). More invidious has been the rise of more subtle means of minimizing interracial contact, which we refer to collectively as **second-generation discrimination.** Often in conjunction with desegregation, school systems have adopted or expanded the scope of ability grouping of students and have concentrated minority students in lower-level academic groups (Meier, Stewart, and England 1989). Such racial concentration might be justified as remedial action for the provision of inferior education in segregated schools, but the evidence from education research shows that "minority students are highly overrepresented in a situation that perpetuates their disadvantage. . . . [They] are resegregated, provided with an inferior educational experience compared to that of their peers, stigmatized by staff and other students—in short, placed in learning environments that do little to close the gap in minority-majority achievement levels" (Simmons and Brady 1981:132).

Likewise, disciplinary practices can be used for purposes other than maintaining order and authority. Such practices are sometimes "a mere pretense for punishing a child for other reasons," including being black, Hispanic, or poor (Children's Defense Fund 1974:130, also 1975). "Black students are punished for offenses allowed white students or given heavier penalties for similar offenses" (Eyler, Cook, and Ward 1983:144).

Affirmative Action in Employment

Affirmative action is one of the most controversial subjects in American politics today. In many ways, this controversy arises from the distinction between individual and institutional racism noted in Chapter 1. Equal opportunity is a concept that treats individuals only as individuals, assumes that if one is discriminated against it is out of prejudice, and assumes that victims of discrimination will act on their own behalf in reaction to this discrimination. Affirmative action, "the expenditure of energy or resources by an organization in the quest for equality among individuals from different discernible groups" (Crosby 2004:5), considers individuals as representatives of demographic groups, allows for the possibility that discrimination may be an effect of nonintentional or unconscious practices, and promotes a proactive stance against discrimination (Crosby 2004). The laws and regulations that concern affirmative action at the federal level—between 150 and 200 in number (Dale 1995) can be traced back to the 1960s. Presidents Kennedy and Johnson used the term in executive orders forbidding discrimination in federally financed construction and on work sites of federal contractors, but its exact meaning was unclear. When Congress weighed in with legislation to establish a federal presence as an antidiscrimination regulator in the private labor market with the inclusion of Title VII of the 1964 Civil Rights Act, it specifically rejected "preferential treatment to any individual or group on account of an imbalance which may exist with respect to the total number or percentage of persons of any race . . . employed by any employer . . . in comparison with the total number or percentage of persons of such race . . . in any . . . or in the available workforce in any community." The specification of what was required was left to an agency, the Office of Federal Contract Compliance Programs (OFCCP), which issued guidelines stating:

> A prerequisite to the development of a satisfactory affirmative action program is the identification and analysis of problem areas inherent in minority employment and an evaluation of opportunities for utilization of

minority group personnel. The program shall provide in detail for specific steps to guarantee equal employment opportunities keyed to the problems and needs of members of minority groups, including, when there are deficiencies, the development of specific goals and timetables for the prompt achievement of full and equal employment opportunities (U.S. Commission on Civil Rights 1971:173).

The move toward increased reliance upon statistical evidence and mandatory goals and timetables received a push from—of all sources—Republican President Richard Nixon. Seeking short-term political advantage, Nixon championed the "Philadelphia Plan" for desegregating that city's trade unions as a model for affirmative action. The plan, which required numerical evidence of minority representation, appealed to Nixon as a way of driving a wedge between two of the Democratic Party's prime constituencies: organized labor and members of minority groups. Thus, over the opposition of both conservative Republicans and southern Democrats, Nixon successfully lobbied for a plan that included racial job quotas (Graham 1990:301–321; Belz 1991:32; Skrentny 1996:182).

The U.S. Supreme Court added to the mix by issuing an opinion in 1971 in *Griggs v. Duke Power Co.* In this case, the plaintiffs, black employees, challenged the company's use of tests that disproportionately screened out blacks for hiring and promotion but that had no demonstrable relationship to job performance. A unanimous Court ruled that if a test or qualification requirement disproportionately disqualified minorities, the employer could be compelled to defend it as a bona fide occupational qualification. This allowed plaintiffs to prevail in employment discrimination cases without proving intent. An easy way for an employer to reduce the possibility of a suit was to make sure that minority group members were not disproportionately underrepresented.

Public Reaction to Affirmative Action

Public acceptance of the idea of affirmative action, as expressed in public opinion polls, has been erratic, often depending upon the wording of the question. Only when respondents are assured that affirmative action does not mean "rigid quotas" do we find support exceeding 50 percent for affirmative action in the job market (Steeh and Krysan 1996). At least part of the opposition to affirmative action arises from the tendency of whites to believe that even if blacks have been discriminated against in the past, they no longer face such impediments. Thus, preferences are viewed as fundamentally unfair (Kluegel and Smith 1986:185).

Incrementalism and Affirmative Action

Despite partisan changes in presidential administrations, the basic infrastructure for applying affirmative action has remained intact.

Perhaps the most likely source for nonincremental change, interestingly enough, is from the branch of government thought to be most insulated from popular opinion—the courts. The U.S. Supreme Court, in 1989, issued two opinions that seemed to undermine affirmative action policy as it had developed. In *Ward's Cove Packing v. Atonio* the Court ruled that it was insufficient for plaintiffs in job discrimination cases to demonstrate a statistical disparity in minority employment. They must also link the disparity to a specific employment practice or practices alleged to cause the disparity. In the second case, *Richmond v. Croson*, the Court said that before a city could designate a certain amount of its contract work to be "set aside" for minority-owned firms, it must show that the program was narrowly tailored, temporary, and linked to established prior discrimination. These decisions threatened to place a greater burden of proof on plaintiffs in affirmative action litigation. Congress, however, reacted with the Civil Rights Act of 1991, a clear effort to counteract the *Ward's Cove* decision. Still, the sentiment against quotas is strong enough to include language in the Act forbidding its interpretation to "require, encourage, or permit an employer to adopt hiring or promotion quotas on the basis of race, color, religion, sex, or national origin, and the use of such quotas shall be deemed to be an unlawful employment practice" (*CQ Almanac* 1991:255).

The Continuing Saga of Affirmative Action

Change seldom occurs in civil rights policy without presidential or judicial involvement, and President Clinton offered at least rhetorical support for affirmative action. Furthermore, a report commissioned by the president set out the parameters of what is to be considered a fair affirmative action program:

1. The avoidance of quotas;
2. An effort to remedy problems first with race-neutral options;
3. Flexibility in the use of race-conscious measures;
4. A program lasting only as long as needed;
5. Demonstration that the effect on nonminorities is "sufficiently small and diffuse so as not to unduly burden their opportunities" (White House 1995).

The Supreme Court, in 2003, handed down two highly publicized affirmative action decisions, *Gratz* v. *Bollinger* and *Grutter* v. *Bollinger*, both related to higher education. In the former, dealing with undergraduate admissions to the University of Michigan, the Court ruled that that by awarding an automatic 20 points (out of 150) to applicants who attended a predominantly minority high school or who were minority group members themselves, the university had committed impermissible racial or ethnic discrimination. On the other hand, in the *Grutter* case, the Court upheld the holistic approach of the University of Michigan Law School in considering all aspects of an individual applicant and stressed the importance of having a critical mass of minority students as important to creating an environment that promotes free expression and ends racial stereotypes.

Thus, it is clear that the issue will not disappear from the national political agenda. President Bush, although indicating his opposition to affirmative action, but his support for what he refers to as "affirmative access," has adopted the concept in his signature education legislation—the No Child Left Behind Act of 2001. Section 441, b(2)(G), of the law calls for including "information [in reports on the effectiveness of the legislation] on special groups, including whenever feasible information collected, cross tabulated, compared, and reported by race, ethnicity, socioeconomic status, gender, disability, and limited English proficiency." As long as affirmative action programs are associated in the popular mind with quotas, they will serve valuable political functions, but the concept is not foreign to public policymaking.

Extension of the Voting Rights Act (VRA)

As discussed in Chapter 2, the VRA has been instrumental in enhancing minority voting rights and office holding. Much of the law continues in perpetuity, unless specifically repealed, but four crucial provisions will expire in August 2007 if Congress does not act to extend them.

Coverage.   Section 4 of the VRA defines the jurisdictions covered by special provisions of the law as those which used a "test or device" to limit voting and in which less that half of the voting-age population (VAP) were registered or voted in either the 1964, 1968, or 1972 presidential elections.

Preclearance.   Section 5 of the VRA, triggered by Section 4, requires preapproval, or "preclearance," by either the Department of Justice or the Federal District Court in the District of Columbia, for any changes in voting laws or procedures in their jurisdictions.

Federal Examiners and Poll Watchers.   Several sections of the act, taken together, and triggered by Section 4, allow the attorney general to assign federal examiners to register voters who must be accepted as qualified by local authorities. Section 8 of the VRA allows the attorney general to appoint federal poll watchers in the jurisdictions in which examiners have been used to attempt to detect irregularities in the conduct of elections.

Bilingual Voting Materials.   Jurisdictions with significant language minority populations who have limited proficiency in English and higher than the national illiteracy rate are required to provide voting materials in the language of the applicable minority group as well as in English. Covered jurisdictions include the entire states of California, New Mexico, and Texas, and hundreds of jurisdictions in Alaska, Arizona, Colorado, Connecticut, Florida, Hawaii, Idaho, Illinois, Kansas, Louisiana, Maryland, Massachusetts, Michigan, Mississippi, Montana, Nebraska, Nevada, New Jersey, New York, North Dakota, Oklahoma, Oregon, Pennsylvania, Rhode Island, South Dakota, Utah, and Washington.

The last extensions, enacted in 1982, were preceded by dramatic hearings about instances of continuing discrimination, and this extension promises to be no different. For example, the ACLU Voting Rights Project recently brought suit in South Dakota, alleging more than 800 violations of the preclearance provision of the VRA between 1975 and 2002.

Conclusion

This chapter provides a glimpse of the different stages of the public policymaking process and the interaction of the various institutional actors, operating within a federal system, in that process. The crucial hurdle for racial and ethnic minority groups has been getting issues placed on the agenda of a government institution, and the presence of minority group representatives within an institution can facilitate that step. Some progress has been made in increasing minority group representation across institutions at all levels of government.

The case study of equal educational opportunity policy reveals the evolution of the policy problem. The problem was originally defined as constituting the legally mandated racial segregation of black and white students in southern schools. It was presumed that once black and white students entered the same school buildings, the equal educational opportunity problem would be solved. Yet it was discovered that students of other racial and ethnic groups were also denied this opportunity.

The complexity of the American public policymaking system is also illustrated here. The courts, prodded by interest groups, took the lead in defining the problem and articulating a policy, but they found themselves so far ahead of the executive and legislative branches that their decisions could not be implemented. The courts provided a forum in which the pro-civil rights coalition could appeal to "right" rather than to political power. And the conflict could be overt because the U.S. legal system is adversarial yet muted because the format of the conflict is stylized.

Changes external to the policy subsystem were definitely of major importance in the outcome of the conflict. If E. E. Schattschneider is correct that "the *audience* determines the outcome of a fight" (1960:2; emphasis in the original), then the mass media served to change immensely the size and composition of that audience. The expansion of the availability and use of mass media meant the audience for the conflict was no longer strictly local and that it was more independently informed than had been the case when similar issues had previously been decided.

Local officials, who had to implement the policy change within the federal system, were able to thwart a momentous Supreme Court decision. Only when the legislature finally adopted a supportive policy, thus empowering the bureaucracy to participate in implementation, did significant policy change occur.

The accomplishments of those who fought the battles are monumental. Yet by defining the policy problem in terms of segregation, a solution was also defined: When schools were desegregated, success would be achieved. Subsequent experience has shown dramatically that segregated schools were only the symptom, not the disease. But in the minds of many, when schools in which de jure discrimination had existed were desegregated, it was time to focus on other policy problems. The results of this evolution of the policy process include an inertia and a lack of consensus about whether equal educational opportunity is being provided in this country and how one would recognize such opportunity if one saw it.

The consideration of affirmative action likewise shows the importance of framing an issue and the proposed solutions. Very different levels of public support for affirmative action can be attained by changing how one defines the term or the program. Thus, the contest between proponents and opponents of affirmative action is a struggle over presentation, which affects the legitimacy of the policy adopted. Change in civil rights policy has been erratic and time-consuming and will continue to be so.

5

....

Coalition or Competition? Patterns of Interminority Group Relations

One of the nation's trendiest clothing stores settled a race and sex discrimination suit by agreeing to pay $40 million to several thousand minority and female plaintiffs and agreed to alter its well-known collegiate, all-American— and largely white—image by adding more blacks, Hispanics, and Asians to its marketing materials.

—New York, November 17, 2004

MANIFEST CHANGES HAVE OCCURRED and continue to occur in the demographics of most major cities in the United States. Whereas we once referred to urban political dynamics in terms of whites versus blacks, today Latinos, increasing numbers of Asians, and—to a lesser extent—Indians have been added to the mix. These demographic changes have not only altered the political dynamics of urban politics but have also created a new context for relationships among the various racial groups that may take the form of coalition, conflict, or mutual nonrecognition. The continuing second dilemma faced by racial minorities in American society is represented by the question posed by Rodney King at his first postverdict news conference in the wake of the 1992 Los Angeles riots—"Can we all get along?" What options within the American political system are available to members of minority groups, and what are the consequences of pursuing each of these options? Is it feasible for blacks, Latinos, Asians, and Indians to form coalitions to attain political outcomes? Or is it more common for the goals and objectives of these groups to be in conflict? The debate over biracial coalition politics has been intense and enduring. The looming questions have always been "should minorities go it alone and bargain with the larger society, or do they need to form alliances to counter their minority status? And if they make alliances, with whom should they link their fate?" (Sonenshein 1993:3)

This chapter focuses once again on aspects of the second dilemma by examining (1) **coalition politics**—the aggregation of groups to pursue a specific political goal—of blacks, Latinos, and Asian Americans; and (2) the increasing tensions among blacks, Latinos, and Asians and between these groups and the white majority. (Although half of the American Indian population consists of "urban Indians," little research has been conducted on their participation in urban politics.) Additionally, we present a case study of Los Angeles that highlights the various patterns of interminority and majority group relations.

Interminority Group Relations

When differences among groups are found regarding political goals and outcomes, the potential for conflict exists. Political coalitions require that groups have similar goals, desire similar outcomes, and be willing to pursue their objectives in a collaborative and cooperative fashion. Coalitions may be loosely or tightly organized, and cooperation may be tacit or explicit. As with coalitions, the form of competition between groups with differing goals may also vary. Competition may be pursued on an "enemies always" basis or on a "not permanent enemies" stance (Eisinger 1976:17–18).

Group competition accounts for some aspects of the discrimination experienced by minorities. Individuals and groups accrue power and status in a variety of ways; thus, some power contests are understood as involving group against group. Competition exists, therefore, when two or more groups strive for the same finite objectives so that the success of one group may imply a reduced probability that another will attain its goals. We could view group competition in terms of power contests that exist when there is rivalry and when groups have roots in different cultures. Furthermore, the greatest perceived competition may occur among groups that are nearly equal in political power (Blalock 1967). This framework, although it is addressed to majority-minority relations, is also useful in examining relationships among minority groups if we recognize that not only status differences but also status similarities may become bases for conflict.

Coalition or Competition Politics?

The presence of multiple minority groups in major metropolitan cities has led to the assumption that shared racial minority group status generates the potential for political coalitions among the various groups. One of the assumptions of coalition theory has been that the relationship among the various racial minority groups will be one of mutual respect and shared political goals and ideals. Another assumption of coalition theory, however, has been that black political assertiveness is incompatible with the existence of biracial political coalitions between blacks and whites (Sonenshein 1993). Although they were referring to African Americans, Stokely Carmichael and Charles V. Hamilton, in their seminal work, *Black*

Power (1967:79–80), offer four bases on which viable biracial coalitions may be formed. These may also apply to coalitions among blacks, Latinos, Asians, and Indians: (1) Parties entering into a coalition must recognize their respective self-interests; (2) each party must believe it will benefit from a cooperative relationship with the other or others; (3) each party must have its own independent power base and also have control over its own decisionmaking; and (4) each party must recognize that the coalition is formed with specific and identifiable goals in mind. Accordingly, *interests* rather than *ideology* provide the most substantial basis for the most productive biracial coalitions. Arguing that "politics results from a conflict of interests, not of conscience," Carmichael and Hamilton (1967:75) suggest that whites—liberal or otherwise—would desert blacks if their own interests were threatened.

Yet the argument of interests versus ideology is at the heart of the debate over a theory of biracial coalitions. One side of the argument sees interests as the ties that bind biracial coalitions together, coalitions that are, at best, short-lived tactical compromises among self-centered groups. Those who emphasize ideology argue that the essential element of biracial coalitions is common beliefs. This perspective of coalition theory holds that preexisting racial attitudes influence one's perception of racial issues and that these attitudes shape political actions. Thus, coalitions form not from objective self-interests but from shared ideology. The most likely coalition will be one between groups that are close in ideology even when another union would be more advantageous.

The interests-versus-ideology distinction for biracial coalitions is not as clear-cut and dichotomized as it may appear. When black and liberal white—primarily Jewish—interests came into conflict in New York City, liberal sentiments were insufficient to hold the coalition together (Sonenshein 1990). Nevertheless, although ideology alone may not hold coalitions together, without a shared ideology biracial and interracial coalitions are unlikely to form in the first place (Sonenshein 1993).

There are numerous instances of coalitions between blacks and Latinos. Common concerns during the 1960s, such as poverty, formed the foundation for unions between blacks and Latinos, especially Mexican Americans (Estrada et al. 1981), and there is clear evidence of coalition building between blacks and Latinos (see, for example, Browning, Marshall, and Tabb 1984, 1990; Henry and Muñoz 1991; Sonenshein 1993). Since the early 1970s in Los Angeles, the mechanism for minority political incorporation has been a tightly knit coalition of African Americans and liberal whites, primarily Jews, with subsidiary support from Latinos and Asians (Sonenshein 1993).

However, the coalitions between blacks and Latinos began to break apart when policies designed to promote equal access and equity for different groups were sometimes in conflict. For example, blacks were concerned that bilingual education would shift resources from the effort toward desegregation and thus were not supportive of it (Falcón 1988:178). Other policy issues of concern to Latinos that were not perceived as being supported by blacks included the English-only movement, employer sanctions, and the extension of coverage to Latinos in amendments to the Voting Rights Act (National Council of La Raza 1990). Furthermore, Latinos began to question whether affirmative action had benefited them as much as it had blacks because they felt blacks had secured more municipal jobs than had Latinos (Cohen 1982; Falcón 1988).

The coalition between blacks and liberal whites in Los Angeles was beginning to show signs of strain during the last years of Thomas Bradley's administration because of divergent economic interests among the primary partners and increasing demands on the part of Asians and Latinos for **incorporation**—the extent to which a group is represented in dominant policymaking coalitions—into city politics (Sonenshein 1990). In Los Angeles, Asians and Latinos differ significantly from blacks and whites in terms of ideology and interests (Henry and Muñoz 1991:329). (These ideological differences among blacks, Latinos, and Asians were discussed in Chapter 3.) Although recognizing—as we stressed—that standard labels of liberal, moderate, and conservative are too simplistic to reflect the range of ideological orientations within racial minority groups, we can safely conclude that African Americans, Mexicans, and Puerto Ricans hold more liberal perspectives on a range of issues than do Cubans and Asians. Within the Asian group, Chinese Americans are far more conservative than are either Japanese or Koreans.

A 1993 *Los Angeles Times* survey of southern California residents—whites, blacks, Asians, and Latinos—found that 65 percent of blacks identified whites as being the most prejudiced group, and 45 percent felt Asians were the next most prejudiced group, an increase from the 19 percent of blacks who expressed this feeling in a similar 1989 survey. Moreover, blacks believed that Asians (39 percent), far more than whites (29 percent), were gaining economic power to an extent that is not good for southern California (UCLA Asian American Studies Center 1993:5). When pressed to be specific about which group of Asians was perceived as causing problems, a quarter of both blacks and Latinos felt all Asians were doing so, although 19 percent of blacks identified Koreans as the source of problems, and a similar percentage of Latinos mentioned Vietnamese. For the most part, blacks did not view Latinos as being prejudiced (11 percent) nor as gaining more economic power than was good for the area (16 percent). These results support the inference that blacks and Latinos are the most likely coalition partners, followed by Asians and then Anglos (Henry and Muñoz 1991:330). Other analysis has found affinities between blacks and Latinos as compared to whites and Asians (Uhlaner 1991). Evidence such as this demonstrates the difficulties in forming coalitions of racial minorities (Sonenshein 1993:263).

Competition may also arise among the various groups when blacks, Latinos, and Asians each have different goals, when there is distrust or suspicion among the groups, or when the size of one group is such that it no longer needs to form coalitions with other minority groups to gain political success (Falcón 1988; McClain and Karnig 1990; Warren, Corbett, and Stack 1990; Meier and Stewart 1991; McClain 1993). There is increasing evidence that in many communities blacks, Latinos, and Asians compete for scarce jobs, adequate housing, and government services (MacManus and Cassell 1982; Welch, Karnig, and Eribes 1983; Oliver and Johnson 1984; Falcón 1988; Johnson and Oliver 1989; Mollenkopf 1990). Moreover, some survey data suggest that a growing hostility and distrust exist among the three groups (Oliver and Johnson 1984; Johnson and Oliver 1989), with a majority of Mexican Americans not in favor of building coalitions with blacks (see also Grebler, Moore, and Guzman 1970; Ambrecht and Pachon 1974; Henry 1980; Browning, Marshall, and Tabb 1984).

A study using data from the 1980s of all 49 U.S. cities with more than 25,000 people and whose populations were at least 10 percent black and 10 percent Latino found that analyses of socioeconomic data—income, education, employment, and percent not in poverty—revealed no harmful competition in general between blacks and Latinos. The results support a positive covariation relationship: When any group (black, Latino, or white) prospers with respect to education, income, and employment, the other groups do significantly better as well. Political outcome data—percent on the city council, proportionality of council representation, black or Latino mayor—present a somewhat different picture. When either blacks or Latinos made political gains, they did so at the expense of whites. Political competition between blacks and Latinos was evident only when controls for white political outcomes were introduced. This suggests that as black and Latino political successes increase, political competition between blacks and Latinos may be triggered, especially as fewer whites reside in minority-dominated cities (McClain and Karnig 1990; McClain 1993a).

Evidence also indicates that competition appears to occur as the size of the black population increases, with negative consequences for Latinos, particularly on several socioeconomic measures. However, increases in the Latino proportion of a city's population do not appear to be related to competition that is harmful to blacks. Moreover, in a small sample of cities in which blacks constitute a plurality or a majority, Latinos seem to fare less well socioeconomically and, in particular, politically (McClain and Karnig 1990).

In the area of municipal employment, black and Latino outcomes are negatively related to white employment outcomes, which indicates a degree of competition for municipal jobs (McClain 1993a). Blacks or Latinos gain at the expense of non-Latino whites. But evidence also indicates that competition in municipal employment appears to occur as the size of the black workforce increases, with consequences for Latinos. The most significant predictor of limits to Latino municipal employment opportunities is the black percentage of the workforce. As the black share increases, Latino opportunities decline. Latino workforce percentage, however, does not appear to have the same effect on black municipal opportunities. Furthermore, in a small sample of cities in which blacks constitute a plurality or a majority, Latinos seem to fare less well in municipal employment outcomes; in cities in which Latinos constitute a plurality or a majority, the consequences for black municipal employment are inconsistent. Clear evidence that blacks suffer deleterious effects in municipal employment outcomes exists in only one city, Miami.

In a follow-up study using 1990s data of the now 96 cities in the United States with more than 25,000 people and whose populations were at least 10 percent black and 10 Latino, McClain and Tauber (2001) found that political competition between blacks and Latinos had increased somewhat—increasing size of the black population had negative consequences for Latino city council representation. Interestingly, the new source of political competition was between blacks and Asians in many urban centers.

The increasing size of Asian populations in cities had significant negative consequences for black city council representation and the election of a black mayor. What these results suggest is that as Asian presence in cities intensifies, blacks may lose their political advantage and indeed see their political outcomes reduced. As the demographic changes continue in urban cities, we are likely to see more rather than less competition among blacks, Latinos, and Asians in the future.

Whereas this summary of research on interminority group relations indicates increasing competition between blacks and Latinos in certain urban areas, we must recognize that both coalitional and competitive behaviors may occur in the same city but between different strata of each group. For example, elites may engage in political coalition-building, whereas working-class and lower-class people may see their interaction with other racial groups as constituting competition for jobs, housing, and city services. Los Angeles, California, is illustrative of this dual pattern of interaction. Moreover, it is also a city in which blacks, Latinos, and Asians are represented in sufficient enough numbers that their political behaviors have consequences for city politics.

Los Angeles[1]

Los Angeles is prototypical of turn-of-the-century western nonpartisan reform cities. It has been described as an **entrepreneurial city**, a city in which electoral politics is organized so that business interests play a significant role and urban bureaucracies are structured so as not to be dominated by either elected officials or local business interests. Moreover, the nonpartisan tradition of California city politics guarantees that political party organizations play a minimal role in Los Angeles city politics.

Los Angeles was founded in 1781 by Mexican settlers consisting of "two blacks, seven 'mulattoes,' one 'half-breed' and nine 'Indians'" (Sonenshein 1993:21). By 1790, blacks and people of mixed black ancestry were outnumbered by Mexican settlers. African Americans arrived in Los Angeles after the United States gained control of California in 1850, but they did not come in significant numbers until the land boom of the late 1800s opened the city to blacks. Blacks bought property and, until 1915, lived wherever they could afford to buy, many amassing significant wealth through resale to developers at substantial profits. By 1880, the Los Angeles schools had been desegregated, and racial tensions were low (Sonenshein

1993:22). Additionally, by applying pressure on city hall, blacks were able to obtain a few political benefits, including the appointment of one black police officer and one black fire fighter in the late 1890s. In 1890, an estimated 34 percent of Los Angeles blacks lived in owner-occupied homes. This figure greatly exceeded home-owning rates for Mexicans and Japanese, approximated the level for whites, and far exceeded levels for blacks in other major cities at the time. Yet despite this home-owning level, blacks were confined to low-paying, low-status jobs.

Although it had been founded by Mexicans and had been part of Mexican territory, Los Angeles was more accepting of blacks than it was of Mexican Americans. With the increased migration of white midwesterners during the late 1800s, Mexican Americans became increasingly less important in the city's economic and cultural arenas. As a result of the need for unskilled labor and the importation of Mexicans to fill that need, by the early 1900s the Los Angeles Mexican American community was dominated by laborers. As a result, the Mexican American and Mexican populations were less well-off economically than were blacks. Both groups were subjected to massive deportations in 1931, which so decimated the city's Mexican American community that it did not restabilize until the return of its veterans at the end of World War II (Sonenshein 1993:24).

California was particularly antagonistic toward Japanese Americans and Chinese Americans, even more so than it was toward Mexican Americans. As long ago as 1880, California was virulently anti-Asian. Chinese immigration was essentially curtailed with the passage of the Chinese Exclusion Act of 1882, yet Japanese migration to Los Angeles increased steadily until restrictive immigration laws were passed in 1920. "Between 1890 and 1930, the Japanese-American population of Los Angeles County grew from an estimated 1,200 persons to 35,390" (Sonenshein 1993:24). Japanese Americans developed a subeconomy that was parallel to the city's main economy, and they were fairly successful. Yet the hostility toward them did not dissipate; on the contrary, it intensified and climaxed with the internment of Japanese Americans in 1942.

Although blacks and, to a lesser extent, Japanese Americans prospered in terms of home ownership (blacks) and business success (Japanese), access by Los Angeles blacks, Mexican Americans, and Asian Americans to long-term socioeconomic opportunities and political power was severely constrained by changes that were about to occur in the political culture of the city.

Puritanical Conservatism

In the late 1800s a tremendous influx of white midwestern immigrants to Los Angeles brought a desire to build a city "freed from the ethnic hetero-geneous influences of eastern and midwestern cities" (Sonenshein 1993:26). "Militant Protestant clergy" were in the vanguard of the cre-ation of a "native, white anglo-saxon Protestant city," a goal that was completed by 1900. By 1920, white Protestants were the ruling class and controlled most of the public offices; moreover, "the new atmosphere was puritanical and ethnocentric" (Sonenshein 1993:26). As a consequence of the new political culture,

> The civic culture and eventually the local economy became increasingly hostile to Blacks and other minorities. The dominant conservative philoso-phy was augmented by the migration of southern whites to the city after 1910. By now, the increased size of the Black community made it potentially threatening. The southern whites were particularly hostile to Blacks, but the white Protestants also sought to preserve their "small town" city. The result was the development of restrictions on Blacks and other minorities, cutting them off from the next stages of the city's system of generating wealth. (So-nenshein 1993:27)

Conservative reformers who were allied with southern whites openly conspired to restrict minority access to political and economic opportuni-ties through a series of legal maneuvers and political changes. Two city charters, in 1911 and 1915, severely limited elected officials' ability to con-trol city government. This action removed the incentive to develop politi-cal party organizations. As many of the reformers remembered, strong political party organizations had provided the mechanism for limited po-litical incorporation of minorities in eastern and midwestern cities. In 1914 there was even an abortive attempt to start a whites-only jitney ser-vice so that whites would not have to share public transportation with blacks. Housing restrictions in the forms of restrictive covenants, which bound home owners not to sell their property to minorities, and block agreements, which bound entire neighborhoods, were introduced, and their legality was upheld by the courts. (The Supreme Court did not de-clare restrictive covenants unconstitutional until 1948.)

Housing restrictions led to the creation of Los Angeles's black ghettos. When thousands of blacks moved into Watts, that city swiftly incorporated into Los Angeles in 1926 to prevent a black-dominated local government. Other communities including Santa Monica, Huntington Beach, Lomita, and Manhattan Beach also made it difficult or impossible for blacks to buy houses. Thus, the natural turnover in neighborhoods—that of poorer blacks moving in as middle-class blacks moved up—did not occur, and blacks, regardless of economic level, found themselves confined to specific areas of Los Angeles. This segregation also produced a severe housing shortage for blacks during World War II, when thousands poured into the city seeking war-related job opportunities (see Map 2.5).

World War II transformed the city into a major center for the production of aircraft and ships. As this sector grew, the need for skilled labor also increased. The federal government declared Los Angeles an area that had an extreme labor shortage, and people—whites and blacks—flocked to the city. Black labor was now needed, and jobs that had once been denied to them were marginally opened—primarily as a result of President Roosevelt's executive order barring racial discrimination in the defense plants. The deportation of tens of thousands of Mexican immigrants in 1931 and the internment of Japanese Americans in 1942 removed major competitors for jobs and housing.

Postwar Los Angeles returned to the prewar rules and attitudes governing and restricting opportunities for blacks.

> The end of the labor shortage became the vehicle for restoring the old rules. Japanese-Americans released from internment obviously wanted to regain their homes and jobs . . . Returning soldiers clogged the labor force. Mexican workers were imported to Los Angeles once again; by 1950, they outnumbered Blacks. The postwar era allowed for the first time in decades the development of a stable Latino community. . . . The city was returning to minority competition for unskilled jobs, while whites gained most of the skilled jobs. (Sonenshein 1993:30)

As a result of the return to discriminatory hiring practices, between 1950 and 1960 blacks lost many of the occupational gains they had made during the war. Yet at the same time, when restrictive covenants were outlawed, blacks were able to expand beyond ghetto boundaries as middle- and upper-class blacks moved into areas vacated by whites who had moved to the suburbs. Consequently, by the 1960s, Los Angeles blacks were in a paradoxical situation—relative to blacks in other urban areas in the East and Midwest, they enjoyed higher levels of socioeconomic success and home ownership. Yet relative to white Angelenos, Los Angeles blacks were falling increasingly behind economically. As late as 1960, an estimated 95 percent of the city's refuse workers, 80 percent of its street maintenance workers, and 95 percent of its custodians were black (Sonenshein 1993:23).

Political Structure

A unique aspect of the conservative reformists' plan for hegemony of the political structure of Los Angeles was the passage by the voters in 1925 of district elections—a system of district elections for city council members in which candidates are elected by voters in defined geographic parts of the city rather than citywide. Despite a campaign by the city's leaders and the conservative *Los Angeles Times* to overturn the vote, the citizens voted in 1927 to maintain the system. The district electoral system provided the opening, albeit a small one, for minority participation in Los Angeles city politics. However, the political culture was hostile toward minority representation, and even in substantial minority councilmanic districts, it was difficult for blacks and Latinos to be elected. In 1960, the three city council districts that had sizable black populations were represented by white council members. Latinos had slightly more success because of the election of Edward Roybal to the city council in 1949. Interestingly, Roybal won the 9th Council District through the efforts of a multiracial coalition made up of Latinos, blacks, and liberal Jews (Sonenshein 1993:31). In later years, the city leaders used gerrymandering to ensure that blacks and Latinos were unable to elect representatives from their racial groups to the city council.

Los Angeles city leaders—by blocking minority access and maintaining their myopic view of the city as a white Anglo-Saxon Protestant city—ignored many of the changes that had occurred throughout the nation since World War II. This approach allowed city hall to pursue a small-town conservatism of fiscal stringency, strong support for the forces of order, and reluctance to participate in federal social programs. The combination of downtown business and the conservative *Los Angeles Times* was a potent power structure, which restricted political debate.

With the backing of the police bureaucracy, this tightly knit leadership could hold back the hands of time (Sonenshein 1993:31).

This conservative reform culture and the resultant absence of strong political party organizations allowed public bureaucracies to cultivate and develop their own constituencies and to resist public control and oversight. The Los Angeles Police Department (LAPD) is an extreme example of bureaucratic independence and resistance to public control. Over time, particularly under Chief William Parker in the 1950s, the LAPD "developed the ability to insulate itself completely from political oversight. The department ultimately developed an independent political power base, which it used to restrict the city's politics. . . . In time, the LAPD became one of the city's main roadblocks to social change, resisting the rise to power of Blacks and liberals" (Sonenshein 1993:32). The LAPD has been a source of anger and frustration for the minority communities of Los Angeles and has been at the heart of some of the city's most violent and destructive civil disturbances, from the 1965 Watts riot to the 1991 beating of Rodney King to the 1992 riots, as well as being at the center of several mayoral elections, such as that of Sam Yorty in 1961 and Tom Bradley in 1973.

As inhospitable as the Los Angeles political culture and structure were regarding the inclusion of blacks, Latinos, and Asians into the political process, the very nature of the system provided the foundation for multiethnic politics in the city. "Modern Los Angeles had never been a melting pot; *everybody* who differed from the white conservative model was excluded. Therefore, a Los Angeles-style melting pot had to be created politically" (Sonenshein 1993:35). Thus, minority exclusion provided the basis for coalition politics among blacks, Latinos, and Asians.

Coalition Politics

By 1960, blacks constituted 13.7 percent of the population of Los Angeles—nearly half a million people—and, propelled by the national civil rights movement, were poised to seek access to the city political system. As a result of overt and de facto residential racial segregation, blacks were concentrated in three councilmanic districts—the 8th, 9th, and 10th Districts. The 9th District was represented by Edward Roybal, who unsuccessfully opposed the city council's 1960 reapportionment plan designed to dilute black voting strength by dividing the city's black population among five districts, thereby protecting incumbents and not allowing the creation of a majority black councilmanic district (Sonenshein 1993:36–38).

Disappointed by the reapportionment plan and upset by Los Angeles Mayor Norris Poulson's lack of responsiveness to the concerns of the black community, particularly brutality by the LAPD, blacks supported Samuel Yorty in the 1961 mayoral race. Yorty fashioned an unlikely coalition of valley home owners and inner-city racial minority groups. Yorty promised white home owners that he would eliminate a complicated trash collection system, which was a volatile issue for them, and promised black and Latino residents that he would fight police brutality and appoint minorities to city commissions. Blacks, especially, and Latinos provided the margin of victory for Yorty, and he did appoint several minorities to city commissions. However, he failed to make good on his promises to reform the LAPD; in fact, following a conversation with Chief Parker, Yorty never again spoke out against the department, and he gave the department whatever it requested (Sonenshein 1993:38, 40).

Shortly after Yorty's victory, to which they felt they had contributed substantially, blacks set their sights on the vacant 10th District council seat. The city council was to appoint an individual, and initially Yorty was supportive of the appointment of a black. City council members Edward Roybal and Jewish liberal Rosalind Wyman openly called for such an appointment. Numerous individuals were nominated, including Thomas Bradley, at the time a retired police officer and lawyer who had broad district support. However, a majority of the city council members wanted the seat to go to Joe Hollingsworth, a white Republican businessman, and despite heavy pressure from Roybal, they appointed Hollingsworth to the seat. Mayor Yorty signed the ordinance certifying Hollingsworth's appointment, which angered the city's blacks. "The regime seemed intent on preventing black representation" (Sonenshein 1993:41).

Irate black community groups started recall proceedings against Hollingsworth. On two separate occasions, the recall organizers collected the requisite number of signatures to trigger a recall election, but each time they were stymied by the city clerk. On the first occasion, the clerk invalidated enough signatures to reduce the total to less than the minimum number required. On the second attempt, after the organizers had collected more than enough additional signatures to set the recall process in motion, the city clerk invalidated the recall on a technicality he had only recently discovered. Despite a challenge to the State Court of Appeals, the clerk's decision was upheld.

While the 10th District appointment was being challenged, Roybal—the only minority council member—ran successfully for the U.S. Congress, thereby opening up the seat from the 9th District. The district's population was about 50 percent black and 50 percent Latino, but Roybal had been successful in representing the interests of both constituencies. Despite the population distribution, Roybal's high visibility and tenure in office had caused the 9th District to be viewed as a "Latino district." Roybal's resignation and the council's authority to appoint a replacement set in motion competition between blacks and Latinos, and the appointment "had a great influence on the development of black and Latino representation at city hall for the next two decades" (Sonenshein 1993:43).

Two candidates emerged—one black, Gilbert Lindsay, and one Latino, Richard Tafoya, who was Roybal's cousin. Fresh from their defeat in the 10th District, blacks were determined to gain the 9th District seat. A black-Latino struggle ensued, with blacks attempting to gain their first seat on the council whereas Latinos sought to retain the only seat they had been successful in winning. Lindsay was eventually appointed in January 1963, becoming the first African American officeholder. His appointment was the beginning of a 23-year period during which Latinos had no elected officials at city hall. "A particular irony of this battle was that Roybal had been the main opponent of the council's various plans to prevent black council representation" (Sonenshein 1993:44).

As the 1963 municipal elections approached, the 8th District seat, which was held by a white, was being contested by a black; the 9th District seat held by Spacey Lindsay was being contested by Tafoya; and Tom Bradley was challenging Hollingsworth in the 10th District. In the March election, Bradley was elected, with runoff elections held in the 8th and 9th Districts. Eventually, the black candidates in those two districts won, placing three blacks on the Los Angeles city council.

Despite the competition for the 9th District seat, Bradley's campaign for the 10th District seat is identified as the beginning of a multiracial coalition in Los Angeles city politics. Liberal whites—especially Jews—blacks, Asians, and Latinos, particularly Roybal, were instrumental in getting Bradley elected. The multiracial coalition that was forged in 1963 and that was fortified through a series of events over the span of a decade eventually propelled Bradley into the mayor's office in 1973.

The 1965 city elections produced a dynamic composed of Bradley and the multiracial coalition, which was opposed to Mayor Yorty; the other two black city council members were allied with Yorty. Although Yorty won, the entrenchment of the conservative regime in Los Angeles city politics and the exclusion of blacks and liberal whites provided the basis for continued cooperation within Bradley's multiracial coalition.

In August 1965, a traffic arrest by the California Highway Patrol escalated into the first major race riot of the 1960s. The behavior of the LAPD and the attitudes of and responses to the violence and destruction by Mayor Yorty and Police Chief Parker caused Bradley to emerge as their chief critic. Despite black leaders' hope that as a result of the deaths (of 31 blacks and three whites) and destruction ($41 million in property damage) that occurred during the riot, more attention to their concerns would be forthcoming, "the riot was an unqualified disaster for biracial politics, creating a durable and powerful backlash among whites and Latinos" (Sonenshein 1993:78). Surveys revealed blacks' optimism that conditions were improving, a position that was not shared by whites and Latinos.

> Large majorities of both groups were profoundly affronted by the violence and expressed strong support for the police. Few thought the riot would improve race relations. Both groups expressed substantial personal fear of attack by Blacks. . . . Some Latino activists expressed resentment at the great attention being paid to Blacks in the wake of the riot, especially in the allocation of anti-poverty funds. The obvious lack of Latino political influence was remarkable considering that Latinos outnumbered Blacks in the county. (Sonenshein 1993:78)

In the aftermath, the riot solidified blacks' resolve to gain more power at city hall.

Bradley's Ascension to the Mayor's Office

In the wake of the changes occurring in the United States, and on the heels of the 1967 election of Richard Hatcher (Gary, Indiana) and Carl Stokes (Cleveland) as black mayors of major cities, Councilman Tom Bradley decided to become a candidate for mayor in the 1969 election. The specter of the Watts riot and the racial polarization that existed in the nation as well as in Los Angeles overshadowed the race between Bradley and the incumbent mayor, Sam Yorty. Bradley hoped to build on the biracial coalition that had helped him win his 10th District seat, but 1969 proved not to be his year.

In the primary, Bradley led the packed field with 42 percent of the vote, just 8 percentage points short of winning the mayor's office outright. Yorty came in a distant second with 26 percent of the vote. Consequently, Bradley and Yorty moved into the general election. Bradley's primary campaign had assumed that a common ideological bond existed among blacks, Jews, liberal gentiles, and Mexican Americans, and to some extent this had been successful. However, in the general election, where Bradley needed to increase the level of his white support, Yorty was able to successfully exploit the weaknesses in Bradley's coalition strategy.

Yorty set about to impede a coalition among blacks, Latinos, and Jews by highlighting the black-Jewish conflict in the Ocean Hill-Brownsville school district in New York City in 1968. He told middle-class Latinos that because Bradley had pitched his campaign toward poorer Latinos, he would ignore their needs. Yorty also directly exploited white fears of having a black mayor by running ads in the real estate section of valley newspapers with Bradley's picture and the caption "Will Your City Be Safe with This Man?" (Sonenshein 1993:91). In addition, Yorty stoked the embers of the conflict between Bradley and the LAPD, who viewed Bradley—despite his previous police career—as an enemy because of his criticisms of the department and its procedures.

In the general election, the three-way coalition among blacks, liberal whites, and Latinos did not come together as well as Bradley had expected. Yorty won the race with 53 percent of the vote to Bradley's 47 percent. Black support for Bradley was high, and Jewish support was moderate, but two-thirds of Latinos voted for Yorty, as did a similar percentage of whites (Sonenshein 1993:93–94). Despite the loss in 1969, the experience set the stage for Bradley's run for and election to the mayor's office in 1973.

With a more professional and reorganized campaign, Bradley emerged from a three-way primary contest in 1973 in first place, with Sam Yorty second and Jesse Unruh, an unexpected Democratic challenger who cut into Bradley's black and Jewish support, in third place. Once again, Bradley and Yorty faced each other in the 1973 general election. Yorty attempted to use tactics similar to those he had used in 1969, but he was less successful. The LAPD also campaigned heavily against Bradley, threatening that if he were elected there would be mass resignations from the department. Despite these attempts, Bradley easily defeated Yorty with 54 percent of the vote. Bradley's victory was achieved with "high black turnout, solid Jewish support, an increasing Latino base, and little countermobilization by conservative whites" (Sonenshein 1993:108). There was evidence of an emerging black-Latino coalition, and Latinos eventually formed the most loyal and supportive faction of Bradley's coalition. Bradley's win exhibited the depth and strength of multiracial coalition politics in Los Angeles—a coalition that was to consolidate power, bring Asian Americans into its fold, and control city hall from 1973 to 1993 when Bradley stepped down as mayor.

Asian Americans and the Bradley Coalition

Asian Americans became full partners in the Bradley coalition after his initial election in 1973; however, there had always been an Asian presence in his campaign organization. George Takei, known for his role as navigator Sulu in the original *Star Trek* television series, was the chair of a subgroup of Asian Americans in Bradley's 1969 and 1973 mayoral campaigns. Following Bradley's election and Takei's narrow defeat in his quest for Bradley's former 10th District council seat, Bradley appointed Takei to the board of the Southern California Rapid Transit District.

Of Bradley's initial appointments to city commissions, 10 of 140 appointees were Asian Americans. Asians fared well under Bradley, increasing their share of public-sector jobs and top-level positions. When Bradley entered office in 1973, Asians constituted 4.0 percent of the city workforce; by 1991 that figure was 7.5 percent. Additionally, in 1973 they represented 3.0 percent of officials and administrators, and in 1991 that proportion had risen to 8.0 percent. Increases in professional public-sector jobs also occurred, with Asians holding 8.0 percent of the professional jobs in 1973 and 15.4 percent in 1991 (Sonenshein 1993:152–153). Bradley became a major fund-raiser within the Los Angeles Asian American community. Over time Asian Americans—along with Latinos—remained the most consistent of the pro-Bradley groups.

Demise of the Coalition

Although Bradley won reelection to a fourth term in 1985 with a record 68 percent of the vote and with victories in all 15 council districts, changes were taking place within his coalition. Economic alignments were changing, and ideological unions between liberal whites and minorities were becoming strained.

There had always been the potential for conflict between minority and white liberal constituencies in Los Angeles. Even though ideology provided an important common bond, differences of class interest and personal ambition started to crystallize after 1985. The threads of the coalition's balancing act—an ideological interracial alliance and an economic coalition between minority leaders and downtown business—began to unravel (Sonenshein 1993:191).

Bradley saw former coalition members and supporters become adversaries. His control over the city council ended when two of his supporters left the council in 1987. Earlier successful strategies, such as being pro-growth, became victims of their own success, giving rise to voices of opposition within the coalition—for example, from those who favored slow growth. Additionally, for the first time in his career, Bradley's sterling image was tarnished by a financial scandal shortly before the 1989 elections. These factors, coupled with a challenge by a black noncoalition member of the city council who siphoned black votes from Bradley, resulted in Bradley's reelection to a fifth term in 1989 with only 54 percent of the vote. The coalition that controlled Los Angeles city politics was splintering. Although it was not disappearing, it was becoming only one of several groups, rather than the dominant group competing within city politics.

These facts, combined with such events as the beating of Rodney King by the LAPD in 1991 and the rioting in 1992 following the acquittal of the four police officers tried for the beating, contributed to Bradley's 1992 decision not to seek a sixth term in 1993. Yet before leaving office, Bradley was able to pull the coalition together to pass Proposition F in June 1992, which reformed the LAPD by removing civil service protection for the police chief, limiting the chief to one ten-year term, and providing more civil authority over the department. "The winning campaign to implement police reform must be considered one of the greatest victories of the biracial coalition that took power in 1973" (Sonenshein 1993:226).

The 1993 mayoral contest pitted Michael Woo, a Democratic Asian American member of the city council and a member of Bradley's coalition, against Richard Riordan, a maverick millionaire Republican businessman. Bradley's coalition had now broken into several different parts, and Woo's defeat signaled the final demise of the multiracial coalition that had governed Los Angeles for two decades. The end of this coalition does not mean multiracial politics is a thing of the past in Los Angeles; it simply means that the structure Bradley built no longer exists in the same form.

The mayoral race in spring 1997 highlighted the changing nature of racial politics in Los Angeles. Richard Riordan, who during his four-year term had built a reputation as a moderate with broad-based bipartisan support, faced Democratic State Senator Tom Hayden. Hayden, considered an outsider to Los Angeles politics, had a difficult time gaining support from the key constituencies in the old Bradley coalition primarily because Riordan was successful in pulling factions of that Democratic coalition to his side. With a booming economy, declining crime rate, and rejection of many of the national Republican Party's policy positions, Riordan defined his administration in terms of policies and programs that were good for Los Angeles. President Clinton's administration rewarded him for this approach by sending federal dollars into the city. Riordan made inroads into all groups except blacks and beat Hayden in the April primary by a two-to-one margin, a record for a Republican in a city that has twice as many registered Democrats as Republicans (Purdum 1997).

The real story of the mayoral contest, however, was the strength of the Latino vote vis-à-vis the black vote this time around. Although Latinos comprise 33 percent of Los Angeles's adult population, they make up only 14 percent of registered voters and typically between 8 and 10 percent of the voting electorate. Blacks, in contrast, are 13 percent of the population but are 18 percent of registered voters. In this election, however, Latinos outpaced blacks in the proportion of votes cast—15 percent to 13 percent, respectively. The presence of a $2.4 billion school bond issue to repair the city's schools, in a system that is 70 percent Latino, galvanized Latino voters, who turned out in record numbers. Whereas three-fourths of black Angelenos voted for Hayden (antagonism to Riordan stemming, in part, from his opposition to the renewal of black Chief of Police Willie Williams's contract), three-fifths of Latinos voted for Riordan (see Table 5.1). Another segment of the old Bradley coalition, Asian Americans, who had overwhelmingly supported Michael Woo in 1993, also cast the majority of their votes for Riordan. Latinos and Asians, two of the most loyal groups in Bradley's coalition, appeared to be voting counter to the black vote. Clearly, the divergence of policy goals is reflected in the changed voting patterns of these three groups in Los Angeles city politics.

TABLE 5.1 Los Angeles Mayoral Election Results by Race, 1993, 1997, 2001, and 2005

	1993 (June runoff)			1997 (April primary)			2001 (April primary)				2001 (June runoff)		
	% of vote	Woo (%)	Riordan (%)	% of vote	Riordan (%)	Hayden (%)	% of vote	Villaraigosa (%)	Hahn (%)	Soboroff (%)	% of vote	Villaraigosa (%)	Hahn (%)
White	72	33	67	65	71	26	52	23	19	30	52	41	59
Black	12	86	14	13	19	75	14	12	71	5	17	20	80
Latino	10	57	43	15	60	33	20	62	7	8	22	82	18
Asian	4	69	31	4	62	35	4	23	32	25	6	35	65

	2005 (March primary)						2005 (May runoff)		
	% of vote	Alarcon (%)	Hahn (%)	Hertzberg (%)	Parks (%)	Villaraigosa (%)	% of vote	Hahn (%)	Villaraigosa (%)
White	52	3	23	36	5	27	50	50	50
Black	16	2	23	5	54	15	15	52	48
Latino	22	9	17	6	3	64	25	16	84
Asian	6	—	59	12	8	19	5	56	44

Source: Los Angeles Times, June 10, 1993; *Los Angeles Times,* April 10, 1997; *Los Angeles Times,* April 12, 2001; *Los Angeles Times,* June 6, 2001; *Los Angeles Times,* March 10, 2005; *Los Angeles Times,* May 19, 2005.

The 2001 Los Angeles mayoral contest represented an effort to pull the remnants of the Bradley coalition back together, but it resulted in high-lighting the fact that the coalition is irretrievably splintered. Six candidates ran in the nonpartisan mayoral primary on April 10, 2001, including two Latino Democrats (Antonio Villaraigosa and Xavier Becerra); Steve Sobo-roff, a white Republican who was the handpicked successor of the current Republican mayor, Richard Riordan; and the white Democratic city attor-ney, James K. Hahn, who is the son of a prominent politician whose polit-ical base was in the black communities of South Central Los Angeles. Villaraigosa and Hahn emerged as the top vote getters in the primary, and the sources of their support underscore the demise of the Bradley coali-tion. Both Villaraigosa and Hahn are Democrats, and Villaraigosa is con-sidered the more liberal of the two. Sixty-two percent of Latinos who voted supported Villaraigosa (Becerra received a substantial portion of the remaining vote), and 71 percent of black voters supported Hahn. About one-third of white voters supported the white Republican, Villaraigosa re-ceived about one-quarter of the white vote, and Hahn about one-fifth. Asians gave a third of their vote to Hahn and a quarter to Villaraigosa.

In order to win the general election, both Villaraigosa and Hahn had to move beyond their respective bases. Riordan endorsed Villaraigosa, and State Senator Richard Polanco, a Latino Democrat who used to be the leader of the State Senate, endorsed Hahn. Riordan's endorsement was ex-pected to pull conservative whites who voted for Soboroff, his hand-picked Republican successor who lost in the primary, to support Villaraigosa. Polanco's endorsement was to say that not all Latinos were supporting Vil-laraigosa and to try to pull supporters of Xavier Becerra to Hahn.

On June 5, 2001, Latinos turned out in record numbers, representing 22 percent of those who voted in the general election, and gave Vil-laraigosa 80 percent of their votes; their numbers were not sufficient to push Villaraigosa over the top. Hahn won, 54 to 46 percent, with an un-usual combination of votes from blacks (80 percent), Asians (65 percent), moderate Democrats (58 percent), moderate Republicans (70 percent), and conservative Republicans (87 percent). In addition to Latinos, Vil-laraigosa also had the support of liberal Democrats (59 percent). Rior-dan's endorsement did not pull conservative whites to Villaraigosa's side as intended, primarily because Hahn was successful in portraying Vil-laraigosa as soft on crime because of Villaraigosa's letter to President Bill Clinton in support of a pardon for a convicted drug dealer, Carlos Vignali.

Mayoral candidates Antonio Villaraigosa, right, and James Hahn shake hands
May 31, 2001, before their final debate at the Museum of Tolerance, Los Angeles,
California. (AP Photo: Kevork Djansezian)

Hahn's ads highlighting the letter were controversial, and some suggested
that Hahn had introduced an element that was intended to draw on
stereotypes of Latinos as drug dealers. Villaraigosa did not answer the ads
directly and was hurt in the polls by the ads. Hahn was able to appeal to
moderate and conservative whites while continuing to maintain support
of his African American base, which he inherited from his father. About
two-thirds of Asian voters also were more trusting of Hahn than they were
of Villaraigosa. Like Tom Bradley's loss in 1969, this was Villaraigosa's first
run for mayor, and given the changed demographics of Los Angeles, it is
only a matter of time before a Latino, Villaraigosa or someone else, is
elected mayor. What was clear from this election, however, was that the

demographic changes in Los Angeles have made it impossible to put the Bradley coalition back together.

The 2005 mayoral race highlights the many changes that have occurred in Los Angeles since Hahn beat Villaraigosa in 2001. In January 2002, Hahn opposed the reappointment of the black Chief of Police Bernard Parks, who had initially been appointed by Mayor Riordan after the non-renewal of the contract of the previous black police chief, Willie Williams. Parks was an LAPD insider, and Hahn cited Parks' unwillingness to budge on issues like police reform, recruitment and retention, and community policing as the basis for his opposition to Parker's reappointment. Although Parks' support within the Los Angeles black community was not strong, he was the highest ranking black public official in the city, and many blacks, especially black elected officials, were concerned about the loss of this highly visible symbol of political power if he were not reappointed. Given the support black voters gave Hahn in 2001, many felt betrayed by his opposition to Parks' renewal. The Los Angeles Police Commission did not renew Parks' contract. Parks, however, ran for a city council seat in late 2002 and was elected to the council from the 8th District. In 2003, Antonio Villaraigosa was also elected to the Los Angeles City Council from the 14th District. With Villaraigosa's election, Latinos held 4 of the 15 council seats, and blacks held only 3.

Five candidates, all Democrats, were running for mayor in 2005—James Hahn, Antonio Villaraigosa, Bernard Parks, State Senator Richard Alacron, and former State Assembly Speaker Bob Hertzberg. Hahn's 2001 coalition of African American and valley voters had collapsed. Blacks were disenchanted with Hahn over his failure to support Parks' reappointment, and valley residents were upset with Hahn over his opposition to the carving out of new cities in the valley and in Hollywood. Many black elected officials and organizations that supported Hahn in 2001 did not endorse either Villaraigosa or Parks, and many of his valley supporters endorsed Hertzberg. Polls indicated that Hahn had only a quarter of black voters supporting him in 2005, while he had 71 percent in 2001 (McGreevy and Levey 2005). The recent shooting of a 13-year-old black male by police officers has not helped Hahn despite his vocal criticism of the police. Going into the March 8, 2005, primary, a *Los Angeles Times* poll found Hahn, Hertzberg, and Villaraigosa tied in their battle for the two runoff slots (Finnegan 2005).

The March 8 primary saw Villaraigosa and Hahn emerge as the two candidates that went into the runoff on May 17, 2005, setting the stage for a rematch of the 2001 election. Villaraigosa pulled 33 percent of the vote to Hahn's 24 percent. Hahn narrowly bested Hertzberg (23 percent) to grab the second spot for the runoff. (Under Los Angeles' election laws, a candidate has to receive 50 percent of the vote in the primary to avoid a runoff and be declared the winner.)

The 2005 rematch would be different, and Hahn would have a more difficult time putting together the coalition of blacks and conservative whites to keep him in office. Fifty-four percent of black Angelenos voted for Bernard Parks, and exit poll data from the *Los Angeles Times* indicated that Parks' firing was an issue for one-half of those blacks who went to the polls (Barabak 2005). Given the antipathy toward Hahn among a substantial portion of the black population, Hahn is going to have a hard time convincing blacks to vote for him over Villaraigosa this time around. Villaraigosa, on the other hand, increased his support among whites, blacks, and independents while taking the bulk of the Latino vote (Barabak 2005). This shift in his ability to reach across racial lines puts him in a much better position to defeat Hahn in 2005 than in 2001. Moreover, in a surprise move just after the primary, County Supervisor Yvonne Braithwaite Burke, a prominent black elected official and former supporter of Hahn in the 2001 election, endorsed Villaraigosa. Shortly after Braithwaite Burke's announcement, Congresswoman Maxine Waters, former mayoral candiate Bernard Parks, former Los Angees Laker Star Earvin "Magic" Johnson, and Reverend Cecil Murray, a prominent black minister, endorsed Villaraigosa. In the May 17 runoff election, Villaraigosa beat Hahn in a landslide—59 percent to 41 percent. The overwhelming support Villaraigosa received from Latino voters, 84 percent, and his ability to attract a significant proportion of the black vote, 48 percent, propelled him to a stunning and convincing victory (*Los Angeles Times*, May 19, 2005). (For complete results, see Table 5.1.)

Competition

At the time of the formation of the Bradley multiracial coalition, tensions still existed among black, Latino, and Asian elites over the ability of Latinos and Asians to elect representatives to the city council while blacks solidified their control of 3 of the 15 council seats. During councilmanic reapportionment activities in 1985 and 1986, Bradley vetoed a plan that would have eliminated the only Asian American district and would have created a Latino district. However, the unexpected death of a council member provided an opening to reapportion districts in a manner that satisfied all of the parties of Bradley's coalition. As a result, by 1986 two Latinos and one Asian American served along with the three blacks on the 15-member Los Angeles city council.

Whereas the elites amicably resolved their reapportionment differences, tensions were rising among lower-income blacks, Latinos, and Asians. Economic and housing market competition was increasing among these groups in Los Angeles. The city's economy was being restructured by the loss of industry and, hence, of jobs. An estimated 70,000 heavy-manufacturing jobs were lost as a result of plant closings, automation, and the movement of companies overseas. Because of their concentration in the heavy-manufacturing sector, blacks experienced tremendous job loss and dislocation. In addition, between 1970 and 1980, poor Latino and Asian immigrants began to move into the formerly all-black South Central area of Los Angeles. Latino immigrants were unable to find housing in the Latino barrio of East Los Angeles and began to settle in increasing numbers in the black South Central region (Johnson and Oliver 1989).

The sharing of residential space was not the only incursion blacks in that region experienced. Asian immigrants, especially Koreans, opened businesses of all types in black areas. In particular, Koreans penetrated the small-business market in South Central Los Angeles. Relations between Korean shop owners and black customers were rocky and filled with tension. Disadvantaged blacks viewed the Korean merchants as "foreigners" who charged high prices, refused to invest in the community in which they conducted business or to hire blacks, and were rude and discourteous to black customers. The killing of a black teenager by a Korean store owner, and the proprietor's light sentence for manslaughter in 1992, only intensified the conflict. This antipathy between blacks and Koreans culminated in the targeting of Korean businesses by blacks during the 1992 Los Angeles riots: "The basic bone of contention, especially between Blacks and members of immigrant minority groups, is the issue of jobs. Given their deteriorating position in the American urban economy, there is a growing perception among inner-city Blacks that the new immigration has hurt them economically" (Johnson and Oliver 1989:455).

Conflict has also occurred over housing and social amenities. Blacks in the South Central region have been concerned that the influx of immigrants into their neighborhoods has had a displacement effect. Blacks have charged that landlords prefer to rent to Latinos or Asians because of the presence of multiple wage earners in those families, thus forcing black families to move outside the Los Angles metropolitan area to areas with lower housing costs. Additionally, blacks have viewed Latino and Asian immigrants as **free riders**, taking advantage of the social services and benefits blacks feel they fought hard for through protests and litigation (Johnson and Oliver 1989:456).

Conclusion

We have used Los Angeles as a case study of the ways in which the second dilemma is manifested. This case shows the way the city's government system was structured to ensure minimal minority participation (shades of the first dilemma) and describes the process by which blacks, Latinos, and Asians were able to gain access to the system. Relations between the three groups and the white majority have taken and continue to take various forms. There have been a number of political successes but also many failures.

Although Los Angeles has been our case study for a discussion of racial minority group coalition or competition politics, elements of these patterns of interaction can be found in other cities as well. Los Angeles is a special case because it is a western nonpartisan city in which political parties play a limited role in local politics. In cities in which political parties are strong and actively involved in city politics, a different dynamic of coalition politics may be present. However, the increasing tension among blacks, Latinos, and Asians in urban politics seems to be present in many cities regardless of government structure and partisan activities. Whereas the competition between whites and various racial minority groups in urban politics is still a reality in some cities, competition among blacks, Latinos, and Asians will continue to increase as the white presence in many urban centers diminishes. Thus, the second dilemma for America's racial minority groups—what options to choose in attempts to gain access to the political process—is continuing and very complex.

6

....

Will We "All Get Along"?

Five police officers and four dispatchers were
suspended and a sixth officer received a written
reprimand for "inappropriate" computer messages
sent after a nightclub, frequented primarily by blacks,
caught fire. The messages included, among others,
"burn baby burn" "the smell of smoke is the smell of
victory," "My nite is made. I just had a lady ask me if
it was burning. I said yep. She was upset. I was
enthralled," and "I have some extra gasoline if they
need it." The police responding to the fire had allowed
some patrons to sit in patrol cars, who then saw these
messages coming across the computer screen and
became very upset.

—Austin, Texas, March 5, 2005

THE EPIGRAPHS THAT BEGIN each chapter in this book are real, although the names, to rephrase the ending of the old television series *Dragnet*, have been withheld to protect the guilty. For many residents of this country, incidents such as these—especially the the garbage truck drivers and fire bombing incidents—are thought to be long past. Even when they did occur, most people think they were limited to "backward" rural areas and southern states. In fact, many citizens argue vociferously that "some people" (that is, racial and ethnic minorities) today make far too much of race and ethnicity. They deny the existence of widespread differences in treatment or opportunities based on race or ethnicity as American moves through the twenty-first century. Sadly, these are only a small sample of interracial conflicts that have been documented in the United States. Indeed, for other individuals, the events depicted here constitute evidence of the continuing salience of race and ethnicity in the American political fabric and of the differential treatment accorded many U.S. residents based solely on the color of their skin.

When the Rodney King incident and the subsequent verdict galvanized the nation, they simply made undeniable what any conscious human would find difficult to deny—the fact that racial and ethnic conflicts are common in the United States as we move through the beginnings of the twenty-first century. Yet, particularly during the Reagan and two Bush administrations, it was popular to think of racism as something long past.

Race has been and is still an enduring piece of the American political fabric. Although the overt signs of segregation and discrimination that were present when we were born are less common today, racism continues and is still practiced. Consequently, gaining an understanding of the politics of America's racial minority groups is essential to our understanding of the American political system in general. One cannot truly be a student of American politics without also being familiar with the politics of race and the political behaviors of America's racial minority groups.

The Dilemmas Revisited

We began this book by identifying the two primary dilemmas racial minority groups have faced and continue to face as participants in the American political process. The first dilemma is the asymmetry of the U.S. commitment to freedom and equality for all and the denial of these rights, first to African Americans and American Indians and then to Latinos and Asian Americans. This contradiction, identified early by Alexis de Tocqueville, has been addressed in part, but problems still exist. African Americans, American Indians, Latinos, and Asian Americans are citizens, and no one questions whether the protections and privileges embodied in the Constitution apply to all citizens. Also, the right to vote is an accepted principle, and denial of the right to vote on the basis of color is prohibited—at least in theory.

Yet the issue of citizenship is still of grave importance for the Latino and Asian American communities. Because of new immigration into the United States of foreign-born Latinos and Asians, some segments of the American electorate see all members of these groups as immigrants. This perception of "immigrant status" has resulted in discrimination against and denial of rights of American citizens of Latino and Asian descent. For example, in November 1997, the Republican attorney general of Arizona issued a report detailing how in July of the same year police from the city of Chandler, with no interference and perhaps even with some assistance from the Border Patrol, detained people on the basis of their skin color and charged them with being illegal immigrants if they did not speak English well or if they could not produce a birth certificate. Whereas the action netted 432 illegal immigrants, it also netted hundreds of U.S.-born Hispanics and legal immigrants, including schoolchildren, threatening them with deportation to Mexico (where they had never been). We are reminded of the video of Cheech Marin's popular song "Born in East L.A.," in which he is mistakenly swept up by the Immigration and Naturalization Services (INS), fails to convince the INS official that he was born in the United States, is sent to Mexico, and spends the remainder of the video trying to convince officials that he really is a native-born U.S. citizen.

Many Asian Americans have been victims of similar injustices. As a result of the recent hearings on foreign campaign contributions to the 1996 election that focused on contributions from Asian foreigners, Asian Americans visiting the White House encountered a Secret Service security guard who changed their citizenship on official entry documents from "United States" to "foreign" based on their Asian surnames. One of the visitors, Yvonne Lee, was a former member of the U.S. Civil Rights Commission. In another recent incident, Matt Fong, a fourth-generation American and Republican California state treasurer, was asked by a reporter whether his loyalty is divided between the United States and China. Clearly, as "foreign-looking" individuals, Latinos and Asian Americans may find themselves called upon at any moment to prove their citizenship. Few American citizens, except for Latinos and Asian Americans, are confronted with this part of the first dilemma in the twenty-first century, although many Americans who change jobs are discovering that they have to prove their identity and employment eligibility to the satisfaction of the INS.

A second part of the first dilemma, the right to vote, is still very much at issue. The debate is no longer over whether everyone has the right to vote—although there are still instances of localities blatantly attempting to deny or to interfere with the voting rights of racial minorities—but is now over the mechanisms used to protect the right to vote or the dilution of the vote of racial minorities. The issue is complex.

Chapter 2 discussed the Voting Rights Act of 1965 and its subsequent amendments. Debates over the intent, scope, and enforcement of the act continue. Some persons are beginning to use the creation of majority minority districts and lack of competitiveness as a veiled attack on the Voting Rights Act. But such an attack ignores the plethora of other, "safe" districts created for incumbents of both parties. Given the centrality of race in American politics, it is easy to attack the creation of majority minority districts as being unfair while ignoring the unfairness of the rest of the process. This is not to say that there are no legitimate debates over whether black people should be congregated in one district rather than spread over more than one. But the use of majority minority districts as a prima facie case of "the horrible things we are doing to the political process" only masks the concern with race rather than with the serious issues of what it means to represent and to be represented.

Relatedly, critics of districts drawn to maximize minority representation voice comparisons with the system of apartheid identified with South Africa. Such comparisons reveal an ignorance of history because apartheid's goals were the exclusion of one race from participation in government and the domination of one race by another. When majority minority districts are drawn, their purposes are the opposite of those of apartheid. In such districts, no one is denied the right to register and to vote for the candidate of his or her choice, to run for office, or to exercise any of the other political or civil rights characteristically denied by apartheid.

The second dilemma, what racial minorities should do to increase their access to the political process, is ongoing. As we live through the twenty-first century, what do we, the authors, see as the future for racial minorities in American politics? Do we envision more coalitions among racial minority groups, or do we anticipate increased tensions? As the numbers of the various minority groups increase in urban centers and, concomitantly, as the size of the white population decreases, tensions are bound to increase. As we have seen throughout this book, African Americans, Latinos, Asian Americans, and American Indians differ in a number of areas— for example, ideology, partisan identification, and policy preferences. Clearly, the old stereotype that "all minorities think alike," a variant of the racist stereotype "they all look alike," has been shown to be totally false. The groups may have some issues in common, but there are just as many issues on which they may disagree.

We must also remember that racial minorities, having been socialized in a society that sees them as inferior to whites, are equally likely to believe in the inferiority of members of racial groups other than their own. Thus, blacks are likely to have stereotypical attitudes toward Asians and Latinos, Asians toward blacks and Latinos, and Latinos toward Asians and blacks. Moreover, immigrants coming to this country have formed their images of African Americans and American Indians from Hollywood films and U.S. television exported by way of satellite and syndication. As a result of all of these factors, tensions among the groups will continue to increase and unless elite members of the communities intervene, will only become worse.

McClain et al. (2005) have studied the effect of Latino immigration into the South on relations with black Americans, using data collected in Durham, North Carolina. North Carolina has the fastest growing Latino population in the nation. Latinos, by and large, are an entirely new population in the South, and the South, for the most part, has had no experience with immigrant populations of Latin American origin. These Latino immigrants have no sense of Southern history and the legacies of slavery and segregation on the social and political environment of the region. McClain et al. found that Latino immigrants in Durham, for the most part, hold negative stereotypical views of blacks, with Latino males holding more stereotypical views of black Americans than do Latina females. Moreover, these negative attitudes do not appear to dissipate the longer Latino immigrants remain in the country. In addition to holding negative stereotypical views of black Americans, Latino immigrants do indeed feel that they have more in common with whites than with blacks. Moreover, living in the same neighborhoods as blacks appears to reinforce the view on the part of Latino immigrants that they have more in common with whites and the least in common with blacks. These findings do not auger well for relations between black Americans and Latino immigrants in the South. As Latino immigration continues at such high rates, this might suggest that Southern blacks will not only have to be concerned with racism and its consequences among whites but also among new Latino immigrants as well.

Another direction in which racial minority group politics may move is toward the formation of voting coalitions with other racial minorities. Such movement, however, depends upon the political context within which these groups interact. In cities in which the various groups are numerical minorities and competition for representation appears to be between minorities and whites, the desire to increase the minority share of favorable political outcomes may represent the basis for coalitions. The opposite may be true, however, in cities where a racial minority has become a numerical majority. In those instances, the majority minority no longer needs to form coalitions with others to maintain electoral domination; thus, coalitions may be formed between other racial minorities and whites. At no time should we presume that the extant white power structure will not act in an attempt to maintain its hegemony. We are not sure what is going to happen in the South, but at the moment it looks as if coalitions between blacks and Latinos in the South might not be possible.

An arena in which access for racial minorities is crucial and to which attention will also be directed in the future is the policy process. Only in recent years have a sufficient number of minority policymakers appeared to allow us to begin to gauge their impact. Obviously, much work remains.

Although the number of minority elected officials contrasts starkly with the small numbers prior to the Voting Rights Act of 1965, the number is still a fraction of what it should be. As more racial minorities are elected to public office—particularly at the state and local level—appointed to significant government decisionmaking positions, and hired in larger numbers as professionals within the public sector, racial minorities' access to

the policy process will improve, which will allow the mobilization and inside access models of agenda setting to be used. However, until the time
when racial minorities have greater input into the policymaking process,
they are likely to remain targets, rather than initiators, of public policy.

Targeting Racial and Ethnic Minorities

Racial and ethnic minorities find themselves the targets of various negative policies. California passed an initiative curtailing public services to illegal immigrants (Proposition 187) in 1994 and an initiative terminating
race- and gender-based affirmative action programs (Proposition 209) in
1996. Analysis of voting on Proposition 187 shows that counties with the
largest Latino populations were strongest in their support of the proposition, despite the fact that statewide, Latinos voted against it 77 percent to
23 percent (Hero and Tolbert 1996:866). The implementation of Proposition 187 was blocked by an appeal, and in November 1997 a federal district court declared all provisions denying services to illegal immigrants
in education, health, social services, and law enforcement unconstitutional. Overwhelming majorities of blacks (74 percent), Latinos (76 percent), and Asians (61 percent) voted against Proposition 209. It was
appealed to the Supreme Court after the Ninth Circuit Court of Appeals
in San Francisco found it constitutional. In November 1997 the Supreme
Court refused to hear the appeal, thereby setting the stage for Proposition
209 to go into effect.

In November 2004, Arizona voters overwhelmingly (56 percent) approved Proposition 200, a scaled-down version of California's Proposition
187. Proposition 200 requires individuals applying for public benefits to
provide proof of citizenship. Additionally, it requires state workers to report to federal officials illegal immigrants applying for benefits; if they do
not, they could be jailed. Support for the initiative was strongest among
whites, but exit polls suggest 47 percent of Latinos in Arizona also supported the measure (Marosi 2004). In late November, the Mexican American Legal Defense and Education Fund filed suit to block implementation
of Proposition 200 and received a temporary restraining order against the
state, keeping the measure from going into effect. In late December, however, a federal judge lifted the restraining order and ruled the measure
should be implemented. The measure was opposed by politicians from
both political parties—Democratic Governor Janet Napolitano and Re-

publican Senator John McCain. Concerns with illegal immigration and the determination of the constitutionality of Proposition 200 has generated efforts in other states, for example, Colorado, to try to get initiatives on the ballot in 2006. Moreover, given the fate of Proposition 187, Republicans in California are collecting signatures to get an initiative patterned after Arizona's Proposition 200 on the California ballot in 2006. The California initiative would block illegal immigrants from access to local and state benefits and from getting driver's licenses. State and local governments could also be sued for failure to enforce the law (Marosi 2004).

VRA: Looking to the Future

We foresee the nature of partisan politics and racial minority group voting undergoing changes. Blacks are not likely to shift dramatically from the Democratic Party to the Republican Party, primarily because the Republican Party is moving further away from the issues of importance to the national black community. Moreover, the intolerance of differences that is seen among some Republicans, which was cultivated during the Reagan and first Bush administrations and exhibited at the 1992 national convention in Houston and in Pat Buchanan's presidential race in 1996, makes it even more unlikely that blacks will find the Republican Party a welcome alternative. Nevertheless, given the trends in the level of partisan identification with the Democratic Party, we foresee a weakening of blacks' attachment to the party and possibly an increase in the numbers who see themselves as political independents, although a very small number of religiously conservative blacks are beginning to align with the Republican Party. Moreover, Donna Brazile, a prominent Democratic strategist and Al Gore's campaign manager in 2000, warned the Democrats not to take black voters for granted. As discussed in Chapter 3, blacks constitute an important voting bloc for the Democrats, and any significant weakening of party attachment is likely to create electoral problems in certain regions of the country.

We also expect that Mexican Americans and Puerto Ricans will essentially remain within the Democratic Party fold, but that in some instances and some regions of the country—for example, parts of the Southwest—they will adopt an independent stance or see the outreach by the Republican Party as inviting. In 2005, members of the Congressional Hispanic Caucus were withholding their Democratic Party membership dues until

House Democratic Party leaders assured them that the party would make concerted efforts to mobilize Latino voters and to address more actively the policy needs of Latino communities. On the other hand, we also predict that Cubans will remain primarily Republican, yet cracks are beginning to appear in the solid Cuban American Republican leanings. The exiled Cuban community appears to consist of three groups—those born in Cuba and who came to the United States before 1980, by far the largest group, who are solidly Republican; those who fled the island since 1980, have closer ties to Cuba, and are slightly more Democratic than Republican in their leanings, a small group; and those who are American-born children of Cubans with no ties to Cuba and who are more heavily Democratic than the other two groups, a smaller group still. In the future, the latter two groups will begin to outnumber the first group, and we may begin to see a more pronounced shift to the Democrats among Cubans.

The groups most susceptible to being recruited by the political parties in the future are Asian Americans and American Indians. The group with the highest proportion identifying themselves as political independents is Asian Americans. Yet voting patterns in the 1996, 2000, and 2004 presidential elections suggest that they are moving toward the Democratic Party. The allegiance and voting patterns of American Indians appear to depend on the policy positions taken by the parties on issues of concern to the various subgroups. The defection of U.S. Senator Ben Nighthorse Campbell from the Democratic to the Republican Party did not significantly move American Indians in the Republican direction. Lest one think the politics and political behaviors of racial minorities are unimportant components of the American political process, the 2000 U.S. Census estimates that by the year 2020, Latinos will constitute 15.7 percent of the population. African Americans will be second, with 13.9 percent of the populace, with Asian Americans third at 7.0 percent. American Indians, although fourth, will also experience a substantial increase to 0.9 percent of the population (Day 1993:xxii). In some regions of the country—for example, California—whites, according to the 2000 census, are already in the minority because the combination of racial minority groups constitutes a majority of the population. Hence, California becomes the first nonwhite majority state in the continental United States. (The majority of Hawaii's population is Asian American and Pacific Islander.) Thus, despite barriers—past and present—to effective participation of these groups in American politics, racial minority groups will become more, rather than less, important to the American political system. And the increase in the numbers and geographic concentration of specific populations will make these minorities more potent political forces—forces with which both Democrats and Republicans will have to contend.

Conclusion

As we end this book, the answer to Rodney King's plea, "Can we all get along?" remains in doubt. Issues of race were at the heart of the beginnings of this nation, and they remain central to the American political system in the twenty-first century. Barriers to the full participation of racial minorities in that system remain. Many school districts are still effectively segregated, and second-generation discrimination issues are moving to the forefront. Racial prejudice does not appear to be waning. Thus, one should not be so smug as to suggest, as some do, that "all that stuff happened in the past and has nothing to do with the situation today." History has a causal effect on the future, and historical effects linger for several generations and, in some instances, perpetuate themselves.

In spite of these ongoing concerns, progress has clearly been made. The authors—one white, one black; one female, one male; one raised in the Deep South, one raised in the West and North—were born in 1950 and 1951, respectively, into a society that was highly segregated. In our lifetimes we have seen a major transformation in the social, educational, and political opportunities of various racial groups. We have seen grandsons and granddaughters of slaves registering to vote for the first time, the signs that designated "colored" water fountains and restrooms removed, the election of the first big-city black mayors, the election of the first black governor in the state that was at the heart of the Old Confederacy, and integrated churches and police forces in the rural Deep South. Progress has been made, although not equitably or swiftly.

We also have seen David Duke, a past and perhaps current Ku Klux Klansman, make a serious run for governor of Louisiana; three highly publicized cases of individuals—Charles Stuart in Boston, Susan Smith in South Carolina, and Jesse Anderson (the man who was killed at the same time and in the same prison as Jeffrey Dahmer)—allegedly murder family members but initially blame the crime on an unknown black assailant; a high school principal in Wedowee, Alabama, cancel (then reinstate) a high school prom in order to prevent interracial couples from attending; teachers label a bored black elementary school student as mentally retarded when he would not (not *could* not) read a passage he had been assigned; members of the U.S. military at Fort Bragg, North Carolina, murder a black couple as an initiation rite into a neo-Nazi group; black churches burned, many for racial hatred reasons; a major oil company's executives tape-recording of racially disparaging remarks about black employees; a black female university professor in Maryland rent a bungalow on her property to a white couple who subsequently terrorized her with racial epithets and threats of physical violence; New York City police officers brutalize an innocent black man with a toilet plunger in a precinct bathroom; black students receive death threats at Pennsylvania State University, necessitating police protection at graduation; a black professor let go after he complained that a white professor hung a portrait of a Klansman on a classroom wall, left a Confederate license plate in the professor's office, and gave him a film showing a runaway slave being hacked to death; a football coach of Marshall University calling the members of the Ohio State University football team, "a bunch of Mandingos"; and three crosses, reminiscent of the terror tactics of the Ku Klux Klan, burned in Durham, North Carolina. Obviously, many issues still need to be resolved, and such resolutions will only come with a great deal of conflict. But given the potential political influence of minority groups, we try to remain hopeful that progress will continue.

Discussion Questions

Chapter 1

1. The authors state that there is "evidence of the continuing salience of race and ethnicity in the American political fabric." Do you agree with this assessment? Why or why not?
2. Thomas Jefferson, a student of classical liberal theory, opposed slavery but owned slaves. Theoretically, given the tenets of that theory, what justification could Jefferson have devised to explain his holding of slaves? Also from a classical liberal framework, what would be the weaknesses of his rationalization?
3. Citizenship is a primary criterion for participation in the American political system. What are the similarities and differences in the barriers to citizenship faced by African Americans, Latinos, Asian Americans, and American Indians? What are the important landmarks in these groups' efforts to attain citizenship? How was the Constitution changed to accommodate the inclusion of these groups?
4. Following citizenship, the ability to vote is central to participation in the political process. Yet gaining the franchise was not easy for racial minorities. How have the requirements for voting eligibility evolved since the ratification of the Constitution? How did blacks, Latinos, Asians, and American Indians each gain the franchise?

Chapter 2

1. A group's size is important in a majoritarian system, but population means different things depending upon the political issue under consideration. How do demographic characteristics affect actual and potential political power?
2. "Minorities" by definition are at a disadvantage in national politics. But in some areas, groups that are in the minority nationally constitute a near majority or a majority. What are the implications of this pattern for minority politics?
3. Why are some political movements successful whereas others fail? Choose a group that suffers from a disadvantage within the U.S. political system and explain how you would design a political movement to try to alleviate this situation.
4. What kind of protection is afforded to racial and ethnic minorities under contemporary voting rights law, and why was such a law thought to be necessary when it was passed and extended?
5. Do you agree with Lani Guinier's questioning of whether a majoritarian system means that 51 percent of the people control 100 percent of the power?

Chapter 3

1. Why is there a conflict within the scholarly literature over the utility of the pluralist framework for explaining the political behaviors of and outcomes for racial minorities in American politics?
2. Which of the approaches to the study of racial and ethnic politics do you find most useful? Why?
3. What are the elements of group cohesion? And why is group cohesion important to the political participation of racial minorities?
4. How would you characterize the ideological orientations of African Americans, Latinos, American Indians, and Asian Americans? Do you feel the terms liberal and conservative are appropriate labels for racial minority ideological and political orientations? Why or why not?
5. What is the history of the relationship of blacks to the two political parties? What is the level of partisan identification among the various minority groups? How strongly attached to the two parties are the various racial minority groups?
6. What reasons would you give for the gender differences in voter registration and turnout within the various groups?

Chapter 4

1. By what process is public policy made, and what potential and what pitfalls does this process have for members of racial and ethnic minority groups?
2. Why is access to the policy process important for the continued incorporation of racial groups into the political system?
3. Because we are all affected by public policy, we are all "targets" of public policymaking. Why might being such a target be of greater concern to a member of a racial or an ethnic minority group than to a member of a majority group?
4. Which of the major political institutions do you think has the greatest impact on public policies that affect minority group members? Defend your position.
5. What has been the effect of Shirley Chisholm's 1972 presidential bid, Jesse Jackson's two presidential campaigns, and now Carol Moseley-Braun's and Al Sharpton's forays into the 2004 presidential primaries on the presidential selection process? On the access of racial minorities to the political system? Or has there been little or no change as a result of these campaigns? Give examples for your position.
6. Why should anyone be concerned about whether members of racial and ethnic minority groups are represented in the executive, legislative, and judicial branches of government?
7. What are the advantages and disadvantages of the federal system of government for members of racial and ethnic minority groups?
8. Fierce political battles have been fought in attempts to attain equal educational opportunity. Why is this goal considered to be so important? What has been achieved? What is left to be accomplished?

9. List the various definitions of affirmative action and discuss the implications of each definition for policymaking and public support.

Chapter 5

1. What is your response to the question, should minorities work alone and bargain with the larger society, or do they need to form alliances to counter their minority status?
2. Why is there a popular assumption that blacks, Latinos, Asians, and Indians will form coalitions? Is this assumption accurate? Under what conditions are multiracial alliances feasible?
3. One pattern of interminority group relations is competition. What are the conditions under which racial minorities view themselves as competitors with other minorities?
4. Would we expect the dual patterns of relations among racial minorities in Los Angeles to be present in other cities? Why or why not?
5. What role did Asians play in Tom Bradley's coalition?

Chapter 6

1. What do you see as the future of racial minority group politics?

Glossary

Adoption is the stage in the public policymaking process in which decisions are made among proposed alternatives for dealing with a problem. This activity is most often conducted by the legislative branch of government.

Affirmative action programs operate on the premise that equal protection of the laws cannot be achieved simply by stopping discrimination but requires positive action to make sure that equality is realized.

Agenda setting is the phase in the policymaking process in which the particular issues gain exposure that is significant enough to cause policymakers either to choose to act or to feel compelled to act on them. The policy output is often determined by which actors are involved in the agenda-setting process. See also **inside access model, mobilization model,** and **outside initiative model.**

Antimiscegenation laws, which existed in more than half the states, banned interracial marriages. Most antimiscegenation laws addressed black and white marriages, although many states included prohibitions on white and Asian marriages and white and Hispanic marriages. Antimiscegenation laws were declared unconstitutional by the Supreme Court's 1967 ruling in *Loving v. Virginia.*

Bilingual education is the concept that purports that non–English-speaking students should be taught in their native language or should be taught to speak English. For Latino activists, **MALDEF** in particular, this issue has surpassed desegregation in importance and, in fact, can conflict with it.

Black and Tan Republicans constituted the wing of the Republican Party that favored Reconstruction and strong enforcement of civil rights laws. The Republican's nomination of Barry Goldwater in the 1964 presidential election signaled the final demise of this faction.

Citizenship is the status of enjoying to the fullest extent the privileges and immunities granted by a sovereign state. At present the Constitution provides citizenship to all those born or **naturalized** in the United States. In the pre-Civil War United States, citizenship was determined by the state in which one resided, and as a means of furthering racial discrimination virtually every state refused to confer citizenship upon nonwhites. The Fourteenth Amendment (1868), at least on paper, mandated that states could not deny citizenship on the basis of race; however, it took more than a century and countless legislative acts and executive orders before all eligible racial minorities were granted full citizenship.

Classical liberalism is the political and economic theory—normally associated with John Locke and John Stuart Mill, among others—that posits that the individual possesses a sphere of rights free from interference by the state. These rights are both civil and economic in nature. Classical liberalism is the primary political theory underlying the U.S.

Constitution. Although it has conferred civil rights on the populace, it was also the justification for perpetuating slavery. The government was not allowed to regulate slavery because the slaves were viewed as their owners' property.

Coalition politics constitutes the way in which a collection of disparate groups come together to fight for a specific political purpose that is shared to some degree by all of the groups. In minority politics, coalitions form among the various racial groups, and controversy exists over how well the groups cooperate versus how much they are in competition with each other.

Congressional Black Caucus is a group of black senators and representatives that was formed in 1971 as a means of concentrating black power in Congress. The purpose of the group is to combine forces to promote issues of special concern to African Americans, and it has been influential on certain minority issues. Latinos followed suit in 1977 with the formation of the Congressional Hispanic Caucus, and in 1994 Asians in Congress formed the Congressional Asian Pacific American Caucus.

Cumulative voting is a voting technique in which each voter can register an intensity of preference. Voters are not required to vote for only one candidate per open seat; they may apply all of their votes to one candidate or choose any other distribution up to the maximum number of positions to be filled. For example, a cumulative voting scheme for a six-person governing body would assign six votes to each voter. A voter, therefore, could vote for six separate candidates, place all six votes for one candidate, apply two votes to one candidate and four votes to another, or any other combination adding up to six. Cumulative voting is important because it allows minority groups—whether racial, religious, or partisan in nature—to concentrate their votes and, thus, to increase their chances for representation. Although controversial, cumulative voting schemes were used by Illinois to elect its state representatives for almost a century, and they have been present in several local jurisdictions throughout the United States.

District elections constitute an electoral system in which the entity in question is divided into a number of subregions, each electing its own official. Conversely, in at-large elections regions are not divided; rather, all officials are elected by the entire entity. For racial minorities, district elections are considered to be advantageous because racial groups can be concentrated into a single district and, thus, elect an official of their own choice. However, with racial gerrymandering, district elections do not guarantee that the group will be able to elect someone of its own choice.

Dominated groups are those groups that have been excluded from participation in the decisionmaking process by which society's resources are distributed. Racial minorities, among others, qualify as dominated groups.

Entrepreneurial city is a city in which electoral politics is arranged so that business interests play a significant role and, in most cases, political party organization plays a very small role. Los Angeles is an example of an entrepreneurial city.

Ethnicity subsumes a set of learned characteristics, often, but not always, associated with nationality. These characteristics, such as language and religion, have frequently been the basis for discrimination against groups.

Evaluation is the final step of the policymaking process in which it is determined whether or not the policy had the intended effect. The methods employed to assess a particular policy are extremely crucial in the final evaluation.

Federalism constitutes the division of powers between the national government and the state governments. Each level exercises some powers exclusively while sharing others.

Formulation is the stage in the policymaking process at which issues on the agenda are converted to actual proposals to be considered for adoption into policy. The formulation stage is characterized by a number of alternatives to be chosen from in reaching a particular policy goal; therefore, a crucial element of the formulation stage is the composition of the institution(s) making the policy choices.

Free riders are those who do not participate in political action because they know they will receive the benefits without incurring costs. Some black activists claim that other minority groups are free riders because they did not struggle to obtain civil rights as blacks did and yet have received the benefits.

Grandfather clause was a device used by southern states in the late nineteenth and early twentieth centuries to prevent black suffrage. By denying the right to vote to those whose grandfathers were slaves, the South effectively denied suffrage to virtually all southern blacks. The grandfather clause is one of many examples of how the South circumvented Reconstruction. In 1915 the Supreme Court, in *Guinn v. United States*, declared that the grandfather clause was unconstitutional.

Group identity or cohesion, in terms of racial politics, refers to the extent of the solidarity expressed by members of a racial minority. Cohesion can be measured by the proportion of minorities who believe that their group experiences discrimination and by feelings of closeness to other members of the group. Cohesion is important because it is a strong predictor of how effectively a minority group can be mobilized for political action.

Group political consciousness is a measure of how individuals in a racial minority view themselves within that minority group—in particular, what they prefer to be called. It is an important gauge of group cohesion.

Implementation involves putting a policy into action after it has been formulated and adopted. As with the other stages of the policymaking process, implementation is subject to numerous influences that are both internal and external to the implementing agency or agencies; consequently, following implementation a policy may or may not resemble the form in which it was actually developed.

Incorporation is the degree to which groups are represented in the dominant policymaking coalitions within a city. Racial and ethnic minority groups have rarely been incorporated.

Inside access (initiative) model is a type of agenda-setting process in which issues arise within the sphere of government and are not extended to the mass public. Until racial minorities' presence within the policymaking elite is increased, this model is the least applicable to setting the civil rights agenda.

Interest group activities are the actions of organized associations of individuals who share the same views on a particular issue or set of connected issues and attempt to influence related government policies. Racial minorities can be classified as interest groups when they solicit the government on racial policies.

League of United Latin American Citizens (LULAC) is an organization formed by middle-class activists to advance the goals of Latinos. The group has been instrumental in fighting segregation of Latinos in education.

Lily White Republicans represent a wing of the Republican Party that did not favor a strong reconstruction or a civil rights platform. By 1964, the Lily White wing had emerged as the leader of the party.

MALDEF. See **National Association for the Advancement of Colored People's Legal Defense and Education Fund**.

Mobilization model is a model of agenda setting that considers issues that are initiated by the policymaking elite, yet for interest in the issue to be sustained, policymakers must extend it to the public at large. As with the **inside initiative model**, the mobilization model's applicability to the civil rights agenda is largely dependent upon the presence of minorities within the policymaking elite.

The National Association for the Advancement of Colored People's Legal Defense and Education Fund (NAACP LDF) is a group of attorneys whose primary goal is to advance the cause of African Americans by using the legal system. Once fused with the NAACP, the LDF, or Ink Fund, is now an independent organization that has won many significant cases involving African Americans—most notably the *Brown v. Board of Education of Topeka* (1954, 1955) case, which outlawed segregation in public schools. Today, in addition to fighting racial discrimination, the LDF works on behalf of death-row inmates and the economically disadvantaged. Other minorities have followed the litigation-oriented model of the LDF, particularly the Mexican American Legal Defense Fund (**MALDEF**) and the Puerto Rican Legal Defense and Education Fund (**PRLDEF**).

Naturalization is the process by which nonnative-born people can become citizens of the United States. In the past, restrictive naturalization procedures have been used to keep racial minorities—particularly Asians, American Indians, and Latinos—from becoming citizens.

Outside initiative model is an agenda-setting model that considers the process by which issues are brought to the agenda through the nongovernmental ranks. The issue is initiated by a particular group, then moves to the public at large, and, finally, reaches the relevant policymakers. This model of agenda setting is the most applicable to the efforts by racial minorities, who have not been present within the policymaking elite, to bring civil rights issues to the agenda.

Partisan identification is the attachment a group or an individual feels to a particular political party. It measures direction toward a particular party and intensity of support. Party identification is a useful indicator in predicting voting behavior. Blacks, Chicanos, and Puerto Ricans are strong Democratic identifiers; Cuban Americans generally identify with the Republican Party; and Asians identify less strongly with either party.

Pluralism is a theory of government that contends that power is group based. Moreover, pluralism claims that because there are multiple points of access within American government, each group possesses an equality of opportunity when competing with other groups for power and resources. In minority politics, pluralism views each minority group as having the ability to compete adequately for power and resources; however, many scholars criticize pluralism for not taking into account systematic racial discrimination that exists within the system.

Political ideology constitutes the underlying beliefs, intentions, and attitudes of a particular social or political group, which in turn shape the group's actions and opinions on political issues. Ideology is traditionally conceived in terms of liberal, moderate, and conservative; however, numerous scholars find that classification scheme to be unsatisfactory. Furthermore, in relation to minority group politics, scholars have experienced difficulty in attributing a particular ideology to each racial group.

Political incorporation constitutes the extent to which a particular racial minority is able to exert influence within a political system. Incorporation goes beyond mere representation; rather, it is based on quality of leadership and coalition building with other racial groups.

PRLDEF. See **National Association for the Advancement of Colored People's Legal Defense and Education Fund.**

Public policies are the result of a purposive course of action by government officials attempting to deal with a problem. They represent what government does, as opposed to what it says it is going to do, about public problems.

Racism is the belief that race is the chief determinant of human characteristics and capabilities and that differences among the races provide for the superiority of one race. Racism is the primary condition that leads to discrimination against one race by another.

Rainbow Coalition is a concept advanced by then-presidential candidate Jesse Jackson in the hopes of forging a majority within the Democratic Party. Jackson sought to build a coalition of blacks, Latinos, Asians, American Indians, poor whites, and liberal whites as a means of pushing the party in a leftward direction. In 1984 the Rainbow Coalition met with limited success in influencing the Democratic Party platform; in 1988, following a more professionally managed campaign, Jackson was able to transform the Rainbow Coalition into a slightly more influential force.

Representative bureaucracy is a concept concerned with the degree to which the public workforce shares the demographic characteristics of the population at large. The presumption is that shared characteristics yield shared attitudes. If this is true, a representative bureaucracy should be a responsive bureaucracy.

Second-generation discrimination refers to a subtle form of discrimination against minority students in public education. Many schools group minority students together under the guise of remedial education, yet evidence indicates that this is in reality a form of resegregation—that is, schools are merely finding ways to keep minority groups separate and to provide them with an inferior education.

Separate but equal doctrine constitutes the interpretation of the Equal Protection Clause of the Fourteenth Amendment articulated in *Plessy v. Ferguson* (1896), which allows for racially segregated facilities as long as they are of equal quality. In reality, however, the facilities for blacks have been inferior to those for whites.

Social movements are efforts by disadvantaged groups to empower themselves. Prerequisites to the formation of social movements include an existing structure of social organizations, a leadership pool, the ability to tap outside resources, and skillful planning.

Socioeconomic status is a measure used in the social sciences that gauges the social and economic condition of a particular group or individual. Some of the indicators include educational attainment, income, unemployment rate, and poverty. For racial minority groups, socioeconomic status is a good predictor of political activity and of the ability of the group to overcome discrimination.

Southern Manifesto was the statement issued by most white southern politicians immediately following the *Brown v. Board of Education* of Topeka (1954, 1955) decision, which outlawed segregation. The statement decried the decision and indicated that the South would be willing to fight its implementation. The Southern Manifesto was one of the first indications that the South would resist integration regardless of national policy.

Suffrage is, simply, the right to vote. Traditionally, the jurisdiction conferring the right to vote, or the franchise, has been the individual state. The states have used their ability to determine suffrage as a means of discriminating against women and racial minorities. Constitutional amendments (Fifteen, Nineteen, Twenty-Four, and Twenty-Six) and federal legislation (e.g., the Voting Rights Act of 1965) have been enacted to ensure universal suffrage to all citizens over age eighteen regardless of race, gender, or financial status.

Three-fifths compromise was the settlement reached at the Constitutional Convention maintaining that slaves would be counted as three-fifths of a person for ascertaining the population to determine representation in the U.S. House of Representatives. This aspect of the Constitution, now rendered void by the Thirteenth and Fourteenth Amendments, demonstrates the fact that slaves were not considered citizens by the framers of the Constitution. At the time of its adoption, the compromise was viewed as a means of cooperation between the North and the South, yet, as the history of the nineteenth century reveals, this harmony between the two regions was short-lived.

Valence issues are the issues on which political candidates compete by claiming to stand for the same universally desired values without specifically explaining how they will achieve those values. For example, many candidates campaign as being antipoverty. Valence issues can have a critical impact on elections by influencing voter support for the candidate who most effectively articulates those values.

Vote dilution impedes the ability of minority voters to translate votes into the election of candidates of their choice. Devices such as at-large elections and racial gerrymandering have been used for this purpose.

Voting behavior is the way people vote in elections and the forces that influence those votes. Contrary to some perceptions, voting behavior varies both among and within minority groups.

White primary was a device used by southern states by which the Democratic Party would claim that as a private organization it could prohibit African Americans and other minorities from participating in primary elections to select its nominees. The South was a one-party region; thus, the primary election almost always determined the eventual winner. As a result of the white primary, blacks and other minorities were effectively disenfranchised. In 1944 the Supreme Court, in *Smith v. Allwright*, ruled that the Democratic Party was a public institution and that, therefore, the white primary violated the Fifteenth Amendment.

With all deliberate speed was a concept formed by the Supreme Court in the 1955 case *Brown v. Board of Education of Topeka* (*Brown II*). The Court ruled that desegregation must be implemented as quickly as possible, although not immediately. The vagueness of this doctrine allowed southern communities to resist desegregation for almost two decades.

Timelines

Timeline of African American Political History

1619   The first twenty indentured servants arrive in Jamestown, Virginia, from Africa.

1641   Slavery is first officially recognized by American colonial law when Massachusetts incorporates slavery into its body of laws.

1776   The Declaration of Independence is issued; southern states force Thomas Jefferson to eliminate antislavery rhetoric from the document.

1777   Vermont becomes the first American territory to abolish slavery.

1780   Seven black residents of Massachusetts petition for the right to vote, arguing "no taxation without representation," and have their claim upheld by a state court.

1781   The Articles of Confederation are ratified, extending citizenship to all free inhabitants. An effort by southern states to limit citizenship to all free whites is defeated; however, the states soon find ways to circumvent this edict.

1787   The U.S. Constitution is drafted. It considers slaves to be three-fifths of a person for apportionment purposes; it leaves citizenship requirements to the states; Article I, Section 9, forbids Congress to outlaw international slave trade prior to 1808 (after ratification, Delaware was the only state to forbid the importation of slaves).

1787   The Northwest Ordinances ban slavery in the Northwest Territory, which later includes Illinois, Indiana, Michigan, Ohio, and Wisconsin.

1793   The Fugitive Slave Law is passed (and is later upheld by the Supreme Court in 1842). It requires that the federal government assist in returning runaway slaves.

1804   Ohio passes a series of laws restricting the rights of freed blacks.

1807   Congress bans the importation of slaves. This action results in an increase in the number of domestic slave laws and in a stepped-up illegal international slave trade.

1820   The Missouri Compromise is passed, representing a settlement between slave owners and abolitionists. The act strikes a balance between the admission of slave states and free states to the union; it later turns out to be a failure.

1829   David Walker, a free black, begins publishing Walker's Appeal, calling for slaves and free blacks to rise up against slavery, using violence if necessary.

1831   The first National Negro Convention convenes in Philadelphia. It marks the first time African Americans from all over the country meet to advance the plight of all blacks (free and slaves) living in the United States.

1848   The Massachusetts Supreme Court, in *Sarah C. Roberts v. City of Boston*, upholds the practice of segregation. The language "separate but equal" appears in common law for the first time.

1850   The compromise of 1850 allows California to be admitted as a free state and halts slavery in the District of Columbia but requires stricter enforcement of the Fugitive

Slave Law. Alabama, Georgia, Mississippi, and South Carolina are disgruntled with the compromise and begin talk of secession.

1854   The Kansas-Nebraska Act rescinds the Missouri Compromise, allowing each state to decide for itself whether to be a free state or a slave state. For many states this decision ultimately leads to violence between the two factions.

1857   The Supreme Court decides *Dred Scott v. Sanford*. The decision, written by Chief Justice Taney, declares that the Constitution recognizes the slave owners' "property" rights regarding slaves above the citizenship rights of blacks; it also declares that any attempt by Congress to regulate slavery in the territories is unconstitutional.

1861   The Confederate States of America commence the Civil War with an attack on Fort Sumter in South Carolina.

1861   The Federal Confiscation Acts call for freeing the slaves; however, they make exceptions in the border states, where the Fugitive Slave Law continues to be enforced.

1863   The Emancipation Proclamation frees all but the 800,000 slaves in the loyal border states.

1865   The Civil War ends, and the Thirteenth Amendment abolishing slavery is ratified.

1868   The Fourteenth Amendment is ratified, requiring states to grant full citizenship to all citizens regardless of race; this includes forbidding states to deny "equal protection of the law" and "due process of law." Section 5 grants Congress broad discretion in enforcing the amendment.

1870   The Fifteenth Amendment, barring states from denying anyone the right to vote because of race, is ratified; the southern states easily circumvent the spirit of this amendment with poll taxes, literacy tests, and even violence.

1875   The Civil Rights Act outlaws racial segregation in public accommodations and in the military; however, in the 1883 *Civil Rights Cases*, the U.S. Supreme Court declares the act to be unconstitutional.

1876   When the presidential race is thrown into the House of Representatives, Republican Rutherford B. Hayes bargains with southern Democrats, exchanging their support for ending Reconstruction. Upon assuming office in 1877, Hayes removes the military from the southern states, leaving blacks unprotected in the process.

1880   In *Strauder v. West Virginia*, the U.S. Supreme Court finds West Virginia's statute mandating all-white juries to be in violation of the Equal Protection Clause of the Fourteenth Amendment.

1881   Tennessee passes a railroad segregation law. Similar laws are passed in other states: Florida (1887); Mississippi (1888); Texas (1889); Louisiana (1890); Alabama, Arkansas, Georgia, and Kentucky (1891); South Carolina (1898); North Carolina (1899); Virginia (1900); Maryland (1904); and Oklahoma (1907).

1883   In the *Civil Rights Cases* the Supreme Court declares the Civil Rights Act of 1875 to be unconstitutional.

1884   In *Ex Parte Yarborough* the U.S. Supreme Court affirms the power of the federal government to enforce the Fifteenth Amendment. This case and several others, such as Strauder, demonstrate that the Court was willing to enforce the Fourteenth and Fifteenth Amendments; however, this willingness was short-lived.

1895   Booker T. Washington delivers his Atlanta Exposition address, expounding the philosophy of his Tuskegee Institute, which purported that blacks should master labor skills and achieve economic independence before attempting to obtain political equality.

1896   In *Plessy v. Ferguson*, the U.S. Supreme Court upholds Louisiana's practice of racial discrimination, declaring that separation of the races is allowable as long as the facilities are equal. This is known as the separate but equal doctrine.

1900   In reaction to the Supreme Court's sanctioning of segregation, southern states begin to officially sanction segregated facilities. Some African Americans combat this unequal treatment with organized boycotts.

1905   W. E. B. DuBois and other black leaders organize the Niagara Movement, a crucial national political convention for the development of the civil rights movement.

1909   Developing out of the Niagara Movement, the NAACP is founded as the lobby organization for black rights. W. E. B. DuBois is the editor of *The Crisis*, the NAACP's official publication.

1915   The Grandfather Clause, a device used by southern states to deny the franchise to those whose grandparents were slaves—thereby effectively circumventing the Fifteenth Amendment—is declared unconstitutional by the U.S. Supreme Court in *Guinn v. United States*; the NAACP is instrumental in sponsoring this litigation.

1919   The Nineteenth Amendment is ratified, giving women the right to vote.

1924   Mary Montgomery Booze is the first woman elected to the Republican National Committee.

1925   The Brotherhood of Sleeping Car Porters and Maids is founded by A. Philip Randolph; this is the first major black labor union, made necessary by the discriminatory practices of the white unions.

1927   Minnie Buckingham-Harper assumes her husband's unexpired term in the West Virginia legislature, thus becoming the first African American female to serve in any legislative body in the country.

1932   In *Nixon v. Condon*, the Supreme Court rules that the Democratic Party in Texas is part of the state government; therefore, its white primary violates the Equal Protection Clause of the Fourteenth Amendment.

1941   A. Philip Randolph threatens a large-scale march on Washington as a means to protest racial discrimination. He calls off the march after the government creates the Fair Employment Practices Commission, which can only investigate instances of discrimination in the government's war industries.

1944   In *Smith v. Allwright*, the U.S. Supreme Court completely invalidates Texas's white primary as violating the Fifteenth Amendment.

1945   The Supreme Court, in *Screws v. United States*, rules that a Georgia sheriff did not violate a black man's Fourteenth Amendment rights by beating him to death "without the due process of law" for stealing a tire.

1946   The Supreme Court rules in *Morgan v. Virginia* that states cannot compel segregation on interstate buses.

1948   The Democratic Party and Harry Truman begin to extend themselves to African Americans by desegregating the military, creating a Commission on Civil Rights, and adopting a pro-civil rights platform at the party's nominating convention. The latter move causes many southern state delegations to abandon the Democratic Party and form the States Rights Party, headed by South Carolina governor Strom Thurmond.

1948 Racially restrictive covenants in housing contracts are declared unenforceable by the Supreme Court in *Shelly v. Kraemer.*

1952 Charlotta Bass is the first African American female to be nominated for the U.S. vice presidency by a major political party (the Progressive Party).

1954 The Supreme Court issues its unanimous landmark ruling *Brown v. Board of Education of Topeka*, declaring that in education, separate facilities are inherently unequal, thereby overturning the precedent set in *Plessy v. Ferguson.* This ruling renders segregated schools unconstitutional.

1955 The Supreme Court issues *Brown II*, which outlines the way the ruling in *Brown I* should be implemented. The Court's standard of "all deliberate speed" is sufficiently vague to allow the southern states to stall in desegregating their schools.

1955 The Reverend Martin Luther King Jr., Rosa Parks, and other civil rights leaders organize the Montgomery bus boycott, which ultimately results in ending discrimination on Montgomery, Alabama, buses.

1957 The first Civil Rights Bill since 1875 passes.

1957 President Dwight Eisenhower, who initially opposes the Supreme Court's *Brown v. Board of Education of Topeka* ruling, dispatches federal troops to Little Rock, Arkansas, to enforce a court order to desegregate its schools.

1960 The Civil Rights Act of 1960 is passed.

1963 The Reverend Martin Luther King Jr. organizes the historic march on Washington, which more than 200,000 people of all races attend to protest racial discrimination; it is here where Reverend King gives his immortal "I Have a Dream" speech. The march on Washington is arguably one of the largest nonviolent protests in U.S. history.

1964 The Twenty-Fourth Amendment to the Constitution bans poll taxes in all federal elections.

1964 As a result of intensive lobbying by civil rights leaders and the keen political skill of President Lyndon Johnson, Congress passes a comprehensive Civil Rights Act; this legislation gives the federal government enormous power in compelling states to end their practices of racial discrimination.

1964 Constance Baker Motley is the first African American female elected to the New York State Senate.

1965 Again as the result of intensive lobbying by civil rights activists and the political know-how of Lyndon Johnson, Congress passes the Voting Rights Act; to ensure fair voting practices, this act places the voting practices of states that lag in ending voting-booth discrimination under the jurisdiction of the federal government.

1966 The U.S. Supreme Court invalidates poll taxes in state elections in *Harper v. Virginia Board of Elections*; this case opens broad access to the polls to many previously disenfranchised African Americans.

1967 Lyndon Johnson appoints Appeals Court judge and former U.S. solicitor general and director counsel of the NAACP LDF Thurgood Marshall to the Supreme Court;

he is the first nonwhite to sit on the Court. The first big-city black mayors are elected—Carl Stokes in Cleveland, Ohio, and Richard Hatcher in Gary, Indiana.

1968   Dr. Martin Luther King Jr., arguably the most important civil rights leader in African American history, is assassinated in Memphis, Tennessee.

1968   Shirley Chisholm, from New York's 12th District, becomes the first African American female elected to the U.S. House of Representatives.

1972   Congresswoman Shirley Chisholm runs for president, becoming the first African American to launch a serious campaign for the U.S. presidency.

1973   Thomas Bradley is elected mayor of Los Angeles. Lelia K. Smith Foley is elected mayor of Taft, Oklahoma; she is the first African American woman mayor in the continental United States.

1976   Barbara Jordan becomes the first African American to deliver a keynote speech at a major political party convention when she does so at the Democratic National Convention. Yvonne Braithwaite Burke, a representative from California, is the first woman to chair the Congressional Black Caucus. Unita Blackwell is elected the mayor of Mayersville, Mississippi, becoming the first African American mayor in that state.

1978   The Supreme Court issues its complicated affirmative action decision in *Bakke v. California*. The Court rules that states may not use quotas as a means to ensure racial diversity; however, the Court does allow states to use race as a "plus" for admissions qualifications to universities and professional schools.

1981   Ronald Reagan takes office as president of the United States; he instantly scales back the federal government's role in protecting the rights of minorities in the name of the "New Federalism."

1981   Liz Byrd is elected to the Wyoming House of Representatives; she is the first African American to be elected to Wyoming's State House.

1984   Reverend Jesse Jackson becomes the first African American candidate to run for president within one of the two major political parties when he enters the Democratic primary. Although his campaign suffers from logistical problems, he still finishes third behind Gary Hart and the eventual nominee, Walter Mondale. At the Democratic Convention Jackson contends that his level of influence does not match the proportion of votes he garnered.

1988   As a result of the liberalized primary process and a better organization, Jesse Jackson runs a more successful presidential campaign; he finishes second behind eventual nominee Michael Dukakis. At the Democratic Convention Jackson delivers his "Quilt Speech." In the general election Republican nominee George Bush employs the racially charged Willie Horton commercial.

1989   L. Douglas Wilder, the grandson of slaves, becomes the first African American to be elected governor of a state when he ekes out a victory over Marshall Coleman in Virginia. In the same month David Dinkins is the first African American elected mayor of New York City.

1989   *Ward's Cove Packing, Inc. v. Atonio* and a series of other cases are decided. The Supreme Court rules that when employees file discrimination suits, the burden of proof is on the employee to show the existence of discrimination; statistics are no longer considered evidence of racial discrimination in the workplace.

1989   General Colin Powell is appointed the twelfth chairman of the Joint Chiefs of Staff, the first black to hold that position.

1990   In response to the *Ward's Cove* decision, Congress passes the Civil Rights Act of 1990, which allows for more statistical evidence to be used in employee discrimination suits. The act is vetoed by President Bush, and Congress is unable to override the veto.

1990   Sharon Pratt Dixon (Kelly) becomes the first woman and the first Washington, D.C., native to be elected mayor of the nation's capital.

1991   Thurgood Marshall retires from the Supreme Court, and President Bush appoints black conservative Clarence Thomas as his replacement. Thomas's nomination faces problems because of his judicial ideology and charges of sexually harassing his employees. His nomination becomes a public show trial, pitting him against his African American accuser, Anita Hill.

1991   Congress passes another Civil Rights Act, virtually identical to the one passed in 1990. President Bush, whose popularity is waning, signs the bill.

1992   Four white Los Angeles police officers are tried for use of excessive force against black motorist Rodney King. The beating was captured on videotape; however, the officers are acquitted by an all-white, all-suburban jury. As a result of the verdict, Los Angeles erupts with racial violence and rioting; the physical, economic, and psychological damage is enormous.

1992   Arkansas Governor Bill Clinton defeats incumbent George Bush as president of the United States; he promises to seek a new racial diversity.

1992   Carol Moseley-Braun from Illinois is elected to the U.S. Senate. She is the first African American female and the first African American Democrat elected to the Senate.

1993   The U.S. government pursues a federal civil rights case against the four Los Angeles police officers accused of beating Rodney King, resulting in convictions and prison terms for two of the officers. The city is peaceful following the verdicts.

1996   Congressman Gary Franks, Connecticut Republican, loses his bid for reelection. Franks was first elected in 1990.

1996   Members of Congress Cynthia McKinney (D–Ga.), Sanford Bishop (D–Ga.), and Corrine Brown (D–Fla.) all survive reelection in their redrawn districts. Their districts were declared unconstitutional and redrawn in *Miller v. Johnson* (1995) and *Johnson et al. v. Mortham* (1996).

1998   Carol Moseley-Braun of Illinois loses her bid for reelection to the U.S. Senate; President Clinton appoints her Ambassador to New Zealand and the Independent State of Samoa.

1998   President Clinton is impeached by the House of Representatives; black Americans provide him the highest level of support of any group in the United States.

1999   President Clinton is acquitted by the Senate on impeachment charges.

2000   A contested presidential election occurs amid charges of black disenfranchisement in Florida and other states.

2001   President George W. Bush appoints Colin Powell as the first black Secretary of State; Condoleezza Rice is appointed the first female and second black National

Security Advisor. Bush also appoints John Ashcroft as Attorney General of the United States, causing outrage from black politicians, civil rights groups, and the black public in general.

2003   The Supreme Court upholds affirmative action in undergraduate admissions at the University of Michigan but strikes down the procedure at their law school.

2003   Reverend Al Sharpton and Carol Moseley-Braun both decide to run for president.

2004   Condoleezza Rice is the first African American female nominated to be Secretary of State.

2004   Barack Obama is elected to serve in the U.S. Senate and was elected over another black candidate, Alan Keyes.

Timeline of American Indian Peoples, All Tribes and All Regions

1000   This is the approximate date of the formation of the Iroquois League, the oldest political alliance in North America.

1638   The first reservation is established in Connecticut; remaining members of the Quinnipiac Tribe are placed on this reservation.

1775   American colonists declare war against England. The colonies' provisional government—the Continental Congress—establishes three Indian commissions (northern, middle, and southern); each commission is charged with preserving amiable relations with indigenous tribes and keeping them out of the violence. However, many Indians ally themselves with the British, and many join forces with the American colonists.

1777   The Articles of Confederation organize the new government of the United States. The articles assume authority over Indian affairs except when the "legislative right of any State within its own limits [is] infringed or violated."

1778   The United States signs its first Indian treaty with the Delaware Nation; in exchange for access to that nation's land by U.S. troops, the United States promises to defend and admit the Delaware Nation as a state.

1789   The U.S. Constitution is adopted. Article I, Section 8, grants Congress power to regulate commerce among foreign nations and Indian tribes.

1789   Congress places Indian affairs under the War Department.

1802   Congress appropriates more than $10,000 for the "civilization" of Indians.

1803   As part of the Louisiana Purchase, the United States acquires lands on which numerous Indian tribes reside.

1815   The United States begins the process of removing Indians to western lands.

1816   Congress restricts licenses for trade with Indians to American citizens.

1824   The Bureau of Indian Affairs is created within the War Department.

1827   John Ross is elected president of the Cherokee Nation; he is the first president since the adoption of the nation's new constitution that year in New Echota, Georgia.

1830   President Andrew Jackson successfully pushes his Indian Removal Bill through Congress.

1831   The U.S. Supreme Court, in *Cherokee Nation v. Georgia*, holds that Indian tribes are domestic dependent nations, not foreign nations.

1832   In *Worcester v. Georgia*, the U.S. Supreme Court, in an opinion written by Chief Justice John Marshall, ensures the sovereignty of the Cherokees; however, President Andrew Jackson refuses to follow the decision and initiates the westward removal of the Five Civilized Tribes (Cherokee, Chickasaw, Choctaw, Creek, and Seminole). The term *Five Civilized Tribes* originated because these five tribes modeled their governments after American and state institutions and had been assimilated into the white culture.

1835   The Treaty of New Echota is signed. Cherokees agree to westward removal.

1838   The Trail of Tears begins. Cherokee Indians are forced to travel almost thirteen hundred miles without sufficient food, water, and medicine; almost one-quarter of the Cherokees do not survive the journey. The Potawatomis in Indiana experience similar hardships on their Trail of Death.

1847   Pueblos in Taos, New Mexico, ally with Latinos to overthrow the newly established U.S. rule.

1848   The Treaty of Guadalupe Hidalgo (see Mexican American timeline) is signed, bringing the Mexican War to an end. As a result of the vast amount of land ceded to the United States, many new Indian tribes fall under U.S. jurisdiction.

1849   The Department of the Interior is created, and the Bureau of Indian Affairs is shuffled from the War Department to the Interior Department.

1853   The Gadsen Purchase (see Mexican American timeline) is completed. More tribes come under the jurisdiction of the United States.

1854   Several southeast U.S. tribes (Cherokee, Chickasaw, Choctaw, Muskogee, and Seminole) form an alliance.

1861   The Civil War begins. Various Indian tribes fight on both sides. Stand Watie, a Cherokee, becomes the only Indian brigadier general in the Confederate Army; he leads two Cherokee regiments in the Southwest.

1864   Approximately eight thousand Navajos are forcibly marched to Fort Sumner, New Mexico, on the Navajo Long Walk; after three years of harsh imprisonment, the survivors are released.

1865   Confederate General Robert E. Lee surrenders to Union General Ulysses S. Grant at Appomattox; at General Grant's side is Colonel Ely S. Parker, a full-blooded Seneca.

1867   The Indian Peace Commission finalizes treaty making between the United States and Indian tribes.

1869   President Ulysses S. Grant appoints Brigadier General Ely S. Parker to head the Bureau of Indian Affairs; he is the first Indian to fill this position.

1871   Congress passes legislation that ends treaty making with Indian tribes.

1884   In *Elk v. Wilkins*, the U.S. Supreme Court holds that the Fourteenth Amendment's guarantee of citizenship to all persons born in the United States does not apply to Indians, even those born within the geographic confines of the United States.

1901   Congress passes the Citizenship Act of 1901, which formally grants U.S. citizenship to members of the Five Civilized Tribes.

1921   Congress passes the Snyder Act, which appropriates money for Indians regardless of the amount of Indian blood or their residence.

1924   Congress passes the Indian Citizenship Act, conferring citizenship on all American Indians.

1934   Congress passes the Indian Reorganization Act, which allows for tribal self-government, and begins the Indian Credit Program; concurrently, the Johnson-O'Malley Act provides for general assistance to Indians.

1939 Chief Henry Standing Bear and other Sioux leaders appeal to Korczak Ziolkowski, who worked on the presidential sculptures at Mount Rushmore in ex-Sioux territory, to create a similar monument to Chief Crazy Horse. Ziolkowski began work in 1947; in 1998 his son Casimir continued to work on the monument.

1944 In Denver, Colorado, the National Congress of American Indians is founded.

1948 Through judicial means, Indians in Arizona and New Mexico win the right to vote in state elections.

1949 The Hoover Commission recommends "termination," which would mandate that Congress no longer recognize Indian sovereignty, thus eliminating all special rights and benefits.

1953 Congress passes a law—introduced by Wyoming Representative William Henry Harrison—that gives California, Minnesota, Nebraska, Oregon, and Wisconsin legal jurisdiction over Indian reservations, thus initiating the termination process.

1958 Secretary of the Interior Seaton begins to retract the termination policy.

1961 More than 210 tribes meet at the American Indian Chicago Conference, where the Declaration of Indian Purpose is drafted for presentation to the U.S. Congress.

1968 Congress passes the American Indian Civil Rights Act, giving individual Indians constitutional protection against their tribal governments. This protection is the same as the protection the U.S. Constitution provides against state and local governments.

1968 The American Indian Movement (AIM) is founded; it is a protest movement based on the model of the black civil rights protest groups.

1969 Indian activists occupy Alcatraz Island near San Francisco in addition to staging sit-ins at the Bureau of Indian Affairs.

1960s From the late 1960s to early 1970s, tribes begin to create tribal colleges to ease the transition from reservation life to mainstream schools. Twenty-seven such colleges are created.

1971 The Alaskan Native Claims Settlement Act is passed; it eliminates 90 percent of Alaskan Natives' land claims in exchange for a guarantee of 44 million acres and almost $1 billion.

1972 In protest of a history of broken promises to Indian tribes, two hundred Indians participate in the Trail of Broken Treaties march, ultimately occupying the Washington, D.C., office of the Bureau of Indian Affairs.

1973 AIM organizes an occupation of Wounded Knee on the Pine Ridge Reservation in South Dakota, near the Nebraska border; the occupation ends with an armed confrontation with the FBI. AIM member Leonard Peltier is still (as of 2005) held in federal prison for the murder of two FBI agents, despite evidence that his trial was unconstitutional and unfair.

1975 The Indian Self-Determination and Education Act is passed, giving Indian tribal governments more control over their tribal affairs and appropriating more money for education assistance.

1979 The U.S. Supreme Court awards the Lakota Nation $122.5 million in compensation for the U.S. government's illegal appropriation of the Black Hills in South Dakota.

1980   The Penobscots and Passamaquoddies accept monetary compensation from the U.S. government for their lands (the Massachusetts colony—now the state of Maine), which the government took illegally in 1790.

1986   Congress amends the Indian Civil Rights Act and grants tribal courts the power to impose criminal penalties.

1988   The Alaskan Native Claims Settlement Act is amended, giving corporations the option to sell their stock after 1991.

1988   Congress officially repeals the thirty-five-year-old termination policy.

1992   Representative Ben Nighthorse Campbell, a Cheyenne from Colorado, is elected to the U.S. Senate.

1993   Ada Deer is appointed assistant secretary for Indian affairs by President Bill Clinton. She is the first Indian woman to hold the position.

1994   Three hundred representatives from the 545 federally recognized Indian tribes meet with President Clinton, the first time since 1822 that Indians have been invited to meet officially with a U.S. president to discuss issues of concern to Indian peoples.

1994   President Clinton signs a law that provides Indians with federal protection in the use of peyote in religious ceremonies.

1996   Laguna Pueblo faces a legal challenge regarding its long-standing tradition of allowing only men on the ballot for tribal office.

1996   The University of Arizona creates the first PhD program in American Indian studies.

1997   For the first time in history, American Indians are included in the presidential inaugural festivities as special and individual participants. American Indians are in the parade and have an American Indian ball.

1997   Alaskan Natives take a case to the Supreme Court regarding their right to tax others on their land (44 million acres in Alaska). The question posed: Does "Indian country" exist in Alaska as a result of the 1971 Alaskan Native Claims Settlement Act?

1997   Tribal constitutional problems in the Cherokee Nation in Oklahoma lead to intervention by federal officials. Tribal Justice Dwight Birdwell calls upon the United States to intervene and reinstate the Constitution of the Cherokee Nation.

1998   Four thousand Alaska Natives march in Anchorage in protest of Alaska legislative and legal attacks on tribal governments and Native hunting and fishing traditions.

1998   In a unanimous decision, the Supreme Court ruled that, in the absence of a reservation, the Venetie Tribe of Alaska does not have the right to tax others on land conveyed under the 1971 Alaskan Native Claims Settlement Act. In essence, the Court decreed that "Indian country" does not exist in Alaska.

1999   President Clinton visits the Pine Ridge Indian Reservation.

2000   The U.S. Supreme Court declines to review a religious freedom case centering around the use of Devil's Tower in Wyoming, a sacred site to several Indian nations. This decision upholds a federal court ruling that supported the religious rights of Indians against challenges from recreational rock climbers.

2000   In *Rice v. Caetano*, the U.S. Supreme Court struck down a restriction that had allowed only persons with Native Hawaiian blood to vote for the trustees of the Office of Hawaiian Affairs.

2000 Assistant Secretary of the Interior Kevin Gover (a Pawnee) issues a startling apology to American Indians on behalf of the Bureau of Indian Affairs, decrying the poor treatment Indians have experienced from his agency.

2001 Census data show that the self-identified population of American Indians increased from 1 million to more than 2.4 million, a 26 percent increase. An additional 4 million Americans claimed at least part Indian ancestry.

2001 President George W. Bush nominates Neal McCaleb, a Chickasaw, to be the Assistant Secretary for Indian Affairs.

2001 Loyal Shawnees gain federal recognition.

2001 A federal appeals court rules that tribal trust funds had been mismanaged by the government.

2002 Senator John McCain introduces legislation to reform the trust fund process.

2002 President Bush declares support for tribal colleges and universities.

2002 Interior Secretary Gale Norton and Assistant Secretary for Indian Affairs Neal McCaleb are placed in contempt of court for continued issues with trust fund reform.

2003 In a major appellate court on Native American sovereignty, the court rules that the Oneida Nation is exempt from having to pay New York State taxes.

2004 The National Museum for the Native American opens.

2005 The Oneida Nation independently pledges $1 million to efforts to help survivors of the Indian Ocean tsunami and earthquake.

Timeline of Mexican Americans

1540   Explorers from Mexico first enter the Southwest.

1821   The Republic of Mexico gains its independence from Spain.

1829   The Republic of Mexico outlaws slavery, thereby creating a conflict with many Anglo immigrants who were invited to settle in northern Mexico (now Texas) to fill a capital void and who wanted to retain the practice of slavery.

1836   Anglos and dissident Mexicans in Texas revolt and secede from Mexico, creating the Republic of Texas, where slavery is legal. The United States instantly recognizes Texas, whereas Mexico does not.

1845   The Republic of Texas officially becomes a U.S. state.

1846   After almost a decade of hostility, the United States declares war on the Republic of Mexico. Many Americans believe Mexico is weak and can be easily conquered.

1848   The Treaty of Guadalupe Hidalgo officially ends the hostilities between the United States and Mexico. Mexico cedes a tremendous amount of territory to the United States. The United States increases its territories by 33 percent, acquiring most of the present states of Arizona, New Mexico, California, Colorado, Texas, Nevada, Utah, Kansas, Oklahoma, and Wyoming. Mexican citizens living in the ceded territories are given the option to go to Mexico or to remain and live under U.S. rule. The United States grants Mexican citizens who elect to stay all guarantees of citizenship and freedom of religion; these guarantees, however, are not fully enjoyed.

1850   The California Foreign Miners Tax Law is passed, barring Mexicans from mining occupations. The hardships of the law are exacerbated by anti-Mexican violence.

1851   All native Mexicans are excluded from the California state senate, and California passes the California Land Law, which strips most native Mexicans of their land. The Mexican American population in California is divided into the rich Chicanos, called Californios, and the poor masses, the Cholos.

1853   The United States dispatches James Gadsen to Mexico to purchase land. Mexico is financially strapped and, therefore, is willing to sell the territory of what are now the southern portions of New Mexico and Arizona (the Gadsen Purchase). The United States wants the land for a rail line to California.

1855   California passes a statute prohibiting vagrancy that is referred to colloquially as "the Greaser Law." The Bureau of Public Instruction in California requires that all schools use English exclusively.

1859   In Texas, Mexican Americans revolt against Anglo leaders; this is known as the Juan Cortinas revolt.

1884   Juan Patrón is murdered in the territory of New Mexico. Educated at Notre Dame University, Patrón had been elected speaker of the New Mexico house at age twenty-four. He was best known, however, for his support of Alex McSween in his battle against Judge Warren Bristol and District Attorney William Rynerson in the Lincoln County, New Mexico, wars, which began as a property feud and ended with a violent shoot-out; other notable participants include Billy the Kid.

1889   In New Mexico Chicano resistance efforts begin. The two predominant groups directing the revolt are the Gorras Blancas and the Manos Negros.

1890   The political party for the Gorras Blancas, the United People's Party, has several candidates in local elections in New Mexico.

1894   One of the first *mutualistas* (community-based support organizations) is formed in Tucson, Arizona. The Alianza Hispano Americano provides insurance and funeral services for Mexican Americans; it soon expands its activities to include political action and publishing.

1902   The United States passes the Reclamation Act, which significantly increases agricultural efforts in the Southwest and thus expands the demand for agricultural labor, which is satisfied by Chicanos.

1903   Two thousand Mexican American laborers march through Clifton-Morenci, Arizona, while striking against the arduous conditions they face in the Clifton-Morenci copper mines.

1907   Ricardo and Enrique Magon found El Partido Liberal Mexicano (PLM); the PLM organizes workers in southern California and, at times, is regarded as militant. The PLM and followers of the Magon brothers spread throughout the United States, organizing Chicano workers.

1912   New Mexico and Arizona are admitted as states in the United States. In Arizona, Anglos control both politics and industry, whereas Chicanos control little of either. In New Mexico, Anglos control industry, but Chicanos are better represented in state government.

1915   The first Latino to serve in the U.S. House of Representatives, Benigno "B. C." Hernandez from New Mexico, takes office; he serves from 1915 to 1916 and from 1919 to 1920.

1917   The Immigration Act of 1917 places a tax on Mexican employees and requires literacy tests. Industrialists and agriculturalists in the Southwest, who rely on this cheap source of labor, eventually pressure the government into repealing the law. Ezequiel Cabeza de Baca is inaugurated as governor of New Mexico after serving as lieutenant governor (1912–1916) but dies after six weeks in office.

1928   The League of United Latin American Citizens (LULAC) is founded in Texas, composed primarily of relatively wealthy Chicanos. LULAC's main function is to compel all Chicanos to learn English as a means of getting ahead in the United States. LULAC is considered assimilationist in focus.

1929   The first Latino U.S. senator, O. A. Larrazola, a Republican from New Mexico, is elected to fill the unexpired term of a New Mexico senator who died in office. Larrazola serves only one year.

1935   Democratic member of Congress Dennis Chavez is appointed to fill one of New Mexico's senate seats, which became vacant when the incumbent was killed in a plane crash; Chavez is reelected five times and dies in office in 1962.

1940 Unity leagues begin to arise in California; their primary objective is to combat segregation and discrimination directed at Chicanos.

1942 The federal government establishes the Bracero Program (Public Law 45) in response to the labor shortages caused by World War II; the program calls for Mexico to send workers to the United States to fill the void, with wages determined by both countries. This program increases the number of Chicanos in the Southwest, and the workers are given legal immigrant status. Chicano labor leaders oppose the program.

1944 The Comite Mexicano Contra el Racismo is founded to provide Chicanos with the necessary legal aid to fight discrimination and racism; its chief publication is *Fraternidad*.

1946 In what is later dubbed "the Lemon Grove Incident," California Judge Paul J. McCormick holds that segregation of Chicano school children violates both California law and the U.S. Constitution (*Mendez v. Westminster School District*).

1948 The American G.I. Forum is founded by Hector Garcia and other Mexican American veterans in response to a Three Rivers, Texas, funeral home's denial to bury a Mexican American killed in the Pacific during World War II. The Forum works to advance political and social causes of Mexican Americans.

1949 Edward Roybal becomes the first Latino to be elected to the Los Angeles City Council since 1881; his victory is in part a result of the Community Service Organization's (CSO) work in registering Chicano voters.

1950 Operation Wetback commences. Since the end of World War II, there has been less need for agricultural labor; thus, many Mexicans are indiscriminately apprehended and deported to Mexico.

1951 The Bracero Program is renewed; many Chicano labor leaders view the Braceros as major hindrances in their unionization efforts.

1954 The Supreme Court acknowledges in *Hernández v. Texas* that Latinos are not being treated as "white" and recognizes them as a separate class of people suffering extreme discrimination. It is also the first U.S. Supreme Court case argued and briefed by Mexican American attorneys.

1960 Chicanos who support John F. Kennedy's candidacy for the presidency form Viva Kennedy clubs. The activity of these clubs significantly aids the Kennedy-Johnson results in California and Texas.

1961 Reynaldo Garza, a native of Brownsville, becomes the first Latino to be appointed to a federal judgeship in Texas by President John F. Kennedy.

1962 Edward Roybal becomes the first Latino from California to be elected to the U.S. House of Representatives when he defeats a white Republican incumbent in the 30th District in Los Angeles.

1962 César Chávez leaves the CSO to form the National Farmworkers Association (NFWA) to unite all farmworkers.

1964 The Bracero Program is ended. Joseph Montoya from New Mexico is elected to the U.S. Senate to the seat previously held by Dennis Chavez, serving until 1976 when he is defeated in his run for reelection.

1965 The NFWA supports the Filipinos in the Agricultural Workers Organizing Committee in their labor dispute with grape growers in Delano, California. This incident helps launch César Chávez to a position of national prominence.

1966 César Chávez negotiates contracts between his NFWA and the Schenley Corporation, Gallo, Christian Brothers, Paul Masson, Almaden, Franzia Brothers, and Novitiate.

1967 Reis Lopez Tijerina enters a courthouse in Tierra Amarilla, New Mexico, and attempts to place the district attorney under citizen's arrest. A shoot-out erupts, and Tijerina escapes. After a long manhunt, he is apprehended but is later acquitted of all charges.

1967 David Sanchez establishes the Brown Berets, a paramilitary group interested in defending Chicano communities.

1967 Elizar Rico, Joe Raza, and Raul Ruiz found *La Raza*, a magazine that serves as a primary chronicler of the Chicano movement.

1968 Chicano students walk out of five Los Angeles high schools, demanding more Chicano administrators and teachers, courses in Mexican American history, and a cessation of discrimination against Chicano students. The walkouts receive national attention. The leaders of the walkouts are indicted by a Los Angeles grand jury, but the indictments are soon dismissed as unconstitutional.

1969 Chicano university students form El Movimiento Estudiantil Chicano de Aztlan; the organization leads the Chicano movement throughout the Southwest.

1969 The Ford Foundation funds the Mexican American Legal Defense and Education Fund as a legal aid group to fight for the rights of Chicanos.

1970 La Raza Unida Party (LRUP) chapters are formed to place candidates in races for office. LRUP's presence is felt in Colorado, Texas, California, Arizona, and New Mexico.

1970 Mexican American Ricardo Romo runs for governor of California on the Peace and Freedom Party ticket.

1971 In Crystal City, Texas (more than 80 percent Chicano), LRUP candidates dominate the elections for the board of education and city council.

1971 The First Chicana Conference is organized. The conference examines the role of women in the Chicano movement.

1972 Brown Berets occupy Santa Catalina Island for twenty-four days to protest illegal land seizure violating the Treaty of Guadalupe Hidalgo.

1972 The Dixon-Arnett Law is passed by the state of California; it provides that any employer who knowingly hires undocumented workers will be fined. The Supreme Court of California deems the law unconstitutional.

1972 Chicano lawyer Ramsey Muniz runs for governor of Texas on the LRUP ticket.

1973 In *San Antonio v. Rodriguez*, the U.S. Supreme Court upholds Texas's school financing system despite claims that its inequities unconstitutionally deprive Mexican American students of their fundamental right to education. The Court reasons that the Mexican American students are not absolutely deprived of education and that education is not a fundamental constitutional right.

1974 Raul Castro is elected the first Chicano governor of Arizona. LRUP does relatively well in California, Texas, and Colorado.

1977 The Congressional Hispanic Caucus is established to monitor legislation and "other governmental activity that affects Hispanics" and to "develop programs and other activities that would increase opportunities for Hispanics to participate in and contribute to the American political system."

1981　Henry Cisneros is elected mayor of San Antonio, Texas, which is 55 percent Chicano; he is reelected in 1983, 1985, 1987, and 1989 and steps down as mayor in 1991.

1983　Federico Peña is elected mayor of Denver, Colorado; he is reelected in 1987.

1986　The Immigration Reform and Control Act, which is a major effort to reduce illegal immigration, is passed. The act increases border patrol activities and provides for harsh sanctions against employers who knowingly hire undocumented workers; additionally, the law provides for legalization of all people who have resided illegally in the United States since January 1, 1982.

1989　President George Bush appoints conservative former New Mexico representative Manuel Lujan as secretary of the interior.

1993　President Bill Clinton appoints Federico Peña secretary of transportation and Henry Cisneros secretary of housing and urban development.

1996　Hector Garcia, founder of the American G.I. Forum, dies. Garcia's G.I. Forum is a veterans' organization that worked to break down discrimination against Mexican Americans.

1996　Bob Dole receives a smaller proportion of the Latino vote than any Republican candidate in twenty-five years. Reagan won almost 40 percent in 1984. Dole received only 21 percent in 1996.

1997　President Clinton appoints Federico Peña secretary of energy, Bill Richardson ambassador to the United Nations, and Aida Alvarez director of the Small Business Administration.

1998　Cruz Bustamante is elected lieutenant governor of California; Antonio Villaraigosa succeeds him as the second Latino Speaker of the California Assembly.

2000　Latinos pick up four seats in the California Assembly, bringing the total to twenty, the largest in California history. Latinos have seven seats in the state senate.

2001　The 2000 U.S. Census indicates that Latinos are tied with blacks as the largest racial minority group in the United States and will surpass them and become the largest minority by the 2010 census.

2001　President George W. Bush appoints Alberto Gonzalez as the White House Counsel.

2001　Antonio Villaraigosa loses the mayoral election of Los Angeles to James Hahn.

2003　Cruz Bustamante is the lead Democratic gubernatorial candidate in the California recall election, but loses to Republican candidate Arnold Schwarzenegger with only 31.6 percent of the vote.

2004　Alberto Gonzales is the first Mexican American nominated as U.S. Attorney General.

2005　Antonio Villaraigosa is elected mayor of Los Angeles, the first Mexican American mayor in 133 years.

Timeline of Puerto Ricans

1493   Christopher Columbus lands on present-day Puerto Rico; he claims it as the Spanish island of Boriquén. Columbus calls the island San Juan Bautista. Approximately thirty thousand Taíno Indians are living on the island.

1508   Ponce de León is appointed governor of the island and founds the first settlement, known as Puerto Rico; he conscripts the Indians to mine for gold. The first school in Puerto Rico is established in Caparra.

1775   The population of Puerto Rico is 70,250, 6,467 of which are black slaves. The Indian population has been completely wiped out.

1873   Slavery is abolished on Puerto Rico.

1897   Spain grants autonomy to Puerto Rico; as a result of immigration, the population approaches 900,000.

1898   The Spanish-American War begins. By July, American forces land on the island.

1899   The Treaty of Paris is ratified, ending the Spanish-American War. The United States annexes the island of Puerto Rico.

1900   The Foraker Act is passed, making Puerto Rico an "unincorporated" U.S. territory. President McKinley appoints a governor to administer the territory. The first fifty-six Puerto Ricans arrive in Hawaii.

1901   Luis Muñoz publishes the first bilingual Spanish-English newspaper in New York City.

1917   The Jones Act grants U.S. citizenship to all Puerto Ricans.

1937   Oscar Garcia Rivera becomes the first Puerto Rican to be elected to the New York state legislature.

1942   Hiram C. Bithorn becomes the first Puerto Rican major league baseball player (with the Chicago Cubs).

1946   The first Puerto Rican governor, Jesús T. Piñero, is appointed by President Woodrow Wilson.

1950   Public Law 600 gives Puerto Rico a chance to draft its own constitution.

1950   Nationalists attack the governor's mansion, killing twenty-seven and wounding ninety. In Washington, D.C., Nationalists attempt to assassinate President Truman, killing a White House police officer. Pedro Albizu Campos and other Nationalist leaders are given lengthy prison sentences.

1952   The Commonwealth of Puerto Rico ratifies its new Commonwealth Constitution. In the first election, the Popular Democratic Party wins the most votes, and the Independence Party finishes second.

1953   The United Nations directs the United States to discontinue classifying Puerto Rico as a non–self-governing territory.

1954   Four Puerto Rican Nationalists begin shooting in the U.S. House of Representatives; five members of Congress are wounded.

1958   Tony Mendez becomes the first Puerto Rican to be appointed Democratic Party district leader in El Barrio, New York.

1966   Herman Badillo becomes the first Puerto Rican to be elected Bronx borough president, New York City.

1970   The 1970 census reveals that 2.8 million people live on the island of Puerto Rico and that 1.5 million Puerto Ricans live in the United States. Herman Badillo becomes the first Puerto Rican member of Congress from the mainland.

1973   Maurice Ferré, a Puerto Rican, is elected the first Latino mayor of Miami. He serves six terms before he is defeated in 1985.

1974   A consent decree is signed between the New York City school system and Puerto Rican plaintiffs represented by PRLDEF mandating bilingual programs in New York City schools.

1978   Olga Mendez becomes the first Puerto Rican woman elected to a major post in the United States, the New York State Senate.

1979   Luis Roviera is appointed Colorado state Supreme Court justice.

1993   Nydia Velazquez (D–N.Y.) becomes the first Puerto Rican woman to be elected to the U.S. Congress.

1997   Federal district court declares the majority Latino 12th district (Nydia Velazquez's congressional district) unconstitutional.

2000   Puerto Rico elects its first female governor, Sila María Calderón.

2001   Three Puerto Rican politicians are sentenced to jail for protesting the U.S. Navy's bombing of Vieques Island in Puerto Rico.

2002   In an effort to increase political influence in the mainland United States, more than 300,000 Puerto Ricans living in strategic areas were registered to vote prior to the 2002 election.

2004   Anibal Acevedo Vila wins an extremely close race for governor of Puerto Rico over a strong showing from the pro-statehood party.

Timeline of Cuban Americans

1801   Spain allows Cuba to engage in open commerce; although the Spanish government withdraws this privilege in 1809, many Cubans still engage in free trade.

1823   The United States issues the Monroe Doctrine, thus indicating U.S. willingness to become involved in Spain's dealings with Cuba.

1885   Vicente Martínez Ybor, who migrated to Cuba from Spain to avoid compulsory military service, purchases a plot of land immediately northeast of Tampa, Florida. On his land he develops a cigar manufacturing operation, which grows at a phenomenal rate. Ybor's development eventually becomes Ybor City, and the Cuban American population in Tampa mainly resides there. Cubans migrate to Ybor City to work on the tobacco farms and in the cigar factories.

1886   Slavery is abolished in Cuba.

1894   José Martí, a Cuban exile living in Florida, and others unsuccessfully attempt to raid Cuba from Jacksonville; the expedition is funded by donations from Cuban tobacco-field workers in Key West and Tampa.

1895   With the support of the U.S. government, Cuba launches a war of independence against Spain.

1898   The U.S. battleship *Maine* is sunk in Havana Harbor, Cuba, which begins the Spanish-American War. The United States ultimately wins the war, thus achieving Cuba's independence from Spain. Cuba, however, remains under U.S. military rule.

1901   Congress approves the Platt Amendment, granting Cuba conditional independence; the United States reserves the right to intervene on Cuba's behalf.

1959   Fidel Castro successfully overthrows General Fulgencio Batista y Zaldívar as president of Cuba. Castro soon becomes prime minister of Cuba, declaring that free elections will be held in four years, after problems are solved. Upper-income and professional Cubans, with financial help from the United States, begin to arrive in Florida.

1961   In the infamous Bay of Pigs operation, 1,500 Cuban American exiles, supported by the U.S. government, attempt to invade Cuba. The invaders are handily defeated, as almost 1,200 (80 percent) of the exiles are captured and imprisoned in Cuba.

1962   U.S. intelligence services spot Soviet missiles in Cuba; President John F. Kennedy blockades the island with air and naval forces. The United States and the Soviet Union are pushed to the brink of nuclear war over the issue. Soviet Secretary Nikita Khrushchev admits that missiles are present and promises to withdraw them.

1973   The "freedom flight," which brought more than 250,000 anti-Castro Cubans to the United States, ceases operations.

1980   President Jimmy Carter publicly announces that the United States will accept 3,500
        Cuban refugees from the port of Mariel, thus beginning an immense wave of
        Cuban immigration to the United States. The United States is deluged with Cuban
        immigrants, many of whom are not political prisoners but ordinary criminals. The
        United States detains the new immigrants for an indefinite period.

1980   President Carter declares a state of emergency in Florida and authorizes $10 million
        for refugee assistance. He also calls up nine hundred Coast Guard reservists to help
        administer aid to Cuban refugees.

1980   Cuba halts the 159-day Mariel boat lift.

1980   A group of politically conservative, anti-Castro Cuban Americans in Miami,
        Florida, form the Cuban-American National Foundation, which functions as a
        trade association and political lobbying organization; Miami construction mogul
        and Cuban American community leader Jorge Mas Canosa is elected the founda-
        tion's first president.

1982   With the support of the Cuban-American National Foundation and the Reagan
        administration, Congress authorizes the Voice of America to initiate Radio Martí,
        an anti-Castro, anti-Communist radio broadcast transmitted to Cuba. Radio
        Martí angers Fidel Castro, who suspends agreements and dialogue with the
        United States.

1984   African American city manager Howard Gray, of Miami, Florida, who is extremely
        unpopular with the Cuban community, is fired. This incident demonstrates the
        emerging political power of Miami's Cuban American community.

1985   Nonideological technocrat Xavier Suarez becomes the first Cuban-born mayor of
        Miami, Florida (although it is important to note that the first Latino mayor of Mi-
        ami was Maurice Ferré, a Puerto Rican). Suarez defeats Democratic incumbent
        Ferré and Raul Masvidal, a Reagan supporter and a member of the Cuban-American
        National Foundation.

1986   The former mayor of Tampa, Bob Martinez (R), is elected governor of Florida;
        Martinez, a Cuban American, is the first Latino governor of the state.

1990   Martinez, who is extremely unpopular, is defeated by former U.S. Senator Lawton
        Chiles (D) in his bid for reelection.

1996   Florida Cuban Republicans support a Cuban Democrat against a black Republican
        for mayor of Dade County.

1996   Florida Cubans give half of their votes to Bill Clinton, putting the state's electoral
        votes in his column. Bob Dole and the Republicans alienated a significant portion
        of the Cuban vote with anti-immigrant rhetoric during their campaign.

2000   The Elián Gonzalez case further strains relations between Cuban Americans and
        the Clinton administration. It also increases tensions between Cuban Americans
        and blacks and non-Cuban Latinos.

2000   Despite anger at the Clinton administration for the removal of Elián Gonzalez,
        close to half of Florida's Cuban American population voted for the Democratic
        candidate, Al Gore.

2001   President George W. Bush appoints Mel Martinez of Florida as Secretary of Hous-
        ing and Urban Development.

2001   In April the first U.S. cargo shipment in forty years left for Cuba, although it failed to dock a few weeks later. This first commercial food shipments since 1963 arrived in December.

2002   Mario Diaz-Balart is elected and his brother Lincoln is re-elected to serve in the 108th Congress.

2002   Former President Jimmy Carter's visit to Cuba marked the first time a U.S. president, current or former, was in the country since the 1959 revolution.

2004   President Bush tightened U.S. restrictions on travel to Cuba.

2004   Mel Martinez was elected to the U.S. Senate.

Timeline of Asian Americans:
Chinese, Japanese, Koreans, Filipinos, East Indians, Southeast Asians

1785   Three Chinese sailors land in Baltimore, Maryland.

1790   The first known native of India is reported in the United States in Salem, Massachusetts.

1790   The Naturalization Act of 1790 grants the right of U.S. citizenship to all "free white persons."

1834   The first Chinese woman in the United States, Afong Moy, is put on display in a New York theater.

1843   The first known Japanese immigrants arrive in the United States.

1848   The *Eagle* docks in the San Francisco harbor, bringing the first reported Chinese immigrants.

1850   Following an influx of Chinese immigration to California as a result of the discovery of gold, the Foreign Miners Tax is imposed on the Chinese to impede further immigration.

1852   Sugar plantation owners in Hawaii bring in 180 Chinese indentured servants.

1868   The first Japanese contract workers are brought to sugar plantations in Hawaii.

1869   The first transcontinental railroad is built with the labor of Chinese immigrants; two thousand Chinese railroad workers go on strike for better working conditions.

1870   The anti-Chinese movement is initiated. Many communities single out Chinese immigrants through discriminatory laws and violence.

1875   The Page Law prohibits prostitution and "coolie" labor in the United States.

1880   The California Civil Code forbids marriage between a white person and a "Negro, Mulatto, or Mongolian."

1882   The Chinese Exclusion Act is passed and signed into law; it bars the immigration of Chinese laborers and prohibits Chinese from becoming naturalized citizens.

1885   The Japanese government allows its workers to go to Hawaii as contract laborers; in the ensuing decade more than 30,000 workers migrate.

1898   The United States officially annexes Hawaii.

1898   The Spanish-American War ends with the signing of the Treaty of Paris. The Philippine Islands are given to the United States. Filipinos are viewed as "wards" of the United States and thus do not need visas to travel there. Filipino women who marry American veterans are allowed to migrate to the United States as war brides.

1898   The Supreme Court rules in *United States v. Wong Kim Ark* that children of Chinese immigrants born in the United States are U.S. citizens despite the Chinese Exclusion Act of 1882.

1905   The Asiatic Exclusion League is formed; it lobbies to prevent the immigration of Asians.

1913   The California Land Act is passed; it bars aliens from owning land. Many Japanese farmers are adversely affected.

1917   The 1917 Immigration Act prohibits immigration of labor from all parts of Asia except Japan.

1918   The Act of May 9 allows all people who served in the U.S. armed forces in World War I, regardless of race, to become naturalized citizens.

1922   The Cable Act rescinds the citizenship of women who marry aliens who are ineligible for citizenship (which includes all Asians except Hawaiians and Filipinos).

1923   The Supreme Court rules in *United States v. Thind* that Indian immigrants are not eligible for U.S. citizenship.

1924   The Immigration Quota Act excludes all aliens who are ineligible for citizenship. It allows the entry of alien wives of Chinese merchants but not of alien wives of U.S. citizens.

1931   Filipinos who served in the U.S. armed forces are eligible for U.S. citizenship.

1934   The ruling in *Morrison v. California* mandates that Filipinos are not eligible for citizenship.

1935   A reparations bill is passed by Congress encouraging Filipinos to return to the Philippines; only two thousand leave.

1942   President Franklin Roosevelt signs Executive Order 9066, which creates zones from which the military has the power to exclude people; consequently, more than 112,000 Japanese residing in these zones are forcefully removed to ten "relocation" camps.

1943   Congress repeals the Chinese Exclusion Acts; however, Congress establishes an annual quota of 105 Chinese immigrants.

1946   Wing F. Ong, the first Asian American to be elected to state office outside of Hawaii, was elected to the Arizona State House of Representatives.

1952   The McCarran-Walter Act upholds the national origin quotas for Asian Americans based on the figures from the 1924 Immigration Quota Act. Aliens previously ineligible for citizenship are subsequently allowed naturalization rights.

1956   The first Asian American—Californian Dalip S. Saund—is elected to the U.S. House of Representatives.

1958   Hiram Fong of Hawaii is the first Asian American to be elected to the United States Senate.

1964   The Civil Rights Act is passed, outlawing all racial discrimination.

1965   The Voting Rights Act is passed, forbidding outright electoral discrimination on account of race.

1965   The Immigration and Naturalization Act eliminates national origin quotas; hemisphere-based quotas are used instead. The Eastern Hemisphere's quota is set at 170,000, limited to 20,000 immigrants per country.

1971   The provisions of the McCarran-Walter Act providing for detention camps are repealed.

1974   *Lau v. Nichols* rules that school districts must provide special education for students who speak little or no English.

1975   Congress establishes the Indochinese Refugee Assistance Program (Public Law 94–23); this act resettles approximately 130,000 Southeast Asians (mostly Vietnamese and Cambodians) to the United States.

1976   *Wong v. Hampton* allows resident aliens to be eligible for federal jobs.

1976   After thirty-four years in existence, Executive Order 9066 is repealed by President Gerald Ford.

1982   Following a racially motivated argument in a Detroit, Michigan, bar, twenty-seven-year-old Vincent Chin is clubbed to death with a baseball bat; the two white assailants receive light sentences. In response, Chinese Americans (with the assistance of other Asian American groups) form the Citizens for Justice. A federal grand jury investigates, and one of the assailants is given a twenty-five-year prison sentence. His conviction is later overturned by the Sixth Circuit Court of Appeals.

1982   A Southeast Asian immigration quota of ten thousand is set by President Ronald Reagan.

1983   With the assistance of the Japanese American Citizens League, the National Committee for Japanese American Redress initiates federal litigation, seeking monetary compensation for the more than 100,000 Japanese Americans who were interned during World War II. Meanwhile, the convictions of Fred Korematsu, Minoru Yasui, and Gordon Hirabayashi, who were convicted of curfew violations during World War II, are reversed.

1985   Michael Woo is elected to the Los Angeles City Council; he is the first Chinese American to serve in that position.

1986   California passes an initiative declaring English as the official state language.

1988   The U.S. Congress, with the reluctant agreement of President Reagan, publicly apologizes for interning Japanese Americans during World War II and authorizes payment of $20,000 to each former internee.

1993   Michael Woo loses his race for mayor of Los Angeles to Richard Riordan.

1996   Asian Americans donate $10 million legally to the Clinton campaign. (Money also was donated illegally by foreign Asians.)

1997   The U.S. Senate holds hearings on illegal foreign Asian contributions. Asian Americans feel that the hearings are creating a backlash against Asian Americans.

1997   Asian American government officials and several visitors have their nationality changed from "United States" to "foreign" on official entrance documents by White House security guards and the Secret Service. The reason later given by embarrassed U.S. officials is that their last names "sounded foreign."

1997   A complaint is filed with the U.S. Commission on Civil Rights by the National Asian Pacific American Legal Consortium, the Organization of Chinese Americans, and other groups alleging that as a result of the campaign finance scandal, public officials, the Democratic and Republican Parties, and the media had evidenced a pattern of bias against Asian Americans based on their race and national origin.

1999   President Clinton appoints Norman Mineta, former congressman from California, as Secretary of Commerce, making him the first Asian American to hold a cabinet post.

2000   Asian Americans, for the first time, give a majority of their votes to a Democratic presidential candidate, Al Gore.

2000   Asian Americans in the California State Assembly form the Asian Pacific Islander Legislative Caucus (APILC), the first in California history.

2001   Elaine Chao is confirmed as Secretary of Labor and is the first female Chinese American to serve in the Cabinet.

2002   Washington Governor Gary Locke signs legislation that bans the use of the word "oriental" in official government documents.

2004   UCLA becomes first major U.S. research institution with an Asian American Studies Department.

2005   Doris Matsui decides to run in the race to fill her late husband's seat in the U.S. House of Representatives and wins.

Notes

Chapter 1

1. This and subsequent epigraphs are drawn from a number of sources. One is taken from an issue of the *Intelligence Report*, a bimonthly publication of the Klanwatch project of the Southern Poverty Law Center in Montgomery, Alabama. Each issue includes pages of such incidents that are only a sample from the project's files. Two incidents were reported in the *Washington Post*, two were reported in *The New York Times*, and one in *The Anchorage Daily News*.

2. The term *civilized* came about because historically, these tribes had associated with whites and adopted the culture of whites—especially their commercial culture. The fertile southeast land coupled with a commercial mindset enabled these tribes to amass great wealth, furthering their image as "civilized." It should be noted that the fertility of the land of the Southeast was not lost on whites, who coveted the territory. Beginning in the 1830s, the U.S. government, especially under the administration of President Andrew Jackson, removed the Five Civilized Tribes from their land to reservations in the relatively barren Oklahoma Territory.

Chapter 3

1. Ralph J. Bunche, the first African American to receive a PhD in political science from Harvard (in 1934), was the founder of the Department of Political Science at Howard University. Bunche later worked for the United Nations and in 1950 received the Nobel Peace Prize for his negotiations with Israelis and Arabs in the Middle East. Mary McLeod Bethune, founder and president of Bethune-Cookman College in Daytona Beach, Florida, was the director of the Division of Negro Affairs of the National Youth Administration. Robert C. Weaver served in the Department of the Interior under Franklin Roosevelt and later became secretary of labor under President Lyndon Johnson. Rayford W. Logan, a pioneer in the development of the study of what he preferred to call "Negro history," served as a consultant to the State Department, particularly on issues related to the Caribbean basin and to Africa.

2. Earl Warren was a former Republican governor of California, and Eisenhower, who was pursuing a southern white strategy, assumed—incorrectly—that Warren would hold the line on civil rights issues. After the 1954 *Brown* decision, when it became clear that the Warren Court was moving forward to dismantle segregation, Eisenhower is

quoted as saying that his appointment of Earl Warren as chief justice "was the biggest damn fool mistake I ever made" (Rodell 1968:12).

Chapter 4

1. These regulations clearly noted that segregation was still mandated for "members of the Negro race or persons of Negro ancestry" but not for "members of any other race" (quoted in San Miguel 1987:126).
2. In Arizona, a similar case banned the segregation of Mexican American students in 1951 (see *Gonzales v. Sheely*).
3. The plaintiffs in this case challenged the local school board's practice of segregating Mexican American students for the first two grades and requiring these students to spend four years in these grades regardless of their academic achievement. Thus, Mexican American youngsters could not enter the third grade until their fifth year of school. The school board countersued, asking that the parents of the children involved in the suit be enjoined from speaking any language other than English in the presence of school-age children and that they keep their children from associating with anyone who did not speak English. The federal judge dismissed the defendants' counterclaim in a terse footnote.

Chapter 5

1. This section draws heavily on the excellent work of Sonenshein (1993).

References

Alexander v. Holmes. 1969. 396 U.S. 19.

Alston v. School Board of Norfolk. 1940. 112 F.2d 992.

Amaker, Norman C. 1988. *Civil Rights and the Reagan Administration.* Washington, D.C.: Urban Institute Press.

Ambrecht, Beliana C., and Harry P. Pachon. 1974. "Ethnic Political Mobilization in a Mexican American Community: An Exploratory Study of East Los Angeles, 1965–1972." *Western Political Quarterly* 27:500–519.

American Friends Service Committee et al. 1970. *The Status of School Desegregation in the South, 1970.* American Friends Service Committee, Delta Ministry of the National Council of Churches, Lawyers Committee for Civil Rights Under Law, Lawyers Constitutional Defense Committee, NAACP Legal Defense and Educational Fund, and Washington Research Project.

Asian American Legal Defense and Education Fund. 1996. "3,200 Asian American Voters in NYC Polled on Election Day; 70% of Asian Americans Support Clinton." Press release, November 7, 1996.

Asian Pacific American Labor Alliance, AFL-CIO. Undated. Membership brochure.

Barabak, Mark Z. 2005. "Déjà Vu Not Quite All Over Again." *Los Angeles Times* (online) 10 March 2005.

Barringer, Herbert, Robert W. Gardner, and Michael J. Levin. 1993. *Asian and Pacific Islanders in the United States.* New York: Russell Sage Foundation.

Baumgartner, Frank R., and Bryan D. Jones. 1993. *Agendas and Instability in American Politics.* Chicago: University of Chicago Press.

Bayles, Tom. 2000. "NAACP Questions Irregularities." *Sarasota Herald-Tribune* 10 November 2000.

Bean, Frank, and Marta Tienda. 1987. *The Hispanic Population of the United States.* New York: Russell Sage Foundation.

Belz, Herman. 1991. *Equality Transformed: A Quarter-Century of Affirmative Action.* New Brunswick, N.J.: Transaction.

Blalock, Herbert M. 1967. *Toward a Theory of Minority-Group Relations.* New York: John Wiley & Sons.

Blauner, Robert. 1972. *Racial Oppression in America.* New York: Harper & Row.

Bobo, Lawrence D., James H. Johnson Jr., Melvin Oliver, James Sidanius, and Camille Zubrinsky. 1992. *Public Opinion Before and After a Spring of Discontent: A Preliminary Report on the 1992 Los Angeles County Social Survey.* Los Angeles: UCLA Center for the Study of Urban Poverty, Occasional Working Paper.

Bositis, David A. 1996. "Blacks and the 1996 Elections: A Preliminary Analysis." Joint Center for Political and Economic Studies. Unpublished paper.

———. 2000. "The Black Vote in 2000: A Preliminary Analysis." Washington, D.C.: Joint Center for Political and Economic Studies.

Boswell, Thomas D., and James R. Curtis. 1983. *The Cuban-American Experience: Culture, Images and Perspectives.* Totowa, N.J.: Rowen and Allanheld.

Bradley v. Milliken. 1975. 402 F. Supp. 1096.

Brischetto, Robert. 1996. "Women Lead the Modest Jump in Hispanic Political Representation." Web article. Copyright Hispanic Business, Inc.

Browning, Rufus P., Dale Rogers Marshall, and David H. Tabb. 1984. *Protest Is Not Enough.* Berkeley: University of California Press.

Browning, Rufus P., Dale Rogers Marshall, and David H. Tabb, eds. 1990. *Racial Politics in American Cities.* New York: Longman.

Brown v. Board of Education of Topeka. 1954. 347 U.S. 483.

Brown v. Board of Education of Topeka. 1955. 349 U.S. 294.

Burstein, Paul. 1985. *Discrimination, Jobs, and Politics: The Struggle for Equal Employment Opportunity in the United States Since the New Deal.* Chicago: University of Chicago Press.

Bush v. Vera. 1996. 517 U.S. 952.

CNN. 2000. "Election 2000." http://www.cnn.com/election.2000.

Cain, Bruce E. 1988. "Asian-American Electoral Power: Imminent or Illusory?" *Election Politics* 9:27–30.

Cain, Bruce E., and D. Roderick Kiewiet. 1984. "Ethnicity and Electoral Choice: Mexican-American Voting Behavior in the California 30th Congressional District." *Social Science Quarterly* 65:315–317.

———. 1986. "California's Coming Minority Majority." *Public Opinion* 9:50–52.

Cain, Bruce E., D. Roderick Kiewiet, and Carole J. Uhlaner. 1991. "The Acquisition of Partisanship by Latinos and Asian Americans." *American Journal of Political Science* 35:390–442.

Calvo, M., and Steven Rosenstone. 1989. *Hispanic Political Participation.* San Antonio, Tex.: Southwest Voter Education Project.

Carmichael, Stokely, and Charles V. Hamilton. 1967. *Black Power: The Politics of Liberation in America.* New York: Random House.

Catawba Indian Tribe of South Carolina v. United States. 1993. 982 F.2d 1564.

Chafe, William H. 1993. *Never Stop Running: Allard Lowenstein and the Struggle to Save American Liberalism.* New York: Basic Books.

Chaudhuri, Joytopaul. 1982. "American Indian Policy: An Overview of the Legal Complexities, Controversies, and Dilemmas." *Social Science Journal* 19:9–21.

Cherokee Nation v. State of Georgia. 1831. 5 Peters 1.

Cheyenne-Arapaho Tribes of Oklahoma v. United States. 1992. 966 F.2d 583.

Children's Defense Fund. 1974. *Children Out of School in America.* Washington, D.C.: Children's Defense Fund of the Washington Research Project.

———. 1975. *School Suspensions: Are They Helping Children?* Washington, D.C.: Children's Defense Fund of the Washington Research Project.

Cisneros v. Corpus Christi Independent School District. 1970. 324 F. Supp. 599, appeal docketed No. 71–2397 (5th Cir. July 16, 1971).

Civil Rights Cases. 1883. 109 U.S. 3.

Clifford, Harlan C. 1992. "Big Ben." *Boston Globe Magazine* 2 August 1992:16, 32–34.

Cobb, Roger W., and Charles D. Elder. 1983. *Participation in American Politics: The Dynamics of Agenda-Building.* 2d ed. Baltimore: Johns Hopkins University Press.

Cohen, Gaynor. 1982. "Alliance and Conflict Among Mexican Americans." *Ethnic and Racial Studies* 5:175–195.

Columbus Dispatch (The). 2005. "Ohio Voting Complaints, Explanations Varied." 7 January 2005:02A.

Congressional Quarterly. *Congressional Quarterly Almanac.* 1991. Washington, D.C.: Congressional Quarterly News Features.

Cooke, W. Henry. 1971. "Segregation of Mexican-American School Children." In *A Documentary History of Mexican Americans,* edited by Wayne Moquin, with Charles Van Doren. New York: Praeger, 325–328.

Crosby, Faye J. 2004. *Affirmative Action Is Dead; Long Live Affirmative Action.* New Haven: Yale University Press.

Cruse, Harold W. 1987. *Plural but Equal: A Critical Study of Blacks and Minorities and America's Plural Society.* New York: William Morrow.

Cumming v. County Board of Education. 1899. 175 U.S. 545.

Dale, C. V. 1995. *Congressional Research Service Report to Robert Dole: Compilation and Overview of Federal Laws and Regulations Establishing Affirmative Action Goals or Other Preferences Based on Race, Gender, and Ethnicity.* Washington, DC: Congressional Research Service, Library of Congress.

Dao, James, Ford Fessenden, and Tom Zeller Jr. 2004. "Voting Problems in Ohio Spur Call for Overhaul." *The New York Times* 24 December 2004:A1.

Davidson, Chandler. 1992. "The Voting Rights Act: A Brief History." In *Controversies in Minority Voting,* edited by Bernard Grofman and Chandler Davidson. Washington, D.C.: Brookings Institution, 7–51.

Davidson, Chandler, and Bernard Grofman, eds. 1994. *Quiet Revolution in the South: The Impact of the Voting Rights Act, 1965–1990.* Princeton: Princeton University Press.

Decker, Cathleen. 1997. "Victories in the State Senate and Assembly Underscore the Future Voting Power of Latinos." *Los Angeles Times* 4 March 1997:B2.

de la Garza, Rodolfo O., Louis DeSipio, F. Chris Garcia, John A. Garcia, and Angelo Falcón. 1992. *Latino Voices: Mexican, Puerto Rican, and Cuban Perspectives on American Politics.* Boulder: Westview Press.

Delgado et al. v. Bastrop Independent School District of Bastrop County et al. 1948. Docket No. 388, W.D. Tex. June 15.

DeSipio, Louis, and Rodolfo O. de la Garza. 1997. "The Best of Times, the Worst of Times: Latinos and the 1996 Elections." Paper presented at the Western Political Science Association Annual Meeting, Tucson, Ariz.

DeSipio, Louis, and Rodolfo O. de la Garze. 2002. "Forever Seen as New: Latino Participation in American Elections." In *Latinos: Remaking America,* edited by Marcelo Suarez-Orozco and Mariela M. Paez. Berkeley: University of California Press.

Doherty, Steven J. 1994. "Native American Voting Behavior." Paper presented at the Midwest Political Science Association Annual Meeting, Chicago.

Dred Scott v. Sanford. 1857. 19 Howard 393.

Eisinger, Peter K. 1976. *Patterns of Interracial Politics: Conflict and Cooperation in the City.* New York: Academic Press.

Elk v. Wilkins. 1884. 112 U.S. 94.

Espiritu, Yen Le. 1992. *Asian American Panethnicity: Bridging Institutions and Identities.* Philadelphia: Temple University Press.

Estrada, Leobardo, F. Chris Garcia, Reynaldo F. Marcias, and Lionel Maldonado. 1981. "Chicanos in the United States: A History of Exploitation and Resistance." *Daedalus* 110:103–132.

Eyler, Janet, Valerie J. Cook, and Leslie Ward. 1983. "Resegregation: Segregation Within Desegregated Schools." In *The Consequences of School Desegregation*, edited by Christine H. Rossell and Willis D. Hawley. Philadelphia: Temple University Press, 126–162.

Falcón, Angelo. 1988. "Black and Latino Politics in New York City." In *Latinos in the Political System*, edited by F. Chris Garcia. Notre Dame, Ind.: Notre Dame University Press, 171–194.

Feagin, Joe R., and Clairece Booher Feagin. 1978. *Discrimination American Style: Institutional Racism and Sexism.* Englewood Cliffs, N.J.: Prentice-Hall.

Fernández, Ricardo R., and Judith T. Guskin. 1981. "Hispanic Students and School Desegregation." In *Effective School Desegregation*, edited by Willis D. Hawley. Beverly Hills, Calif.: Sage, 107–140.

Finnegan, Michael. 2005. "Poll Shows Three-Way Mayor's Race." *Los Angeles Times* (online) 28 February.

Foner, Eric. 1992. "From Slavery to Citizenship: Blacks and the Right to Vote." In *Voting and the Spirit of American Democracy*, edited by Donald W. Rogers. Urbana, Ill.: University of Illinois Press, 55–65.

Franklin, Frank George. 1906. *The Legislative History of Naturalization in the United States.* Chicago: University of Chicago Press.

Franklin, John Hope. 1969. *From Slavery to Freedom.* 3d ed. New York: Vintage Books.

Gallup Organization. 2000. "Black Americans Feel 'Cheated' by Election 2000." Poll, December 20, 2000.

Goldman, Sheldon, and Elliot Slotnick. 1997. "Clinton's First Term Judiciary: Many Bridges to Cross." *Judicature* 80 (May–June):254–273.

Goldman, Sheldon, and Matthew D. Saranson. 1994. "Clinton's Nontraditional Judges: Creating a More Representative Bench." *Judicature* 78 (September–October):68–73.

Gomes, Ralph, and Linda Faye Williams, eds. 1992. *From Exclusion to Inclusion: The Long Struggle for African American Political Power.* Westport, Conn.: Greenwood Press.

Gong Lum v. Rice. 1927. 275 U.S. 78.

Gonzales v. Sheely. 1951. 96 F. Supp. 1004.

Graham, Hugh Davis. 1990. *The Civil Rights Era: Origins and Development of National Policy, 1960–1972.* New York: Oxford University Press.

Gratz v. Bollinger. 2003. 539 U.S. 244.

Grebler, Leo, Joan Moore, and Ralph Guzman. 1970. *The Mexican American People.* New York: Free Press.

Green v. New Kent County School Board. 1968. 391 U.S. 390.

Griggs v. Duke Power Co. 1971. 401 U.S. 424 91 S.Ct. 849, 28 LEd 2d 158.

Griswold del Castillo, Richard. 1990. *The Treaty of Guadalupe Hidalgo: A Legacy of Conflict.* Norman, Okla.: University of Oklahoma.

Grofman, Bernard, Lisa Handley, and Richard Niemi. 1992. *Minority Representation and the Quest for Voting Equality.* New York: Cambridge University Press.

Grutter v. Bollinger. 2003. 539 U.S. 306.

Guadalupe Organization, Inc. v. Tempe Elementary School District. 1978. 587 F.2d 1022.

Guinier, Lani. 1994. *The Tyranny of the Majority: Fundamental Fairness in Representative Democracy.* New York: Free Press.

Guinn v. United States. 1915. 238 U.S. 347.

Gulick, Sidney L. 1918. *American Democracy and Asiatic Citizenship.* New York: Charles Scribner's Sons.

Gurin, Patricia, Shirley Hatchett, and James S. Jackson. 1989. *Hope and Independence: Blacks' Response to Electoral and Party Politics.* New York: Russell Sage Foundation.

Gutiérrez, José Angel. 1998. *The Making of a Chicano Militant: Lessons from Cristal.* Madison: University of Wisconsin Press.

Hart v. Community School Board of Brooklyn District #2. 1974. 383 F. Supp. 699, aff'd 512 F.2d 37, 1975.

Henry, Charles P. 1980. "Black and Chicano Coalitions: Possibilities and Problems." *Western Journal of Black Studies* 4:222–232.

Henry, Charles P., and Carlos Muñoz Jr. 1991. "Ideological and Interest Linkages in California Rainbow Politics." In *Racial and Ethnic Politics in California*, edited by Byran O. Jackson and Michael B. Preston. Berkeley: Institute of Governmental Studies, 323–338.

Hernandez v. Driscoll Consolidated Independent School District. 1957. 2 Race Relations Law Reporter 329.

Hero, Rodney E. 1992. Latinos and the U.S. Political System. Philadelphia: Temple University Press.

Hero, Rodney E., and Caroline J. Tolbert. 1996. "A Racial/Ethnic Diversity Interpretation of Politics and Policy in the States of the U.S." *American Journal of Political Science* 40 (August):851–871.

Higham, John. 1963 [1955]. *Strangers in the Land: Patterns of American Nativism 1860–1925.* Westport, Conn.: Greenwood Press.

Hirschfelder, Arlene, and Martha Kreipe de Montaño. 1993. *The Native American Almanac: A Portrait of Native America Today.* New York: Prentice-Hall General Reference.

Hochschild, Jennifer L. 1984. *The New American Dilemma: Liberal Democracy and School Desegregation.* New Haven: Yale University Press.

Hoffman, Thomas J. 1998. "American Indians: Political Participation and Political Representation." Paper presented at the American Political Science Association Annual Meeting, Boston, 1998.

Holloway, Harry. 1969. *The Politics of the Southern Negro.* New York: Random House.

Holt, Len. 1966. *The Summer That Didn't End*. London: Heinemann.

Hong, Y. C. 1995. "A Brief History of the Chinese American Citizens Alliance." *Centennial Celebration and 43rd Biennial National Convention* (Conference Program). San Francisco: Chinese American Citizens Alliance.

Hopwood v. Texas. 5th Cir. 1996. 78 F. 3d 932.

Ichioka, Yuji. 1988. *The Issei: The World of the First Generation Japanese Americans, 1885–1924*. New York: Free Press.

Independent School District v. Salvatierra. 1930. 33 S.W.2d 790, cert. denied, 284 U.S. 580, 1931.

In re Wallace. 1959. 4 Race Relations Law Reporter 97.

James, Marlise. 1973. *The People's Lawyers*. New York: Holt, Rinehart and Winston.

Jarvis, Sonia R. 1992. "Historical Overview: African Americans and the Evolution of Voting Rights." In *From Exclusion to Inclusion: The Long Struggle for African American Political Power*, edited by Ralph Gomes and Linda Faye Williams. Westport, Conn.: Greenwood Press, 17–33.

Johnson et al. v. Mortham. 1995. 915 F. Supp. 1529, N.D. Fla.

Johnson, James H., Jr., and Melvin L. Oliver. 1989. "Interethnic Minority Conflict in Urban America: The Effects of Economic and Social Dislocations." *Urban Geography* 10:449–463.

———. 2001. *Black Elected Officials: A Statistical Summary, 2001*. Washington, D.C.: JCPES Press.

Johnson v. Miller. 1997. 117 S.Ct. 1264.

Joint Center for Political and Economic Studies (JCPES). 1993. "Political Trend-letter." *Focus* 21:n.p.

Judd, Dennis R. 1979. *The Politics of American Cities: Private Power and Public Policy*. Boston: Little, Brown.

Kaufmann, Karen M., and John R. Petrocik. 1999. "The Changing Politics of American Men: Understanding the Sources of the Gender Gap," *American Journal of Political Science*, 43, July, 864–887.

Keyes v. School District No. 1, Denver, Colorado. 1973. 380 F. Supp. 673.

Kitano, Harry H. L. 1981. "Asian-Americans: The Chinese, Japanese, Koreans, Filipinos, and Southeast Asians." *Annals of the Academy of Political and Social Sciences* 454:125–138.

Kleppner, Paul. 1990. "Defining Citizenship: Immigration and the Struggle for Voting Rights in Antebellum America." In *Voting and the Spirit of American Democracy*, edited by Donald W. Rogers. Urbana, Ill.: University of Illinois Press, 43–53.

Kluegel, James R., and Eliot R. Smith. 1986. *Beliefs About Inequality*. New York: Aldine de Gruyter.

Koplinski, Brad. 2000. *Hats in the Ring: Conversations with Presidential Candidates*. North Bethesda, Md.: Presidential.

Kousser, J. Morgan. 1992. "The Voting Rights Act and the Two Reconstructions." In *Controversies in Minority Voting*, edited by Bernard Grofman and Chandler Davidson. Washington, D.C.: Brookings Institution, 135–176.

Lau v. Nichols. 1974. 414 U.S. 563.

Leadership Education for Asian Pacifics. 1996. *Facts About LEAP.* Los Angeles: Leadership Education for Asian Pacifics.

Leal, David L., Matt A. Barreto, Jongho Lee, and Rodolfo O. de la Garza. 2005. "The Latino Vote in the 2004 Election." *PS: Political Science and Politics* 37:1 (January): 41–49.

Lewis, Anthony. 1965. *Portrait of a Decade.* New York: Bantam.

Lindblom, Charles E. 1980. *The Policy-Making Process.* 2d ed. Englewood Cliffs, N.J.: Prentice-Hall.

Lineberry, Robert L., and Ira Sharkansky. 1978. *Urban Politics and Public Policy.* New York: Harper & Row.

Liptak, Adam. 2004. "Justice Lets Ohio Ruling on Monitors Stand." *New York Times* 3 November 2004:P6.

Logan, Rayford Wittingham. 1954. *The Negro in American Life and Thought: The Nadir, 1877–1901.* New York: Dial Press.

Los Angeles Times Survey, June 1993.

Los Angeles Times Survey, April 1997.

Loving v. Virginia. 1967. 388 U.S. 1.

Low, Victor. 1982. *The Unimpressible Race: A Century of Educational Struggle by the Chinese in San Francisco.* San Francisco: East/West Publishing.

Marosi, Richard. 2004. "Arizona Stirs Up Immigration Stew." *Los Angeles Times* 6 November 2004:A11.

Márquez, Benjamin. 1989. "The Politics of Race and Assimilation: The League of United Latin American Citizens." *Western Political Quarterly* 42:355–377.

Mayer, William G. 1992. *The Changing American Mind.* Ann Arbor: University of Michigan Press.

McClain, Paula D. 1993a. "The Changing Dynamics of Urban Politics: Black and Hispanic Municipal Employment—Is There Competition?" *Journal of Politics* 55:399–414.

McClain, Paula D., ed. 1993b. *Minority Group Influence: Agenda Setting, Formulation, and Public Policy.* Westport, Conn.: Greenwood Press.

McClain, Paula D., and Albert K. Karnig. 1990. "Black and Hispanic Socioeconomic and Political Competition." *American Political Science Review* 84:535–545.

McClain, Paula D., and John A. Garcia. 1993. "Expanding Disciplinary Boundaries: Black, Latino, and Racial Minority Group Politics in Political Science." In *Political Science: The State of the Discipline, II,* edited by Ada W. Finifter. Washington, D.C.: American Political Science Association, 247–279.

McClain, Paula D., and Steven C. Tauber. 2001. "Black, Latino, and Asian Socioeconomic and Political Resources and Urban Electoral Outcomes: Complementary, Competitive or Independent?" Unpublished manuscript.

McClain, Paula D., Niambi M. Carter, Victoria M. DeFrancesco, Monique L. Lyle, Shayla C. Nunnally, Thomas J. Scotto, J. Alan Kendrick, Jeffrey D. Grynaviski, Gerald F. Lackey, and Kendra Davenport Cotton. 2005. "Racial Distancing in a Southern City: Latino Immigrants' Views of Black Americans." Unpublished manuscript.

McCool, Daniel. 1982. "Voting Patterns of American Indians in Arizona." *Social Science Journal* 19:101–113.

————. 1985. "Indian Voting." In *American Indian Policy in the Twentieth Century*, edited by Vine Deloria Jr. Norman, Okla.: University of Oklahoma Press, 105–133.

McDonald, Laughlin, and John A. Powell. 1993. *The Rights of Racial Minorities: The Basic ACLU Guide to Racial Minority Rights*. 2d ed. Carbondale, Ill.: Southern Illinois University Press.

McDonnell, Patrick J., and George Ramos. 1996. *Los Angeles Times* 8 November 8:A1.

McGreevy, Patrick, and Noam Levey. 2005. "Supervisor Endorses Villaraigosa." *Los Angeles Times,* online edition, 12 March.

Meier, Kenneth J., and Joseph Stewart Jr. 1991. *The Politics of Hispanic Education*. Albany, N.Y.: State University of New York Press.

Meier, Kenneth J., Joseph Stewart Jr., and Robert E. England. 1989. *Race, Class, and Education: The Politics of Second-Generation Discrimination*. Madison, Wis.: University of Wisconsin Press.

Mendez v. Westminster School District. 1946. 64 F. Supp. 544, aff'd 161 F.2d 774, 1947.

Michel, Karen Lincoln. 1998. "Fielding a New Clout: Indian Power and Party Politics." *Native Americas* 15:3 (Fall):11.

Miller v. Johnson. 1995. 515 U.S. 900, 115 S.Ct. 2475, 132 LEd, 2d 762.

Mintz, John, and Dan Keating. 2000. "Fla. Ballot Spoilage Likelier for Blacks." *The Washington Post* 3 December 2000.

Missouri ex rel. Gaines v. Canada. 1938. 305 U.S. 337.

Mollenkopf, John H. 1990. "New York: The Great Anomaly." In *Racial Politics in American Cities*, edited by Rufus P. Browning, Dale Rogers Marshall, and David H. Tabb. New York: Longman, 75–87.

Moore, Joan, and Harry Pachon. 1985. *Hispanics in the United States*. Englewood Cliffs, N.J.: Prentice-Hall.

Morgan v. Hennigan. 1974. 379 F. Supp. 410.

Morris, Aldon D. 1984. *The Origins of the Civil Rights Movement: Black Communities Organizing for Change*. New York: Free Press.

Morrison, Peter A., and Ira S. Lowry. 1994. "A Riot of Color: The Demographic Setting." In *The Los Angeles Riots: Lessons for the Urban Future*, edited by Mark Baldassare. Boulder: Westview Press, 19–46.

Muñoz, Carlos, Jr. 1989. *Youth, Identity, Power: The Chicano Movement*. New York: Verso.

Myrdal, Gunnar. 1944. *An American Dilemma*. New York: Harper and Brothers.

Nagel, Joanne. 1982. "The Political Mobilization of Native Americans." *Social Science Journal* 19:37–45.

Nakanishi, Donald. 1991. "The Next Swing Vote: Asian Pacific Americans and California Politics." In *Racial and Ethnic Politics in California*, edited by Byran O. Jackson and Michael B. Preston. Berkeley: Institute of Governmental Studies, 25–54.

————. 1998. "When Numbers Do Not Add Up: Asian Pacific Americans and California Politics." In *Racial and Ethnic Politics in California*, vol. 2, edited by Michael B. Preston, Bruce E. Cain, and Sandra Bass. Berkeley: Institute of Governmental Studies, 3–43.

National Asian Pacific American Legal Consortium. Undated. Membership brochure.

National Association for Asian and Pacific American Education. Undated. Membership brochure.

National Association of Korean Americans. Undated. Membership brochure.

National Association of Latino Elected Officials (NALEO). 1996. "Newly Naturalized Latinos Inspired by Opportunity to Vote and Are Ready to Participate." Press release, October 28, 1996.

———. 2000a. 2000 National Directory of Latino Elected Officials. Los Angeles: NALEO.

———.2000b. "Latinos Grab Seats in State House Nationwide." NALEO News 9 November 2000.

———. 2004. *National Directory of Latino Elected Officials*. Los Angeles: NALEO.

National Center for Education Statistics. 1978. *The Children's English and Services Study*. Washington, D.C.: Government Printing Office.

National Conference of Christians and Jews. 1993. *Taking America's Pulse: The Full Report of the National Conference Survey on Inter-Group Relations*. New York: National Conference of Christians and Jews.

National Council of La Raza. 1990. "Background Paper for Black-Latino Dialogue." Unpublished paper.

National Institute of Education. 1977. *Conference Report: Desegregation and Education Concerns of the Hispanic Community*. Washington, D.C.: Government Printing Office.

Native American Rights Fund (NARF). 1993. *Annual Report*. Boulder: NARF.

Native American Studies Association (NASA). 2001. "Native American Policy Network Newsletter" 17 (Spring):3.

New York Times. 1992. "Portrait of the Electorate, 1992." 5 November 1992. Available online at http://www.nytimes.com/library/politics/elec-port.html.

———. 1996. "Portrait of the Electorate, 1996." 7 November 1996. Available online at http://www.nytimes.com/library/politics/elec-port.html.

———. 2004. "Playing with Election Rules." 30 September, A28.

Niquette, Mark. 2005. "Blackwell Under Fire; Letter Asks for Illegal Money." *The Columbus Dispatch* 8 January 2005:B01.

Nolan, Martin F. 1992. "Candidates Offer Vivid Contrast in Biographies." *Boston Globe* 18 October 1992:A19.

O'Connor, Karen, and Lee Epstein. 1984. "A Legal Voice for the Chicano Community: The Activities of the Mexican American Legal Defense and Educational Fund, 1968–82." *Social Science Quarterly* 65:245–256.

Oliver, Melvin L., and James H. Johnson Jr. 1984. "Inter-Ethnic Conflict in an Urban Ghetto: The Case of Blacks and Latinos in Los Angeles." *Social Movements, Conflicts, and Change* 6:57–94.

Olsen, Marvin C. 1970. "Social and Political Participation of Blacks." *American Sociological Review* 35:682–697.

Orfield, Gary W. 1969. *The Reconstruction of Southern Education: The Schools and the 1964 Civil Rights Act*. New York: Wiley Interscience.

———. 1978. *Must We Bus?* Washington, D.C.: Brookings Institution.

Orfield, Gary W., with Sara Schley, Diane Glass, and Sean Reardon. 1993. *The Growth of Segregation in American Schools: Changing Patterns of Separation and Poverty Since 1968*. National School Board Association, Council of Urban Boards of Education.

Organization of Chinese Americans. 1997. "Image." Summer.

Panetta, Leon E., and Peter Gall. 1971. *Bring Us Together: The Nixon Team and the Civil Rights Retreat*. Philadelphia: Lippincott.

Peltason, Jack W. 1971. *Fifty-Eight Lonely Men: Southern Federal Judges and School Desegregation*. Urbana, Ill.: University of Illinois Press.

Pinderhughes, Dianne M. 1987. *Race and Ethnicity in Chicago Politics: A Reexamination of Pluralist Theory*. Urbana, Ill.: University of Illinois Press.

Plessy v. Ferguson. 1896. 163 U.S. 537.

Pohlman, Marcus. 1991. *Black Politics in Conservative America*. New York: Longman.

Population Projection Program. 2000. "Population Projections of the United States by Age, Sex, Race, Hispanic Origin, and Nativity: 1999 to 2100." Washington, D.C.: Population Division, U.S. Bureau of the Census.

Powell, Michael, and Peter Slevin. 2004. "Several Factors Contributed to 'Lost' Voters in Ohio." *Washington Post* 15 December 2004:A01.

Provance, Jim. 2005. "Blackwell Questioned about Ohio's Election Performance." 22 March. Toledoblade.com.

Purdum, Todd. 1997. "Los Angeles Mayor Is Reelected: Hispanic Voters Emerge as Factor." *New York Times* 10 April 1997:A1, A22.

Rangel, Jorge C., and Carlos M. Alcala. 1972. "Project Report: De Jure Segregation of Chicanos in Texas Schools." *Harvard Civil Rights-Civil Liberties Law Review* 7:307–392.

Reeves, Keith. 1997. *Voting Hopes or Fears? White Voters, Black Candidates, and Racial Politics in America*. New York: Oxford University Press.

Richmond v. J. A. Croson Co. 1989. 488 U.S. 469, 109 S.Ct. 706, 102 LEd 2d 854.

Ritt, Leonard. 1979. "Some Social and Political Views of American Indians." *Ethnicity* 6:45–72.

Robertson, David B., and Dennis R. Judd. 1989. *The Development of American Public Policy: The Structure of Policy Restraint*. Glenview, Ill.: Scott, Foresman and Little, Brown.

Robinson, Donald L. 1971. *Slavery in the Structure of American Politics, 1765–1820*. New York: Harcourt Brace Jovanovich.

Robles, Frances, and Geoff Dougherty. 2000. "Ballot Errors Rate High in Some Black Precincts." *Miami Herald* 15 November 2000 (online edition).

Rodell, Fred. 1968. "The Complexities of Mr. Justice Fortas." *New York Times Magazine* 28 July 1968:12.

Rodgers, Harrell R., Jr. 1984. "Fair Employment Laws for Minorities: An Evaluation of Federal Implementation." In *Implementation of Civil Rights Policy*, edited by Charles S. Bullock III and Charles M. Lamb. Monterey, Calif.: Brooks/Cole, 93–117.

Rodgers, Harrell R., Jr., and Charles S. Bullock III. 1976. *Coercion to Compliance*. Lexington, Mass.: D. C. Heath.

Romero v. Weakley. 1955. 131 F.Supp. 818.

Rose, Harold M. 1971. *The Black Ghetto: A Spatial Behavioral Perspective*. New York: McGraw-Hill.

Ross v. Eckels. 1970. 434 F.2d 1140.

Ruffin, David C. 2004. "The Verdict's in on Black Judges." blackenterprise.com, 26 October.

Saito, Leland Tadaji. 1992. *Politics in a New Demographic Era: Asian Americans in Monterey Park, California*. Unpublished PhD dissertation, Department of Sociology, UCLA.

San Miguel, Guadalupe, Jr. 1987. *"Let All of Them Take Heed": Mexican Americans and the Campaign for Educational Equality in Texas, 1910–1981.* Austin, Tex.: University of Texas Press.

Schattschneider, E. E. 1960. *The Semi-Sovereign People.* Hinsdale, Ill.: Dryden.

Seelye, Katherine Q. 1995. "Democrats Lose 1 in Senate with Switch by Coloradan." *New York Times* (national edition) 4 March 1995:8.

Serna v. Portales Municipal Schools. 1974. 499 F.2d 1147.

Shaw v. Hunt. 1996. 517 U.S. 899.

Shaw v. Reno. 1993. 509 U.S. 630.

Sigelman, Lee, and Susan Welch. 1991. *Black Americans' Views of Racial Inequality: The Dream Deferred.* Cambridge: Cambridge University Press.

Sigler, Jay A. 1975. *American Rights Policies.* Homewood, Ill.: Dorsey Press.

Silver, Christopher, and John V. Moeser. 1995. *The Separate City: Black Communities in the Urban South, 1940–1968.* Lexington, Ky.: University Press of Kentucky.

Simmons, Cassandra A., and Nelvia M. Brady. 1981. "The Impact of Ability Group Placement Decisions on the Equality of Educational Opportunity in Desegregated Elementary Schools." *Urban Review* 13:129–133.

Skrentny, John David. 1996. *The Ironies of Affirmative Action.* Chicago: University of Chicago Press.

Slaughterhouse Cases. 1873. 16 Wallace 36.

Smith, Robert C. 1990. "From Insurgency to Ward Inclusion: The Jackson Campaigns of 1984 and 1988." In *The Social and Political Implications of the 1984 Jesse Jackson Campaign,* edited by Lorenzo Morris. New York: Praeger, 215–230.

Smith, Robert C., and Richard Seltzer. 1992. *Race, Class, and Culture.* Albany, N.Y.: State University of New York Press.

Smith v. Allwright. 1944. 321 U.S. 649.

Smyth, Julie Carr. 2005. "Hearing on Election Turns Heated." *The Cleveland Plain Dealer* 22 March 2005 (online article).

Sonenshein, Raphael J. 1990. "Biracial Coalition Politics in Los Angeles." In *Racial Politics in American Cities,* edited by Rufus P. Browning, Dale Rogers Marshall, and David H. Tabb. New York: Longman, 33–48.

———. 1993. *Politics in Black and White: Race and Power in Los Angeles.* Princeton: Princeton University Press.

Southwest Voter Research Institute. 1997. Website. State Latino Voting and Registration Data. http://www.wcvi.org/svrep.

Spickard, Paul R. 1989. *Mixed Blood: Intermarriage and Ethnic Identity in Twentieth Century America.* Madison, Wis.: University of Wisconsin Press.

Spring, Joel. 1989. *The Sorting Machine Revisited: National Educational Policy Since 1945.* updated ed. New York: Longman.

Steeh, Charlotte, and Maria Kyrsan. 1996. "The Polls-Trends: Affirmative Action and the Public, 1970–1995." *Public Opinion Quarterly* 60 (Spring):128–158.

Stokes, Bruce. 1988. "Learning the Game." *National Journal* 20:2649–2654.

Sugrue, Thomas J. 1996. *The Origins of the Urban Crisis: Race and Inequality in Postwar Detroit.* Princeton: Princeton University Press.

Sundquist, James L. 1968. *Politics and Policy: The Eisenhower, Kennedy, and Johnson Years.* Washington, D.C.: Brookings Institution.

Takaki, Ronald. 1993. *A Different Mirror: A History of Multicultural America.* Boston: Little, Brown.

Tate, Katherine. 1993. *From Protest to Politics: The New Black Voters in American Elections.* Cambridge, Mass.: Harvard University Press and Russell Sage Foundation.

Teitelbaum, Herbert, and Richard J. Hiller. 1977. "Bilingual Education: The Legal Mandate." *Harvard Educational Review* 47:138–170.

Thernstrom, Abigail M. 1987. *Whose Votes Count? Affirmative Action and Minority Voting Rights.* Cambridge, Mass.: Harvard University Press.

Therrien, Melissa, and Roberto R. Ramierez. 2001. "The Hispanic Population in the United States: Population Characteristics." *Current Population Reports* March. U.S. Bureau of the Census. P20–535.

Thielemann, Gregory S., and Joseph Stewart Jr. 1995. "A Demand-Side Perspective on the Importance of Representative Bureaucracy: AIDS, Ethnicity, Sexual Orientation, and Gender." *Public Administration Review* 56: 168–173.

Tocqueville, Alexis de. 1966 [1835]. *Democracy in America.* Edited by J. P. Mayer and Max Lerner. New York: Harper and Row.

Torry, Jack. 2005. "Blackwell in D.C. but Won't Be Testifying at Elections Hearing." *The Columbus Dispatch* 9 February 2005:A08.

Tuck, R. 1946. *Not with the Fist.* New York: Harcourt Brace and World.

Tushnet, Mark V. 1987. *The NAACP's Legal Strategy Against Segregated Education, 1925–1950.* Chapel Hill, N.C.: University of North Carolina Press.

Ueda, Reed. 1997. "Historical Patterns of Immigrant Status and Incorporation in the United States." Paper presented at the Workshop on Immigrants, Civil Culture, and Modes of Political Incorporation: A Contemporary and Historical Comparison. May 2–4, Santa Fe, N. Mex.

Uhlaner, Carole J. 1991. "Perceived Prejudice and the Coalition Prospects of Blacks, Latinos and Asian Americans." In *Ethnic and Racial Politics in California*, edited by Byran O. Jackson and Michael B. Preston. Berkeley: Institute of Governmental Studies, 339–371.

Uhlaner, Carole J., Bruce Cain, and D. Roderick Kiewiet. 1989. "Political Participation of Ethnic Minorities in the 1980s." *Political Behavior* 11 (September):195–231.

United States Bureau of the Census. 1990. "General Population Characteristics of Urbanized Areas."

———. 1993. *Asians and Pacific Islanders in the United States.* Series 1990 CP–3–5, August.

———. 1994. "Selected Characteristics of the Population, by Region and Race: March 1994." www.census.gov/population/socdemo/race/api/tab1.txt.

———. 1996. "Distribution of the Population, by Region, Residence, Sex, and Race: March 1996." www.census.gov/population/socdemo/race/black/tabs96/tab03–96.txt.

United States Commission on Civil Rights. 1968. Political Participation. Washington, D.C.: Government Printing Office.

———. 1971. *One Year Later.* Washington, D.C.: Government Printing Office.

United States Office of Personnel Management. 1996. *Annual Report to Congress on the Federal Equal Opportunity Recruitment Program* (Fiscal Year 1996). January. Washington, D.C.: Employment Service Office of Diversity.

United States Senate. 1969. *Indian Education: A National Tragedy—A National Challenge.* Report of Special Subcommittee on Indian Education, Committee on Labor and Public Welfare, 91st Cong., 1st sess., S. Rep. No. 501.

United States v. Cruikshank. 1876. 92 U.S. 542.

United States v. Georgia. 1969. Civil No. 12972, N.D. Ga.

United States v. Harris. 1883. 106 U.S. 629.

United States v. Reese. 1876. 92 U.S. 214.

United States v. Texas Education Agency. 1972. 467 F.2d 848.

United States v. Wong Kim Ark. 1898. 169 U.S. 649.

UCLA Asian American Studies Center. 1993. "CrossCurrents" (Fall/Winter):1, 5.

UCLA Asian American Studies Center. 1996. "CrossCurrents" (Fall/Winter):1.

UCLA Asian American Studies Center. 2000. *2001–2002 National Asian Pacific American Political Almanac 10.* Los Angeles: UCLA Asian American Studies Center.

Verba, Sidney, and Norman Nie. 1972. *Participation in America.* New York: Harper and Row.

Vigil, Maurilio E. 1987. *Hispanics in American Politics: The Search for Political Power.* Lanham, Md.: University Press of America.

———. 1996. "The Political Development of New Mexico's Hispanas." *Latino Studies Journal* 7 (Spring):3–28.

Vose, Clement E. 1958. "Litigation as a Form of Pressure Group Activity." *Annals* 319:20–31.

———. 1959. *Caucasians Only: The Supreme Court, the NAACP, and the Restrictive Covenant Cases.* Berkeley: University of California Press.

Wards Cove Packing Inc. v. Atonio. 1989. 490 U.S. 642, 109 S.Ct. 2115, 104 LEd 2d 733.

Warren, Christopher L., John G. Corbett, and John F. Stack Jr. 1990. "Hispanic Ascendancy and Tripartite Politics in Miami." In *Racial Politics in American Cities*, edited by Rufus P. Browning, Dale Rogers Marshall, and David H. Tabb. New York: Longman, 155–178.

The Washington Post. 1994. 22 May 1994:A10.

Wei, William. 1993. *The Asian American Movement.* Philadelphia: Temple University Press.

Weinberg, Meyer. 1977. *Minority Students: A Research Appraisal.* Washington, D.C.: National Institute of Education, Government Printing Office.

Welch, Susan, Albert K. Karnig, and Richard A. Eribes. 1983. "Changes in Hispanic Local Employment in the Southwest." *Western Political Quarterly* 36:660–673.

Welch, Susan, and Lee Sigelman. 1992. "A Gender Gap Among Hispanics? A Comparison with Blacks and Anglos." *Western Political Quarterly* 45:181–199.

Weyler, Rex. 1982. *Blood on the Land: The Government and Corporate War Against the American Indian Movement.* New York: Everest House.

White House. 1995. Report on the Review of Federal Affirmative Action Programs. http://www.whitehouse.gov/white_house/EOP/OP/html/aa/aa/aa01.html.

Wilkins, David E. 2002. *American Indian Politics and the American Political System.* Lanham, Md.: Rowman & Littlefield.

Williams, Linda F. 1987. "Black Political Progress in the 1980s: The Electoral Arena." In *The New Black Politics: The Search for Political Power*, 2d ed., edited by Michael B. Preston, Lenneal Henderson, and Paul Puryear. New York: Longman, 97–135.

Wollenberg, Charles M. 1978. *All Deliberate Speed: Segregation and Exclusion in California Schools, 1855–1975*. Berkeley: University of California Press.

Worcester v. Georgia. 1832. 6 Peters 515.

Younge, Gary 2003. "It's Time to Take the Men-Only Sign off the White House Door." *The Guardian,* March 3, 3.

Index